TERENCE MacSWINEY

Dave Hannigan is a columnist with the *Sunday Tribune* in Dublin, the *Evening Echo* (Cork) and the *Irish Echo* (New York), and a regular contributor to the *Daily Mail* (Ireland). A former Irish Young Journalist of the Year, he is the author of *De Valera in America* (2008), *Giants of Cork Sport* (2005), *The Big Fight* (2002), *The Garrison Game* (1998), and a children's book, *Kicking On* (2010). He is also an adjunct professor of history at Suffolk County Community College on Long Island. Born and reared in Cork, he now lives in Rocky Point, New York with his wife Cathy, and sons, Abe and Charlie.

Terence MacSwiney

THE HUNGER STRIKE
THAT ROCKED AN EMPIRE

DAVE HANNIGAN

THE O'BRIEN PRESS
DUBLIN

First published 2010 by The O'Brien Press Ltd.
12 Terenure Road East, Rathgar, Dublin 6, D06 HD27, Ireland.
Tel: +353 1 4923333; Fax: +353 1 4922777
E-mail: books@obrien.ie
Website: www.obrien.ie.
Reprinted 2019, 2021.
The O'Brien Press is a member of Publishing Ireland.

ISBN 978-1-84717-182-5

4 6 8 7 5 3
21 23 22

Picture Credits: Photographs on front and back cover and in picture section 1 by kind permission
of the MacSwiney Brugha family, except for page vii, and page viii (top), courtesy of the
Evening Echo, Cork. Photographs in picture section 2 courtesy of the *Evening Echo*, except
for page ii (top) and page vii, by permission of UCDA, and page iii, from
the *London Evening News*, 1920.

Editing, typesetting and design: The O'Brien Press Ltd

Printed and bound in Ireland by Sprint Print.
The paper used in this book is produced using pulp from managed forests.

Published in
DUBLIN
UNESCO
City of Literature

DEDICATION

To the memory of my sister Anne

ACKNOWLEDGEMENTS

Growing up in the Cork suburb of Togher, St Finbarr's Cemetery in Glasheen was part of our extended playground, a place where we hung out, played, and, all the while, tripped through history. From boyhood, we knew that the Republican Plot at the entrance contained, amongst others, a triumvirate of rebel icons in Tomás MacCurtain, Donncha de Barra and Terence MacSwiney. Thirty years later, I came across stories in the *New York Times* archive about the worldwide impact of MacSwiney's hunger strike and, for allowing me to revisit that epic protest now, I'd like to thank my publisher Michael O'Brien.

Elsewhere at The O'Brien Press, Mary Webb did a fine and patient editing job, and Emma Byrne's exceptional design work is evident in your hands right now.

As the cliché goes, it's impossible to list here all the people who contributed in different ways to this project but it would be remiss of me not to express my gratitude to a select few. For starters, Emmet Barry and Denis Walsh were fervent supporters of this project; Professor Clare Frost (Stony Brook University) and Dr Gary Murphy (Dublin City University) improved early drafts with their keen eye for detail, literary and historic; Diarmuid O'Donovan went above and beyond the call of friendship in an exhaustive quest for photographs from the archives of the *Evening Echo*.

In January, 2010, I enjoyed a wonderful and informative afternoon in the company of Máire MacSwiney Brugha at her home in Dublin. As custodian of her father's immense legacy, I thank her, and her sons Ruairí and Cathal

Brugha, for offering me so much assistance with my task.

I would also like to express gratitude to Gavin O'Connor, for friendship and for ferrying me around Dublin and making my research trip there so enjoyable. Special thanks as well to Mark Penney for doing some heavy lifting on my behalf at the National Archives in London.

Since moving to America ten years ago, George and Clare Frost have treated me like one of the family (which technically I suppose I am!), and been a constant source of encouragement. For love, affection and support of that kind over a much longer period, I am very grateful to my brother Tom, sister Denise, niece Kadie, and aunt Christine.

My father Denis died shortly before I began work on this project but his spirit informs every page. For putting books into my hand as a child and teaching me the value of education, I owe him and my remarkable mother Theresa a debt I can never properly repay. They have always inspired.

My wife Cathy battles physical adversity of her own on a daily basis with the sort of equanimity and courage that makes book deadlines seem unimportant and offers a true definition of heroic. Without her love, patience and understanding, none of this would be worthwhile and very little of it even possible.

I would also like to thank her for giving me my sons Abe and Charlie, a pair of scoundrels whose ability to break into a locked office marks them out as two boys with very bright futures ahead of them. You are the lights of my life.

CONTENTS

PROLOGUE   9

1. FREEDOM OF THE CITY   13

2. COURT OF PUBLIC OPINION   31

3. THE POWERLESSNESS OF KING GEORGE   52

4. LABOUR PAINS AND ACCUSATIONS   71

5. WILD GEESE CHASES   91

6. FORTY DAYS AND FORTY NIGHTS   110

7. GOD AND THE GUN   127

8. DOCTORS DIFFER, PATIENT REFUSES TO DIE   145

9. 'THE PLAY'S THE THING...'   162

10. FROM A WHISPER TO A SCREAM   179

11. FORCING THE ISSUE   198

12. A PERFECT MARTYR   218

13. BODY AND SOUL   236

14. THE LONG JOURNEY HOME   256

15. IN LIVING MEMORY   276

BIBLIOGRAPHY   297

SOURCE NOTES   301

PROLOGUE

In the early hours of 20 March 1920, members of the Royal Irish Constabulary, their faces painted black, burst through the door of 40 Thomas Davis Street in Blackpool, Cork and assassinated Tomás MacCurtain. Just seven weeks before these men shot him in his own home, MacCurtain, Commandant of the Cork No. 1 Brigade of the IRA, had been elected the city's Lord Mayor. Befitting the municipal office he held, his body was taken to lie in state at the City Hall. There, the people of Cork duly teemed in to pay their respects to their fallen leader.

When it finally came time to close the door to the public mourners that Saturday evening, MacCurtain's friend Terence MacSwiney stayed behind. He wanted to spend the night beside the coffin he had earlier shouldered up the steps. Over the course of two decades, the pair had forged such a bond of friendship that MacSwiney was godfather to MacCurtain's son Tomás Óg. Their relationship was so close indeed that Eilis MacCurtain used to joke that if Terence had been a girl, she'd have been jealous of the amount of time he spent with her husband.

At the North Cathedral the following day, MacSwiney again could not tear himself away from the casket of his friend. Long after the church had emptied, he remained in a kneeling position, praying before the altar like somebody transfixed. On Monday, after the elongated funeral procession had wound its way through the grieving city to St Finbarr's Cemetery in Glasheen, he steeled himself to deliver an oration by the graveside. His short speech culminated in the line: '... no matter how many lose their lives in the cause of their duty, as did the Lord Mayor, another will always be found to take the lead.'

Just eight days later, MacSwiney was elected unopposed to replace his friend as Lord Mayor. Nominated for the post by Liam de Róiste, seconded by Tadhg Barry, and supported by Sir John Scott, leader of the unionist representatives, the announcement of his appointment caused uproarious cheering and celebrations in the city chambers and beyond. After the chain of office was formally placed around his neck, MacSwiney, who had also succeeded his friend as Commandant of the Cork No. 1 Brigade of the IRA, stood and delivered an acceptance speech that was equal parts stirring tribute, political manifesto and militaristic call-to-arms.

'The circumstances of the vacancy in the office of Lord Mayor governed inevitably the filling of it. And I come here more as a soldier, stepping into the breach, than an administrator to fill the first post in the municipality ... We see in the manner in which our late Lord Mayor was murdered an attempt to terrify us all. Our first duty is to answer that threat by showing ourselves unterrified, cool and inflexible ... I wish to point out again the secret of our strength and the assurance of our final victory. This contest of ours is not on our side a rivalry of vengeance but one of endurance – it is not they who can inflict most but they who can suffer most will conquer – though we do not abrogate our function to demand and see that evildoers and murderers are punished for their crime.'

'*It is not they who can inflict most but they who can suffer most will conquer.*' Within a matter of months, those very words would, in so many ways, become his own epitaph.

CHAPTER ONE

Freedom of the City

But it is because they were our best and bravest that they had to die. No lesser sacrifice would save us. Because of it our struggle is holy, our battle is sanctified by their blood and our victory is assured by their martyrdom. We, taking up the work they left incomplete, confident in God, offer in turn sacrifice from ourselves. It is not we who take innocent blood, but we offer it, sustained by the example of our immortal dead, and that Divine Example which inspires us all for the redemption of our country. Facing our enemy, we must declare our attitude simply ... We ask no mercy and we will accept no compromise.

Terence MacSwiney, inaugural speech as Lord Mayor, 30 March 1920.

Shortly before 5pm on Thursday, 12 August 1920, the postman delivered a letter to 4 Belgrave Place, the home of Annie and Mary MacSwiney. The envelope was addressed to their brother Terence, the Lord Mayor of Cork.

In his absence Mary opened it and found an anonymous note, scrawled in what looked like deliberately bad handwriting, requesting that the IRA assassinate a policeman in Tipperary by the name of Quinn. Helpful details were included about where this RIC officer might be most easily found and shot.

Mary MacSwiney reread the letter a couple of times, then promptly tore it up and burnt it. She'd been long enough in the game to sense when something wasn't quite right. Here was the first ominous sign something was up that day.

Half an hour later, Terence walked in the door, as he nearly always did at that time of the day. She mentioned the special delivery but they didn't dwell on it. This sort of thing was happening so often by then that nobody took much notice. It was after six when Terence finally pushed away from the table, thanked his sisters for the food and the *cupán*, and announced his intention to return to work. Fleeting visits had become the way of it with him and the family home. He could never stay too long in any one house for security reasons, and, in any case, he was always anxious to get back to his desk at the City Hall. Much to do and so little time.

He wasn't to know then that he'd just enjoyed his last supper.

At the top of the steps in Belgrave Place, the city of Cork sprawled out beneath him. A troubled city in a troubled country. His troubled city. His troubled country. More than once in the four and a half months since being elected Lord Mayor, his home town had thrummed with rumours of his own assassination. When friends brought up these stories of his supposed demise, he enjoyed laughing them off, but more often than not, he now travelled with a bodyguard. Everybody assumed that in the War of Independence he was as much a target for killing as his predecessor and friend, Tomás MacCurtain.

Forty-one-year-old MacSwiney cut a dashing figure as he strode purposefully down Belgrave Avenue to begin the short walk across the River Lee that summer's evening, along the very same streets and roads he'd traversed all his life. The same streets and roads he would never stroll again. A tall, dark-haired man with a rebellious lock of hair constantly falling over his face, he was helming a municipality struggling to assert its political independence from British authority, representing the constituency of Mid-Cork in the rebel government that was Dáil Éireann, and serving as commandant of the Cork No. 1 Brigade of the IRA. One man. Three full-time jobs. Some schedule.

'Meals were snatched hurriedly and in the shortest possible time,' wrote his friend P S O'Hegarty. 'In those days it was hardly possible for any of his friends to see him on anything but business. From 10am until 10pm, with short intervals for dinner and tea, he was at the City Hall, working, interviewing, directing. And there was no seeing him there except on business. To an old friend who during a short holiday in Cork at this period liked to see him every day, he used to say: "Come here at 12.45. I'll be going to dinner then and you may as well walk up to the house with me and have some." At 1.30, he would return and plunge into work once more. It was simply phenomenal courage and endurance.'

Befitting a man carrying that sort of immense workload for too long, MacSwiney had been beseeched to take some type of holiday and was scheduled to head off that Saturday. A proposed week away from the routine that might even stretch into ten days, it was hoped that this break would recharge the batteries, stop him from falling sick due to overwork, and, most importantly of all, allow him to spend precious time with his wife Muriel and their two-year-old daughter, Máire.

More and more the dictates of these peculiar and turbulent circumstances were preventing him from seeing them both with any degree of regularity. The fear that the Black and Tans or the RIC might come to arrest or shoot him under cover of darkness meant that he only ever got to snatch a stolen evening here or there with Muriel. Such was the bounty on his head that he never slept in the same bed for two consecutive nights.

'I saw my husband sometimes, because I was in the house of friends but indeed, very, very seldom and always at a very great risk,' said Muriel MacSwiney. 'Sometimes he would come up after dark, because it was a little out-of-the-way place, a little outside of the city. And then he would come after dark and go away the first thing in the morning. The only meal I could have him for was breakfast, and that on rare occasions. I hardly ever saw my husband at all, to tell the truth.'

Their domestic situation was so gravely compromised by the difficult and dangerous environment that the chief means by which he communicated with his family for much of his time as mayor had been the telephone. A perk of the job, his daughter came to regard the device as so synonymous with the voice of her absent father that even when Muriel was making other calls Máire would grab the handset and shout for her daddy.

When MacSwiney returned to his office at the City Hall on this particular evening, there was no time for calls to his wife and child. The headquarters of the municipal government was a busy place, with all the various strands of the struggle, violent and non-violent, coalescing beneath its roof.

Downstairs, one of Dáil Éireann's national arbitration courts (which had in many places usurped the crown's faltering legal system) was holding a hearing involving the Prudential Insurance Company. That one of London's most respected corporations was participating in a court overseen by the outlaw regime in Dublin's Mansion House was a graphic illustration of how the shadow government was trying to adhere to proper judicial structures in order to legitimise its cause.

On a less legal track, MacSwiney was supposed to have a 7pm sit-down with Liam Lynch, Commandant of the IRA's Cork No.2 Brigade, who had travelled into the city especially to see him. Then, he was supposed to meet with the council of his own No.1 Brigade an hour later. His schedule was so tight it had been decided the best thing to do was to have his colleagues gather around his desk for the eight o'clock pow-wow.

As a consequence of that itinerary, the corridors were now teeming with some of the most wanted men in the whole country. Even worse, and unbeknownst to MacSwiney, officers from the Irish Republican Brotherhood, the more exclusive, secretive and older forerunner of the IRA, had also chosen to get together at the City Hall that evening. A decision motivated by the centrality of the location, it would play a crucial role in the denouement of the rest of the night and the remainder of his life.

'A British raid on local mails at one point on 9th August gave them an indication of the possibility that some (IRB) officers would meet at the City Hall three days later,' wrote Florence O'Donoghue, head of intelligence for the Cork No. 1 Brigade.

'It was an accident of war which gave the Intelligence Officer of the British 6th Division at Cork a slight lead which he fully utilised. He had a stroke of luck and he made the most of it.'

The British good fortune was compounded by the fact that nobody in the IRB had taken steps to cancel the compromised meeting. This was why not long after MacSwiney made it back to his office that evening, a convoy of six lorries and six armoured cars departed Victoria Barracks and began trundling down through the northside of the city, heading towards City Hall, eager to act on its freshly-harvested intelligence.

Just moments before the troops swarmed from their vehicles to surround the building, word finally reached those inside of the impending raid. Escape plans were hastily pressed into action. The inevitability of this kind of raid had prompted elaborate security measures to be put in place and the fabric of the building altered to help anybody trying to leave in a hurry.

In the room next to the Lord Mayor's office, a trapdoor in the ceiling led through a series of other trapdoors all the way to the roof. In one corridor, a door had been camouflaged into the wall in order to allow only those in the know to gain egress. Crucially, on this night, MacSwiney had left the key to that door in his sisters' house in Belgrave Place.

'I rushed upstairs to warn the Lord Mayor,' wrote Cornelius Harrington, his personal secretary. 'Between the top of the stairs on my western side of the building and the Lord Mayor's suite on the other side was an open corridor about sixty yards long. As I ran along the corridor I saw Dan Donovan [known as Sandow] come from the Lord Mayor's Room and rush down the main stairs leading to the vestibule. About halfway on this stairs, there was a landing at which was an entrance door to the balcony of the Assembly Hall. Through this door, Sandow disappeared. As I reached the end of the corridor, I met Terry. He was rolling a piece of twine. He knew what was going on. I asked him if he had anything on him that I could take. He said he had not.'

By then, the soldiers had occupied the bottom floor and were on the move. With this avenue out sealed off, MacSwiney and Harrington made for the back stairs on the eastern side. When they reached the bottom steps, they were met by a soldier, his rifle and fixed bayonet extended, shouting: 'Halt!' At this juncture, Harrington decided rather selflessly to try to distract the soldier by walking towards the vestibule. The rifle-holder took the bait and followed him. This allowed MacSwiney to head for the back door.

'When I got to the top of the wall, I saw some civilians coming out the back door of the hall,' said Lieutenant WM Gillick of the 2nd Hampshires, the officer in charge of the detail sent to cover the rear of the building. 'We ran around the path and found them in a hut, a workshop place. There were eleven men in that hut. I sent the private back to the sergeant for some more men and then put a guard over the civilians in the hut.'

The Lord Mayor had made it no farther than the corrugated iron works area behind the City Hall. He was now under arrest. When his fellow prisoners asked him what they should do now that they were heading to jail, he replied: 'Hunger strike.' It was an extreme reaction but also a kind of inevitable one. Just the previous day, eleven Republican prisoners at Cork Jail had started refusing food to call attention to the fact that they were being held there indefinitely without trial.

Whether or not MacSwiney's decision was motivated by his belief that the new intake of inmates should publicise their colleague's plight by acting in sympathy with them, it was certainly a spontaneous move. No prior approval had been sought for such a drastic action from within the IRA.

'It was clear that MacSwiney had determined his own line of action,' said Florence O'Donoghue. 'No one opposed the suggestion and all refused food from the time of their arrest.'

An hour and a half after the raid began, the British soldiers had sorted the wheat from the chaff. Those involved in the Prudential case and all other accidental tourists were released. Only a dozen men remained in custody, all now corralled inside the hut out back. Among them were MacSwiney, his vice-commandant, Sean O'Hegarty, Joseph O'Connor (Quartermaster, Cork No.1 Brigade) and Liam Lynch. At one point, MacSwiney and two others were separated from the main group after the soldiers spotted them surreptitiously trying to tear up and dispose of sheets of paper.

By ten o'clock, the first pangs of hunger hitting, and darkness finally starting to fall on late summer Cork, MacSwiney and his cohorts were on the back of lorries and being driven up to Victoria Barracks. It was quite a haul of elite prisoners, but the lack of an RIC officer in the raiding party meant that the British soldiers didn't even realise how many senior IRA figures they'd just arrested. Perhaps too smitten by the idea of having the Lord Mayor, they ended up releasing the other eleven, including the prized Lynch, without charge just four days later.

When MacSwiney was being taken into formal custody by the military that night, Sergeant-Major Bailey, the officer in charge of the detention facility, asked him to remove his chain of office from around his neck.

'I would rather die than part with it,' said the Lord Mayor. Bailey did not push the matter any further.

At Belgrave Place, the MacSwiney sisters grew frantic when they heard about their brother's arrest. Annie's first reaction had been to pace the floor of their home, lambasting the British and swearing vengeance. They soon had even more problems.

'At midnight that [Thursday] night, two military officers and a large body of men came to our house to raid it,' said Mary MacSwiney. 'They were sent for that letter. They wanted it for evidence against my brother. If that letter had been found he would have been charged, not with the charges that were proffered against him, but on being the leader of a conspiracy to murder policemen. And they searched my house very thoroughly that night to get evidence of his complicity in the murder of policemen. They did their best to manufacture it beforehand.'

The first Muriel MacSwiney knew of her husband's travails was early on Friday morning. Shortly after seven o'clock, a friend knocked at the door of the house where she was staying in the seaside town of Youghal, brandishing a newspaper with the story of his arrest. Her absence from the city made the situation even more complicated and draining.

'What could I do?' she asked. 'There was nobody to mind the baby except myself. I had nobody to take her except strangers and she would not go to them.'

Closer to the action, Mary MacSwiney set about getting in to see her brother, but by the time she gained access he'd already been transferred to another facility.

'I saw him in Cork Gaol that Saturday morning, and that was the first intimation I had that he was hunger-striking,' said Mary MacSwiney. 'He looked very bad then, although it was only his third day.'

That was the bulletin Mary brought to Youghal when she headed down to help Muriel with the baby later that day. On Sunday, the family received unofficial word that a court-martial, to be held under the Defence of the Realm Regulations, had been set for Monday morning. Muriel headed back to Cork and, accompanied by Annie, went to the prison to try to see him right before the trial began. They caught a glimpse, and that was enough of a sight to behold.

'A big military lorry came up, a very large one,' said Muriel MacSwiney. 'I never saw so many soldiers in a military lorry in my life before. My husband was sitting in the centre of them on a chair ... I need not tell you that he was very weak. It seemed such a cruel thing to have so many armed men guarding a weak and absolutely unarmed man ... He was in very great pain. He looked it. I think that was one of the worst times for me ... I knew he was in pain and it was an awful thing that I could not give him anything to eat, for of course, it was part of my duty that I should look after all his wants.'

Despite his debilitated condition, the authorities were taking no chances with the journey to bring MacSwiney from the jail back up to Victoria Barracks, the location for the hearing. Apart from the soldiers flanking him on the back of the truck, there was a convoy of other vehicles, including an armoured car. Every precaution was taken for fear that the IRA might try an audacious rescue attempt. The security measures included rigorously searching every person who wished to attend the hearing, requiring each one to sign his or her name and address in a recording book, and having soldiers stationed throughout the room.

By the time the visibly weakened MacSwiney entered the courtroom that 16 August, Day 4 of his hunger strike, with riflemen on either side of him, there were plenty of familiar faces present. Apart from his wife, with whom he'd managed to snatch a brief conversation in Irish before the start, and Annie, there was Father Dominic O'Connor OSFC, chaplain to the Cork Brigade of the IRA, deputy mayor Donal O'Callaghan, the town clerk Florence McCarthy (who had also visited him in Cork Jail), and a number of other high-ranking officials from the City Hall.

'First of all, they took him up very high stairs to a place where they were going to try him; and then they changed and took him down again,' said Muriel MacSwiney. 'I saw by his face that he was suffering, and I said to one of the soldiers, could they not give him a chair, because he had been without food for so long. I was speaking to him in Irish and they did not interfere. He told me that he felt himself he would be sentenced, and that he would be deported to England and that others arrested with him would get out. But of course he was pleased with that. He wanted to suffer for everybody else's wrongs.'

With Lieutenant-Colonel James (South Staffordshire Regiment) the presiding officer, the other members of the court were Major Percival (Essex Regiment) and Captain Reeves (Hampshire Regiment), and Under the Defence of the Realm Regulations, MacSwiney, by now sitting in a chair, was formally charged with:

- 1. Possession of a numerical cipher that belonged to the RIC
- 2. Having this cipher under his control
- 3. Possession of a document containing statements likely to cause disaffection to his Majesty [which was actually an amended version of the resolution passed by the Cork Corporation acknowledging the authority of and pledging allegiance to the First Dáil]
- 4. Possession of a copy of his own inaugural Lord Mayor's speech from earlier that year [which had been widely publicised at the time it was made]

Before the start of evidence, Colonel James asked MacSwiney if he was represented by legal counsel. His strident response ignored the question, focusing instead on the legitimacy of the entire affair and setting the belligerent tone for his approach to the rest of the day.

MacSwiney: I would like to say a word about your proceedings here. The position is that I am Lord Mayor of Cork and Chief Magistrate of this city. And I declare this court illegal, and that those who take part in it are liable to arrest under the laws of the Irish Republic.

James: Mr. MacSwiney, you will be able to say that afterwards. Do you object to being tried by me, as President, or any of the officers whose names you have heard?

MacSwiney: What I have said already refers to this. You are all individually liable for any action you take in the court.

James: Are you guilty or not guilty?

MacSwiney: Without wishing to be in any way personal to you, I wish to point out that it is an act of presumption to ask me that question. I say this whole proceeding is illegal.

James interpreted that as a refusal to plead. Captain WC Gover OBE then began the case for the prosecution by announcing his regret that the defendant had chosen not to recognise the validity of the court and wasn't going to be professionally represented in the proceedings. In his approach to arguing his brief, Gover's main aim appeared to be proving that the numerical cipher had been in MacSwiney's possession or control on the evening of his arrest.

Private Norris (Hampshire Regiment) testified that while standing guard over eleven prisoners in the hut behind City Hall on the evening of 12 August, he witnessed three of them, including the Lord Mayor, trying to rip up papers. When he reported this information to his superior, the trio was then moved away from the others and a subsequent search of the area where they had been standing revealed two letters (one addressed to the Commandant, First Cork Battalion, IRA) and a coded RIC message. With no knowledge of RIC codes, neither Norris or the officers on duty realised the import of that message at the time of its discovery.

A Lieutenant Koe then gave evidence of participating in a further search of City Hall at 11.30 on the same night. In a roll-top desk in the Lord Mayor's Room, he claimed to have unearthed MacSwiney's private diary and a host of papers including letters and the key to the cipher. This latter batch of material formed the substance of the charges brought against MacSwiney, and County Inspector Maunsell of the RIC was brought in to explain the significance and to establish the veracity of the cipher.

Having confirmed that the key to the cipher was one that had come into operation on 28 July that year for use by RIC officers when transmitting messages, Maunsell also verified that the coded message discovered behind the hut was a note he had sent to the Inspector General in Dublin regarding Republican prisoners on 11 August. Asked whether it was an especially complicated cipher to figure out, he replied: 'I consider that it would be impossible to decipher without a key.'

MacSwiney spoke up at this juncture.

'I have something to say to this, gentlemen,' he said. 'The only thing relevant about this code is this – any person in possession of such a code who is not a member of the Irish Republic is evidence of a criminal conspiracy against the Irish Republic. Therefore, in giving that evidence you do not indict me, but yourself.'

The prosecution having rested its case, Colonel James asked MacSwiney if he intended to call any witnesses in his own defence. He didn't. As he laboured to stand up out of the chair, the presiding officer then offered him the option to speak while seated. He declined.

'I believe I will be able to hold my feet until after the close of these proceedings, and then it is quite immaterial.'

From there, he revisited his earlier attack on the legality of the proceedings and delivered a speech that was more like a soliloquy in praise of the Irish Republic established by Dáil Éireann at the Mansion House in January 1919, rather than an attempted refutation of the charges against him. Having reiterated that his comments were not to be considered an effort at proffering a defence, he did point out inconsistencies in the prosecution case. For starters, Captain Gover had neglected to mention a document seized from MacSwiney's desk that was a resolution regarding the inquest which found the British government and the RIC guilty of the murder of Tomás MacCurtain.

'And now it must be obvious to you that if that were an invention, it would be so grave a matter that it would be the chief charge here today, even in this illegal court. But that document is put aside.'

He then addressed the main charges against himself by alleging that the soldiers involved in the raid hadn't testified truthfully regarding the whereabouts of the cipher.

'Lt. Koe has committed perjury, for the code was not in my desk though I know where it was and am sure that it was put in my desk. I do not know who separated it from other documents; but it must have been done to make two charges against two individuals. No one is responsible but me. I know where that paper was and where it was sworn to be. My respect for your army, little though it was, owing to happenings in this country of late, has now disappeared. It is a document that ought to be only in my possession. No one else should have it without my consent, without committing an offence. Anyone who used such a cipher to transmit messages about the Irish people is guilty of a crime against the Irish Republic.'

The allegation that the cipher was placed in his desk was revisited by Moirin Chavasse in her biography.

'While waiting in the shed, (Quartermaster) O'Connor had succeeded in tearing up the cipher key, and when he and the other prisoners were called out of the shed to be searched he pushed the pieces between some boards,' wrote Chavasse. 'It was found by the military later on, and at the trial, was sworn to have been discovered in the Lord Mayor's desk, and this became the

chief charge against him. When O'Connor found that possession of the cipher key was to be brought against MacSwiney he
offered to make a deposition to the Courtmartial that it had been
in his own possession. MacSwiney refused to allow him to do
this, saying it would be useless and that the Courtmartial would
never allow such a deposition to be published.'

On the day in question, MacSwiney continued to use the
public platform afforded him. Having emphasised that the most
complete rebuttal of this court was contained in the inaugural
speech which formed the basis for the fourth charge against him,
he sought to highlight more inconsistencies in the prosecution
case. Why no mention of other documents they'd seized from
his desk, such as a letter to Pope Benedict XV about the beatifi-
cation of Oliver Plunkett, or a missive received from the president of the municipal council of Paris regarding the port of
Cork? Should these now be considered seditious materials too?

If those sort of comments made good copy for the press
reports on the following morning, MacSwiney, just before his
finishing remarks, revisited his inaugural speech, quoting the
first and last paragraphs from it before concluding: 'This is my
position. I ask for no mercy.'

The military tribunal took just fifteen minutes to consider the
evidence. As the deliberations were going on, MacSwiney and
his wife chatted briefly. They did so in Irish, an age-old tactic
used to prevent the soldiers eavesdropping on their conversation.
Then it came time for Colonel James to read out the verdict: not
guilty on the first charge of having possession of the cipher but
guilty on the second, third and fourth. Again, the defendant was
moved to speak.

MacSwiney: I wish to state that I will put a limit to any term of imprisonment you may impose. I have taken no food since Thursday, therefore I will be free in a month.

James: If sentenced to imprisonment, you will take no food?

MacSwiney: I have decided the term of my imprisonment. Whatever your government may do, I shall be free, alive or dead, within a month.

James announced a sentence of two years without hard labour.

'None of us dreamed that it would be a month,' said Muriel MacSwiney. 'I certainly did not think it would be more than a fortnight at the outside, and I did not think it would be that much.'

With their intention to deport him to England being well-known enough that it was reported in *The Times* of London on the previous Saturday, the authorities kept him in Victoria Barracks that night. While being processed there, MacSwiney complained about the cell to which he was assigned. He made the case that when holding Brigadier General Lucas captive earlier that summer, the North Cork IRA had afforded their prisoner treatment commensurate with his high rank. Apparently swayed by this argument, the British transferred the Lord Mayor to a cell with a better bed and gave him an officer as his guard.

It was there that his sister Mary and younger brother Sean, both of whom hadn't attended the trial, visited him later that Monday evening. They found him huddled for warmth inside an enormous overcoat and Mary immediately tried to find out the planned time for his transfer to England. None of the officers would give any information on that.

'This thing is rather important to us,' pleaded Mary to the soldiers. 'My brother has only the clothes he has on. If you are going to send him out of the country, we want to send him a suitcase with clothes.'

The soldiers would only answer that it might be best to bring the suitcase along. They knew. Just as the family suspected. He was going sooner rather than later.

At three o'clock the next morning, MacSwiney was taken from his cell. He was driven under heavily-armed guard through the streets of his still-sleeping city to Custom House Quay. There, a British naval sloop was waiting to bring him away. As he walked onto the gangplank, his legs unsteady now from four and a half days without food, the Lord Mayor departed his home town for the final time.

CHAPTER 2

Court of Public Opinion

'Taking up another, a living Irishman's poems [the work of Philip Francis Little], this day of watching, one may read:-

A PILGRIM from beyond the sea
Upon a lowly pallet lies,
A love, surmounting agony
Bright gleaming in his tranquil eyes;
So shall the Rose in deserts bloom
When Faith irradiates the Tomb.
EXULTANT NOW, who underneath the rod
Of Tyranny, oppression's yoke had borne,
Exultant…
Flawless those brows were now, and radiant
As is the sun, which shineth in his strength:
A steadfast peace expressed those cloudless eyes.
WHO SAYS they died in vain?
'Tis an irony, a lie!
They have taught us how to live,
Who have shown us how to die.'
Professor WFP Stockley's letter to the *Irish Independent*, 23 August 1920.

So the story goes, twenty-seven-year-old John MacSwiney left Ireland in 1862 because he wanted to go to Rome to enlist in the Papal Guard in order to help protect the Pontiff from the encroaching Italian nationalist forces of Giuseppe Garibaldi. By the time he reached the Vatican, however, the conflict was over. His quest for adventure continued to London where he forged a career as a schoolteacher, and met and married Mary Wilkinson, whose family had emigrated from Cork generations before.

After the birth of their third child, the couple decided to move back to Ireland where John wanted to open a tobacco factory in his home town in partnership with his brother-in-law, John Buckley. By the time another son, Terence James, was born, on 28 March 1879, the business had bankrupted both families and caused major upheaval. The child with the jet black hair would only be six when his father emigrated to Australia, never to return. The boy's abiding memory of his dad would be of learning a poem, usually with a rebel flavour, to recite in front of him on Sunday afternoons.

The bookish kid showed real academic promise at school in the storied North Monastery but left at the age of fifteen so that he could contribute to the upkeep of the family home. He began training as an accountant with Dwyer and Company, and though disillusioned with the drudgery of the work from an early stage, he remained there past his thirty-third birthday. Having graduated with a degree in Mental and Moral Science from University College Cork while working, he snagged a job teaching business methods at the Cork Municipal School of

Commerce. This role eventually led to him traversing the county as Commercial Instructor for the Joint Technical Instruction Committee for Cork.

The upward tick of his professional career was matched by a surge in his interest in Irish nationalism. A curiosity first piqued around the time of the centenary of the 1798 rebellion, it had drawn him into the Young Ireland Society and the Cork Celtic Literary Society, and caused him to use his writing talent towards political ends with opinion journalism, plays and poetry. When the Cork City Corps of the Irish Volunteers was formed in 1913, MacSwiney was immediately nominated onto its Provisional Committee, quickly assumed a lead part in the organisation and was centrally involved in Cork's controversial failure to rise in Easter 1916.

Over the turbulent years that followed the Rising, he was imprisoned for his activities and, along the way, he married, despite the objections of her wealthy family (the owners of a Cork distillery), Muriel Murphy. That the wedding took place under armed guard while he was interned by the British at Bromyard, Herefordshire, perfectly captured how almost every facet of his life had become secondary to and subsumed by his commitment to Irish independence.

By the early hours of Wednesday morning, 18 August, this turbulent journey had brought him to the port of Pembroke, Wales, a prisoner aboard the British naval destroyer, *Salmon*. Still under heavy guard, he was escorted onto a train bound for London. That night, the newly-registered Prisoner No. 6794 was placed in the hospital wing of Brixton Prison, in an airy room that contained six other unoccupied beds, and which reeked of history. This was the same ward where Roger Casement had been detained while on remand in the facility back in 1916.

'This man is not to be released,' wrote Geoffrey Whiskard, assistant-secretary at Dublin Castle, in a telegram dispatched to the Home Office shortly after MacSwiney reached London. 'It is intended to forcibly feed him. You are aware that he is entitled to be treated as a political prisoner.'

Once he arrived in Brixton, there began a daily ritual of physical examinations. Dr WD Higson was the medical officer on duty that week and on Thursday morning, 19 August, Day 7 of the hunger strike, he conducted his first tests on the patient. Having found his pulse to be 54 beats per minute, Higson then wrote the first daily briefing to the Home Office: 'The prisoner is not hostile in any way and states his only objection to taking anything in the way of nourishment is that it would mean prolonging his detention.'

It was only that day the MacSwiney family back in Cork received notification as to where exactly he had been taken. After initial reports that he was headed to Wormwood Scrubs, Art O'Brien, Vice-President of the Irish-Self Determination League of Great Britain, eventually wired them with an update as to his exact location. By the time that information reached Belgrave Place, Mary MacSwiney was already en route to London.

With Friday, 20 August marking the start of his second week without food, Dr Treadwell, the Medical Commissioner of Prisons came to the prison that day to conduct another check-up, an obvious sign that the authorities were concerned about the possible wider implications of his fast. Afterwards, he warned

MacSwiney that due to the lingering damage done by a bout of pleurisy earlier in life, he was especially poorly-equipped to subject his body to this kind of extreme ordeal.

That information had about as much impact on him as the commissioner's subsequent reading of a letter from the Home Secretary, Edward Shortt. This missive reminded him that he would not, under any circumstances, be released on account of his hunger strike. MacSwiney informed prison officials that he fully understood the document, and then dictated a reply. It was transcribed for him by Mr Morris, the prison schoolmaster, who also did clerical work for prisoners. During the dictation, he had to stop several times when he felt like he was going to faint with weakness.

'He [Dr Treadwell] impressed on me the gravity of my state then read a document from you, informing me that I would not be released,' wrote MacSwiney to Shortt. 'And that the consequences of my refusal to take food would rest with myself. Nonetheless, the consequences will rest with you. My undertaking on the day of my court-martial that I would be free or dead within a month will be fulfilled. It is clear from your communication my release is to be in death. In that event, the British government can boast of having killed two Lord Mayors of Cork in six months, an achievement without parallel in the history of oppression. Knowing the revolution of opinion that will be thereby caused throughout the civilised world and the consequent accession of support to Ireland in her hour of need, I am reconciled to a premature grave. I am prepared to die.'

Later in the day, Mary MacSwiney and Art O'Brien walked up to the prison gates for the first time. Only Mary was allowed in because O'Brien didn't have the required permit. Emerging very soon after, she told reporters her brother looked unwell yet expressed himself determined to pursue his protest right to the end. Her stay by his bedside had lasted only fifteen minutes, and had been cut short due to his lack of strength.

'I have just seen him and his condition is even worse than I had anticipated. I found him in bed in a very weak condition. He was so weak that it was with the greatest difficulty I could catch what he was saying. He tried to give me a message for somebody but I could not understand him and had to leave without understanding it. I cannot, therefore, unfortunately, deliver the message. He however made himself clear on one point. He expressed his determination to continue the hunger strike until he was released or died. There was no mistaking his determination on that matter. A warder was in the cell when I was speaking to my brother. He was very kind. So was the priest and doctor.'

If she put on a brave face for the journalists, Mary was actually distraught by what she'd seen. To her mind, her brother looked like a man in so much physical distress that he might not last a week. This notion had been confirmed to her by Dr Higson when he gave a personal assurance that he would contact her immediately once the Lord Mayor reached the brink of death, just so that the rest of the family back in Cork could be advised to travel over.

Obviously motivated by what she'd seen and heard, Mary went to the Home Office that afternoon to seek an audience with the Home Secretary. As a former Chief Secretary for Ireland, Edward Shortt knew well the situation in Cork but on this day he was unavailable to receive her. The only ranking official to speak to Miss MacSwiney was the under-secretary Sir Ernley Blackwell. He also boasted an Irish pedigree. As chief legal adviser to the Foreign Office in 1916, he'd been involved in leaking details of Roger Casement's homosexuality during the latter's trial for his role in the planning of the Easter Rising, an event he was actually hoping to get cancelled at the time of his arrest.

As might have been expected then, Blackwell wasn't exactly a sympathetic ear. He merely reiterated the government's steadfast position about not releasing the hunger striker.

'Do you mean that you are going to let him die in prison?' asked Mary.

He did.

Moreover, Blackwell went on to contend that the responsibility fell on the shoulders of herself and the rest of her family to persuade the mayor to do the sensible thing and accept food before it was too late. She countered that no relative would proffer advice like that, nor would he take it. Hopeless as this meeting may have sounded when she conveyed the details to reporters afterwards (the appetite for MacSwiney news was then intensifying), it didn't deter her any from tilting at more bureaucratic windmills.

Her quest for more positive responses from the highest echelons of the British government would continue for months yet and, before she left the Home Office that day, she handed in a written request for an interview with Shortt.

Behind the public bravado, the British authorities were becoming increasingly worried about the situation. Some were already trying to figure out ways to circumvent the strike. On 20

August, JCC Davidson, a prominent Conservative MP, wrote, on behalf of Andrew Bonar Law, his own party leader, to Alexander Maxwell at the Home Office: 'Mr Bonar Law has noticed that MacSwiney is taking water. Would it not be possible to introduce into it some additional "vitamins" or some substance containing them which would keep him going?'

Maxwell replied that such a manoeuvre might cause him to get suspicious enough to give up the water too, and, in any case, it really wouldn't do much good anyway. That Bonar Law and Davidson were discussing MacSwiney's regimen even after just one week, though, is an indication of how his protest had already begun to impact.

On Saturday, 21 August, Day 12, Muriel MacSwiney arrived at Paddington Station in London. Immediately she set off for the prison with Father Dominic. Even before entering her husband's room for the first time she had an audience with the doctor during which he implored her to try to intervene and to stop the strike.

'You will see your husband in a few minutes,' said Dr Higson. 'And will you not try to get him to take food?'

Higson laboured his point by emphasising the long-term damage the strike would do to the mayor's health if he did manage to survive.

'I told him I understood that, and it was perfectly true, and I understood the harm of going without food, and of course from a health point of view, I quite agreed with him,' said Muriel. 'But I did not interfere with my husband in anything, especially in matters of conscience of what he should do.'

This was the truth. Three years earlier, just months after the couple was married, she had watched her husband and a number of his Volunteer colleagues embark on a hunger strike in Cork Jail as they campaigned for better conditions. Later, she admitted to not believing in that particular protest. Crucially, she didn't tell him this until long after it was over. This time around, though, she declared herself four-square behind her spouse even if she was taken aback by the appalling sight that greeted her from the bed.

'I saw my husband then. I saw a great change in him. He looked very badly indeed. Dreadfully bad.'

Father Dominic's assessment of the situation was more detailed but no less disturbing.

'I found the Lord Mayor considerably worse than when I had last seen him on the Monday before. He was wan, wasted, and haggard-looking, but clear in mind and fully determined to force open the gates of his prison, even though he should die in the attempt.'

That much was reiterated the following morning when, during a chat with Mary MacSwiney, he now had the strength to whisper one more message of defiance. 'My death will do Ireland good and that is all that matters.' His sister wasn't prepared to accept this fate just yet even though she had already received a stern rebuff from the Home Secretary.

'I have received your letter of the 20th instant, asking for an interview with regard to your brother, Mr. Terence MacSwiney, and can only say that an interview would serve no good purpose,' wrote Shortt. 'It is the final decision of His Majesty's Government that Mr. MacSwiney will not be released from prison because he refuses to take food. Owing to the state of his health,

Mr. MacSwiney cannot be fed forcibly. For any consequence that may ensue from his refusal to take food, Mr. MacSwiney alone is responsible.'

Definitive as that communiqué may have sounded, it didn't stop a rumour sweeping London and Cork on Saturday that Shortt had actually ordered an immediate release of the prisoner. Whether maliciously or innocently circulated, this erroneous information reached Father Dominic and caused him to fetch up at the gates in Brixton that night, looking to accompany MacSwiney on his walk to freedom. At that point, the guards assured the Capuchin that nobody had ordered anything, and he departed alone.

This wasn't the only falsehood doing the rounds that weekend. The Sunday papers carried a report from the Press Association that MacSwiney had himself petitioned the Home Secretary for his release. A rather serious distortion of his letter to Shortt that culminated in him asserting his willingness to die prematurely ('I am reconciled to a premature grave'), this was vehemently denied by his wife.

That weekend, MacSwiney's first in London, also marked the beginning of the daily ritual wherein Father Dominic, the family, and a close coterie of friends held vigil by the bedside. They worked out the scheduling as best they could so that somebody was present as often as the prison governor would allow.

'After a bit he did not like to be there without some one of us,' said Muriel. 'My brother-in-law [Sean] came over, and his other sister [Annie] afterwards. For of course they were afraid that he would die at any moment. Nothing but his faith kept him alive. There is no doubt about that. He did not like to be left alone, so one of us would go in the morning, and another at noon, and another in the evening.'

Realising very early on that international publicity might be the best hope for gaining his release, no visit went unreported to the press. Thrust into the spotlight in the middle of London, where suddenly they found themselves fielding inquiries from reporters from all over the world, Mary, Muriel, and Annie morphed quickly into spokespersons for the Lord Mayor, offering eyewitness and often poignant updates on his condition.

'His spirit is as strong as ever,' said Muriel to the *Daily Mail* outside the prison gates on Sunday afternoon. 'Although he could scarcely speak above a whisper, his determination to resist is unchanged. I support him in everything.' The reporter noted that she looked relaxed and cheerful among the many well-wishers already gathering around the jail to pray for her husband. That his detention was now the talk of the country can be gleaned by the fact that on Monday, 23 August, less than a week after his arrival in London, MacSwiney's case warranted an editorial in the *Times*.

'He has appealed to the weapon of the hunger strike, and now, in weakened health, confronts the Government with an embarrassing, though a familiar, dilemma. In our view one course alone is open to them in this instance. Had the Lord Mayor of Cork been tried and sentenced for complicity in murder or in serious outrage, we should have held them justified in permitting him to suffer the full consequences of his action. But his offences are not of this character; and in the eyes of his fellow countrymen, bear no moral stigma. If he dies, the majority of the Irish people will conscientiously regard him as a martyr, and the

Government as his murderers. We can scarcely conceive that Ministers, if they remember the storm which followed the death of Thomas Ashe [an Irish volunteer who died from force-feeding while in custody in 1917], and the shipwreck towards which it first drove the Irish Convention, should desire such a result. Even if they are gambling on the eventual surrender of their prisoner, the game is perilous. Such advantage as might accrue to them were Alderman MacSwiney, from religious or other motives, to yield, would be, at the best, unreal; whereas the detriment, if he persist to the end and by his death stir the angriest depths of Irish feeling, may well be irretrievable. True statesmanship avoids such issues ...'

Strong words from the *Times* that Monday morning set the tone for an action-packed day. After his examination of the prisoner, Dr Higson warned him again of how serious his condition was becoming. Having failed to persuade MacSwiney to eat by pleading that he'd surely be of more use to Ireland alive than dead, Higson also informed him that once he became unconscious the doctor's own medical duty would be to feed him liquids in order to try to keep him alive.

Among the visitors to Brixton Prison on the afternoon of Day 11 was a high-powered religious delegation led by Archbishop Daniel Mannix of Melbourne, Australia. A native of Charleville, County Cork, and a former President of St Patrick's College in Maynooth, Mannix was a polemical figure whose outspoken nationalism had led the British to forcibly prevent him from landing in Queenstown earlier that month. Banned from setting foot in Ireland, he had been basically 'quarantined' in England.

His visit to the jail, accompanied by Bishop Fogarty of

Killaloe and Bishop Foley of Ballarat, was only sanctioned on condition that they undertook not to encourage MacSwiney to continue abstaining from food.

'Could sane Englishmen do nothing to stay the hands of those who were sending him to his grave?' asked Mannix shortly after departing the jail.

'He is very prostrate,' warned Fogarty.

Prostrate he may have been but defiant he remained. From his prison bed, MacSwiney dictated a message he wanted made public that day. 'We must be prepared for casualties in the last battle for Irish independence. Let every man offer his life and the future of the Irish Republic will be safe. God is with us.'

Others were on his side too. At a demonstration calling for 'Peace with Russia' held at Trafalgar Square in London that Monday afternoon, George Lansbury, editor of the left-wing *Daily Herald* and a former MP for Bow and Bromley, told an audience of 7,000 people that the Lord Mayor of Cork was currently being murdered in Brixton Prison by the British government. He even went as far as to ask his fellow agitators what they were going to do about this outrage.

Back at Brixton, Mary MacSwiney didn't like what she saw of her brother's disimproving condition. After passing on his call to arms, she urgently telegrammed Annie back in Cork. 'Just returned from Terry. Much weaker. Be ready to cross tomorrow.' Annie and Sean MacSwiney were on their way to London within hours.

His condition deteriorated further on Tuesday when he was visited by his wife and sister, and a delegation of two colleagues from Cork Corporation, Aldermen Liam de Róiste (who had proposed his election as mayor) and Professor William Stockley. The chair of English at UCC, where he first met MacSwiney, and the victim of an attempted assassination earlier in the year, Stockley's presence sparked an odd confession from MacSwiney: in his current predicament, his mind was still full of remembered lines from Shakespeare's *Macbeth*.

'I am for ever saying them to myself,' he said. 'I never could have thought they were so true.'

Stockley offered a detailed description of the scene he discovered in the ward.

'He lies on a prison bed in pain and restless, panting often and moving parched lips, his voice a whisper,' said Stockley of what he witnessed in the prison that day. 'One can indeed nearly always hear, but only if one places one's ear very close to his mouth which utters no complaint, but which lets his thoughts be known that "the authorities will hold on to me as long as they can, even if they ever let me go". It is bitter irony but it contains truth to say that our hero-victim is fighting for England's "war aims", those fine words belied by base words in Ireland ...

'Terence MacSwiney greets his friends affectionately, gratefully, and has even a nobler and more beautiful smile of kindliness for those coming to see him now in his helplessness than when he was amongst us in all the manly vigour and untiring energy of his work for others, for friends not to say for the poor foe too blind to see that all the world is saved by the man who is ready to lose his mortal life, who dies for justice, indifferent to this passing show unless its actors are seen in the light of the things that are eternal.'

Now almost two weeks without food, MacSwiney's physical

state had already diminished so much that had an order for his immediate release been issued that very day, he would not have been strong enough to be moved. All around him, though, the maelstrom continued to whirl.

Moved by the sight of his friend's suffering, and perhaps motivated by his softly-spoken admonition to him to 'do everything you can for the cause', Professor Stockley sat down in the Cosmo Hotel later that day and wrote a long letter to the *Manchester Guardian*. In a typically literary piece, he invoked Tennyson's Iron Duke ('who never spoke against a foe'), the example of Calvary, and the persecution of Christians in ancient Rome. Having compared what he called MacSwiney's moral tour de force in Brixton to that of Sir Thomas More in the Tower of London, he emphasised again that the mayor was dying for the same cause for which so many Englishmen had died in the Great War.

'But if you Englishmen of the better hopes still and of the old honour, if you wish for inspiration, kneel by that bed in Brixton Prison, watch that panting form on your rack, hear his whispered resolve to die for his country. I say he dies for yours. He dies for what makes life worth living in your country, in every country... If the victim dies for the good cause, for the cause of every soul's right, he has won.'

Meanwhile, Mary MacSwiney was a little more prosaic in the telegram she sent to Prime Minister Lloyd George, then on his summer holidays in Lucerne, Switzerland, on Tuesday, 24 August, Day 12.

'My brother, Lord Mayor of Cork, at point of death in Brixton Prison,' she wrote. 'Home Secretary says Cabinet decision to allow him to die. In event of death his relatives and people of Ireland will hold you and your Government responsible for murder.'

Others were doing their bit to highlight his plight. Back in Cork, workers downed tools for an hour that day and many used the stoppage to attend masses being said for his release. Labour leaders also warned their members to be ready for further calls to action. In quick succession, institutions like the Cork Harbour Board, the Board of Guardians, the Cork Trades and Labour Council, and the County Insurance Committee passed resolutions protesting MacSwiney's deportation and subsequently sent wires of complaint to the Home Office. As a gesture of support, the Cork County Board cancelled all forthcoming GAA fixtures and adjourned indefinitely.

Beyond Cork, public bodies were offering their expressions of solidarity too. The Dublin and Rathdown Boards of Guardians, and the Waterford and North Tipperary County Councils all adopted resolutions demanding his release and echoing the warning that the British government would be responsible for murder if he died. In Dundalk, a thousand employees of the Great Northern Railway stopped work at noon on Wednesday morning and marched to the Dominican Church where Very Rev. Flood recited the rosary for 'a man lying prostrate in an English dungeon'.

Amid this growing clamour, Lloyd George was forced to interrupt his holidays and to give an official response. Having spent most of the morning of the 25th reading various communications he'd received about the case, he dictated the following statement to be distributed to the press.

'I have received several communications here concerning the Lord Mayor of Cork. I deeply regret his decision to starve himself and the suffering he thus, of deliberate choice, is inflicting, not only on himself but on his relations and friends; but the Cabinet are responsible for preserving to the best of their ability the machinery upon which the protection of life and good order depend in the country. If the Lord Mayor were released, every hunger-striker, whatever his offence, would have to be let off. A law which is a respecter of persons is no law. If the Cabinet, therefore, departed from its decision, a complete break-down of the whole machinery of law and government in Ireland would inevitably follow. Whatever the consequences it cannot take that responsibility.

'The release some weeks ago of hunger-strikers in Ireland [at one point nearly 200 Irish internees had been fasting in Wormwood Scrubs] was followed by an outburst of cruel murder and outrage, one defenceless man being shot within sight of the altar of his church, and no expression of protest or regret ever came, even in that case, from the political organisation to which the Lord Mayor belongs. The very crime for which he was convicted indicates that he was concerned in the conspiracy against the constabulary, who are the defenders of order in Ireland. It is the first duty of the Government to afford every protection to these brave men, who are discharging their difficult duty in the face of grave peril. I may add that every invitation to discuss with those who are, for the moment, the spokesmen for Irish Nationalism a peaceable settlement of Ireland, has been spurned by them. The latest offer of the Government made in Parliament on the date of its adjournment has been scornfully rejected by their leader, and we are driven to fight against a claim for the complete secession of Ireland, North and South, from the British Empire. This claim we can never recognise.'

Predictably, this wasn't sufficient for Mary MacSwiney who made public her reply.

'I made no appeal to you for exceptional treatment for my brother. I warned you of your responsibility in the event of his death. He and his comrades [those striking in Cork] demand their freedom as a right. If my brother or any of his comrades must die to win that freedom, they do so willingly, and we are proud of them, but their death lies on you and your Government. Self-determination, for which you say England went to war, is as much Ireland's right as Poland's. We claim it and will have it, even if you have decided that my brother is to die.'

As the Prime Minister was making his position unequivocally clear, Dublin Castle released a statement, wishing to clarify that MacSwiney was arrested at a meeting of the Cork Brigade of the IRA, not, as had been reported in many outlets, at a Sinn Féin arbitration court. It was hoped that educating the British public about his role in the paramilitary campaign rather than the legal affairs of the municipality would stay the burgeoning sympathy for his plight.

Oblivious to all the politicking, MacSwiney continued to ebb away. On 25 August, Day 13, his condition suddenly deteriorated. During a visit from the newly-arrived Sean and Annie, he collapsed and received the last rites from Father Dominic. Not for the last time, it looked like he would not live through the night and, perhaps inevitably, rumours that he had died reached Ireland almost immediately.

'He is facing death with a brave and Christian spirit,' said Fr Dominic to reporters outside the prison. 'The Lord Mayor is in a very critical condition. I was with him at five o'clock this evening when he collapsed. He rallied afterwards after medical treatment. He was not unconscious when I left; he was resigned to his fate. I am afraid it is too late to hope for his recovery now.'

So poorly indeed had he looked that day that the following telegram from Mary MacSwiney was read out at a meeting of the Cork Corporation's Law and Finances Committee that night.

'Lord Mayor much weaker: collapsed this afternoon; wife sent for urgently. Lloyd George's answer is impertinence; I made no appeal and asked for no exception; the right claimed for Lord Mayor is claimed equally for each of his comrades.'

Those lines cast a pall of gloom over the room inside City Hall. Councillor Sean O'Leary moved that they adjourn the meeting because, given the time it took for the message to be delivered from London, there was a chance the Lord Mayor might already be dead, and if he wasn't, it seemed he soon would be.

His proximity to death had begun to swell the crowds gathering around the prison each day. Some prayed. Others shouted pro-Sinn Féin slogans to annoy the police. All were outnumbered on Wednesday night by newcomers, who'd come to attend what was billed as a 'Labour Rally' to protest the government's treatment of MacSwiney and to demand his immediate release. Organised by the *Daily Herald* and its editor George Lansbury, a couple of thousand people heard speeches lambasting the British government's policy delivered from a platform located in a side street near the jail.

What began as a peaceful demonstration (though one punctuated by regular chants of 'Up Sinn Féin' and 'Up the Rebels') eventually degenerated into a riot. As the majority of the crowd were readying themselves to head away from the prison in a formal procession, their pro-Sinn Féin banners still aloft, a squadron of police came from the direction of the jail, marching towards Brixton Hill. Stones were thrown at the new arrivals and soon batons were drawn and all hell broke loose.

Windows of nearby houses were shattered in the mêlée and every movable object was pressed into service as a missile by the protestors. Loose bricks were prised from walls, railings hastily removed from gardens, and even walking canes flew through the air. Soon, mounted police came charging along to try to clear the area. They found the going tough too. One of the riders was felled by a projectile to the skull, another was, as the newspapers put it, also 'unhorsed'. Reinforcements arrived to supplement the police presence and finally, after the cavalry succeeded in dispersing the crowd by ushering them in small groups down nearby side-streets, order was restored.

Despite the injuries sustained by both policemen and civilians, no arrests were made that night. That may explain why, on the following evening, another crowd of several thousand people lined the streets of Brixton. Suitably chastened by the previous debacle, the authorities were better prepared and took no chances of a repeat performance. When the mounted police emerged onto the streets, most spectators took refuge in nearby gardens. This led to the bizarre situation where horses were being manoeuvred onto the front lawns in order to persuade the protestors to keep moving and to leave the area near the prison.

In an unrelated incident, Charles Barry, a sixty-one-year old surgeon from South Lambeth, approached the prison earlier that day, knocked on the door, and demanded to be granted an audience with the Lord Mayor of Cork. He was refused entry and then arrested for being drunk and disorderly. In court, Barry claimed he'd been so concerned about the mayor that he'd purchased a bottle of meat juice and went to the jail in the hope of persuading MacSwiney to take some nourishment. After one of his maids testified that Barry had left his house perfectly sober just half an hour before his arrest, the judge discharged the case, stating that his 'excitement might have been mistaken for drunkenness'.

CHAPTER 3

The Powerlessness of King George

SEE, though the oil be low more purely still and higher
The flame burns in the body's lamp! The watchers still
Gaze with unseeing eyes while the Promethean Will,
The Uncreated Light, the Everlasting Fire
Sustains itself against the torturer's desire
Even as the fabled Titan chained upon the hill.
Burn on, shine on, thou immortality, until
We, too, have lit our lamps at the funeral pyre;
Till we, too, can be noble, unshakable, undismayed:
Till we, too, can burn with the holy flame, and know
There is that within us can triumph over pain,
And go to death, alone, slowly, and unafraid.
The candles of God are already burning row on row:
Farewell, lightbringer, fly to thy heaven again!
'Terence MacSwiney', a poem by AE, published in
***The Times*, 31 August 1920.**

On the morning of Tuesday, 24 August 1920, almost 600 delegates convened in Dublin for what was titled the Irish Peace Conference. Drawn largely from the Anglo-Irish communities around the island, the gathering was speckled with Protestant and Catholic clerics, and also included veteran politicos such as Sir Horace Plunkett and Sir Thomas Esmonde. Even before the official start of business under the chairmanship of Sir Nugent Everard, Lord-Lieutenant for County Meath, a resolution was passed that a message be immediately sent to Downing Street requesting the release of the Lord Mayor. Having received a tepid response to that particular missive, the meeting went one step further two days later and wrote directly to King George V himself.

'We, the undersigned, being members of the Standing Committee appointed by the Irish Peace Conference at its session on Tuesday, August 24, most respectfully implore your Majesty by the exercise of your royal prerogative to release the Lord Mayor of Cork, now at the point of death in Brixton Gaol. We base our prayer in circumstances of unparalleled national emergency upon the highest of all grounds of public policy, the necessity of a great act of conciliation to open the path to the peace which we are seeking to achieve, domestic peace in Ireland and international peace between Ireland and Great Britain. We submit that this great object immeasurably transcends in importance any question of mere administrative principle.'

By the last days of August, just three weeks into the hunger strike, King George V was being inundated with letters and telegrams of this type. They came from all over Britain and Ireland, from all walks of life, and each had the same theme, pleading for the monarch to intervene, to show clemency, and to spare MacSwiney's life. Famously described by AN Wilson as 'a strange mixture of cowardice and bravery, the petty and the grand', the king had come under fire in the preceding years for not doing more to save the life of his cousin Tsar Nicholas II and the rest of the Romanovs after the Russian Revolution. Little wonder then that this sudden barrage of requests worried him greatly.

On 26 August, the king dispatched a telegram to the Home Office, apprising them of the growing demands being made upon him and indicating his desire to do something to appease the baying crowd.

'I am receiving appeals from many quarters, including the editor of the *Manchester Guardian*, to exercise my prerogative. The government knows my views and while appreciating difficulty of their position, I still advocate clemency.'

The reply from Edward Shortt was brief and to the point. 'Mr. Sec. Shortt deeply regrets decision must stand. Irish Chief Secretary informed Mr. Shortt release of Lord Mayor would have disastrous results in Ireland and probably lead to mutiny of both police and military in Ireland.'

Obviously concerned at the sudden royal interest in the hunger strike, Shortt quickly brought the matter to the attention of Lloyd George. 'The King telegraphs to me that he is receiving many appeals to himself to exercise his prerogative and he advocates clemency. I have informed him what [Hamar] Greenwood [Chief-Secretary of Ireland] told me as to the effect of release on military and police in Ireland and said the decision of the cabinet must stand. I discussed the position with Balfour and Churchill. I have also referred the King to your statement.'

Shortt's summit with cabinet members AJ Balfour and Winston Churchill had taken place on 25 August at 10 Downing Street. It can be taken as a measure of the impact events at Brixton Prison were already having that this trio of cabinet heavyweights, one past Prime Minister, one future, debated 'the effect on the country of the apparent climb-down of the government if he [MacSwiney] were to be released.' At one point, they discussed the possibility of authorising his release on medical grounds but decided to hold off on doing anything concrete until they could first enlist the advice of General Macready, commanding officer in Ireland.

After breaking for dinner, the trio discovered that the London evening papers were carrying Lloyd George's unequivocal statement from Lucerne regarding the impossibility of allowing MacSwiney to leave prison. If that, as much as Macready's subsequent counsel against any release, made their own pondering rather moot, their conflab showed how much consternation the Lord Mayor was causing in the upper levels of the British administration.

'I am very sorry that we differ on the subject of MacSwiney,' wrote JCC Davidson, private secretary to Bonar Law, in a letter on 30 August to Lord Stamfordham, the king's private secretary, with whom he was also good friends. 'Regrettable as his death will be, I believe that when he dies, in this country at any rate, the Lord Mayor of Cork will pass into limbo.'

Whatever the unanimity of opinion among the ministers, this conflict between the head of state and the cabinet had re-opened old wounds. This wasn't the first time King George V had antagonised the government by questioning the wisdom of its conduct in Ireland.

'The issue became a major source of friction between the king and his government, and another manifestation of the king's displeasure with the conduct of the government's Irish policy,' wrote Francis Costello. 'Previously, in questioning the efficacy of their policy of coercion and reprisals, the king asked the chief secretary for Ireland "if this policy of reprisals is to be continued and if so where it will lead …?"'

That question bothered the king more and more as summer drew to a close, his frustration compounded by the fact that he wasn't even receiving an official briefing on the hunger strike. Just like those writing to him on a daily basis, he was forced to rely on the newspapers for updates about MacSwiney's condition. Stamfordham voiced the king's concern about being out of the loop to Balfour, who apologised for not keeping him 'adequately informed', before dismissing the concerns of the public regarding MacSwiney.

As a compromise solution, King George was also advocating the idea of putting MacSwiney under a type of house arrest.

'The King feels that the probable results arising from MacSwiney's death will be far more serious and far-reaching than if he were taken out of prison,' wrote Stamfordham on 28 August, 'and moved into a private house where his wife could be with him, but kept under strict surveillance so that he could not escape and return to Ireland.'

Even his wife, Queen Mary, herself the recipient of pleas on behalf of the Corkman, wished to issue a statement about the case, expressing hope that 'King's Ministers who have the power and are humane men may see their way to spare Ireland from additional sorrow.' Even this bland expression of concern was deemed too politically-charged a sentiment to be released at that time.

A revealing glimpse of the goings-on at Balmoral that summer can be gleaned from Dr Norman MacLean, a Scottish churchman who was a guest of the royal household at that time. MacLean was yet another to request that the monarch do his bit to effect MacSwiney's release, a suggestion that prompted the following response from George V.

'I have for some days been trying to save the Lord Mayor of Cork but I have so far found nobody to agree with me. You have said only what I have thought. No doubt I have authority sufficient to save MacSwiney. If I sent a telegram to Brixton tonight, he would be released in the morning. But I have to consider what would happen if I exercised that authority.'

While the king sought solace in a cigarette, MacLean pressed him further.

'May I venture to ask, Sir, what would happen if your Majesty exercised the Royal prerogative of mercy?'

'This is what would happen,' replied the king. 'I would not have a single Minister by noon tomorrow – not even Mr Balfour. Where can I find another Ministry with the Opposition only a handful? I have a power which I cannot exercise. Knowing as I do, the discomforts of the constitutional monarch, I am thankful that I am not an absolute one.'

His fear of using the royal prerogative and losing his cabinet was no secret. In a letter to Horatio Bottomley MP that was also

released to the newspapers, Stamfordham captured the constitutional difficulties facing his boss.

'Even if the King were in favour of such a course, it could only
be effected by the sovereign's personal action in face of the advice
of his Ministers, and with the presumable result of their resigna-
tion, and also the further risk that the country at large might
regard the price paid as too high for the object attained and
blame his Majesty for creating a grave political crisis at a time of
special national stress and anxiety.'

Meanwhile, the king continued to take flak from all sides. The
Westmeath branch of the Comrades of the Great War sent a
telegram to him asking for the release as an act of clemency. The
Roscommon chapter of the Discharged Soldiers' and Sailors'
Federation voiced a protest about his treatment. Sir James Long,
chairman of the Cork Harbour Commission and member of the
governing body of UCC, wrote to Buckingham Palace, respectfully requesting 'that your Majesty remove the title conferred on
me in 1910'. Redmond Howard, nephew of Major John Redmond, made an appeal to the throne in which he invoked the
contribution made by his uncle to the effort of improving relations between the two countries.

'In thanking you for your telegram of yesterday to the King, I
am commanded to express his Majesty's appreciation of your
assurances of hopefulness that, in spite of the very grave condition of affairs in Ireland, the work of reconciliation between the
two races may yet be accomplished,' wrote Stamfordham to
Howard. 'The King fully realises the services rendered and sacrifices made by your family in this cause, and regards with all the
more consideration your appeal, which will receive immediate

and careful attention.'

It didn't matter how much attention this request and all the others were receiving in the royal household. The government had set its course and no amount of complaining from George V was going to effect a change of direction.

'The King is an old coward,' complained Lloyd George in Lucerne. 'He is frightened to death and is anxious to make it clear that he has nothing to do with it.'

Through all this politicking, MacSwiney's condition was worsening on a daily basis. As August came to a close, he was visibly weaker, had begun to cough a lot more (Redmond Howard would cite the lung problems in a personal note dispatched to the queen asking her to use her influence to gain his release), and had developed neuritis in his arms. He was still accepting visitors, however, and though his voice was noticeably faltering, continued to express defiance to all who came to sit by the bedside.

'Your lordship, my conscience is quite at ease about the course I am taking,' said MacSwiney to the Bishop of Cork, Daniel Cohalan. 'I made a general confession this morning; I receive Holy Communion every morning; I might never again be so well prepared for death; I gladly make the sacrifice; they are trying to break the spirit of our people; my death will be an example and an appeal to our young men to make every sacrifice for Ireland.'

The pair had history. MacSwiney had once asked the bishop to intervene on his behalf and to try to persuade Muriel's recalcitrant mother to bless their forthcoming marriage, a union of which she did not approve. Cohalan spoke to Mrs Murphy but to no avail. Now, he sat next to MacSwiney in a London prison and was so moved by his experience in the prison that he wrote a lengthy and quite extraordinary letter to the *Times* of London.

Apart from calling for self-government for Ireland, he castigated the British government for its failure to properly investigate the assassination of Tomás MacCurtain and also blamed them for the IRA's subsequent murder of RIC District Inspector Swanzy in Lisburn. Swanzy had been killed a few days earlier because it was believed he'd organised the attack on MacCurtain, and Cohalan reasoned that the authorities should have removed him from Ireland when they had the chance.

'... the offences imputed to the Lord Mayor, as stated, have no substance,' wrote Cohalan. 'The tribunal was a military tribunal. The sentence of two years' imprisonment has no moral sanction; it is a manifest injustice. And as the sentence has no moral sanction, the Lord Mayor should not be left to die in gaol; the Lord Mayor should be released at once. May I ask you Sir, is it just to prolong the suffering of such a noble specimen of our humanity?'

On the same page of the newspaper that day came a remarkably similar if less elongated plea from the Reverend FB Meyer, a legendary Baptist preacher and evangelist at Christ Church in London. Dubbed 'the Christian socialist', Meyer urged every minister of religion throughout the country to telegraph an appeal 'to the Prime Minister in Lucerne, and to the Secretary for Ireland, urging for the release of the Lord Mayor of Cork.'

The *Times* was suitably impressed by the ecumenical storm now brewing on its own letters page to devote editorials on 28 and 30 August to the MacSwiney case. In the first of these pieces (they were reputedly written by RJB Shaw, an Irish barrister based in London), Lloyd George was taken to task and the entire conduct of British policy in Ireland called into question. The second of them succinctly addressed the pressure being brought to bear on the king from so many different quarters.

'… the Christian conscience of this country must question instinctively the morality of the Government's decision. The voice of protest has been loud and unmistakable. There has been an appeal to the Crown. The King has, in accordance with his own wise practice and that of his immediate predecessors, adhered strictly to constitutional usage. Nevertheless, the country is aware that, within a sphere undoubtedly his own, he has acted with promptness and due sense of the gravity of the issue involved. Moreover, even though the Lord Mayor of Cork may have failed to divert settled condemnation from the acts for which he has been sentenced, he has, by the very quality of his courage, appealed directly, and most dramatically, to the mercy of a strong and generous people.'

With the case now front and centre in the English capital, garnering massive amounts of column inches in the most influential papers there, it was little wonder that Liam de Róiste, one of Cork Corporation's official representatives in London, wrote in his diary that week: 'If released alive he will have won, if released in death, he shall still win … MacSwiney in Brixton. Lloyd George on the Swiss Mountains. Was there ever material for an epic such as this?'

Whatever about an epic, there was a soap operatic element to the daily parade of visitors walking through the throng of onlookers at the prison gates. On the afternoon of Saturday, 28

August, Day 16 of the hunger strike, de Róiste himself strode the gauntlet, accompanied by Professor Stockley and Bishop Cohalan. Afterwards, the two city councillors issued a joint statement.

'Terence MacSwiney is as calm, as thoughtful for others, as affectionate in his friendliness as of yore, and he does not forget the Irish work going on in the world, and he encourages each of us to go away through the country and to do anything that may help right action for our country's good. He said the doctor thinks him little changed for the moment. He is thinner and more sunken in the face. The doctor adds that at any moment may come the change which will put our sufferer beyond hope of bodily release.'

The fact that almost everybody who went in made some sort of pronouncement when they came out illustrated that the propaganda war was ongoing. That week's edition of the *Spectator* magazine was accusing MacSwiney of trying to commit suicide, and so the provision of updates and stirring quotes to journalists was as much about countering the negative spin from opponents as it was about promoting MacSwiney's own cause.

The same day that Stockley and de Róiste were giving their impressions to the press, helpfully mentioning that they witnessed a variety of food being placed upon his pillow to tempt him from his fast, Mary MacSwiney followed up her daily visit with an emphatic denial of malicious reports that the prison doctor was administering proteins to her brother in his drinking water.

'I told the doctor that nothing of that sort should be done, and that it was absolutely against the wishes of his friends, and also said that if the Government wished to release my brother it should do so before the eleventh hour,' she said. 'The Government should either release him or let him die. It would not be fair to keep him lingering in pain by artificial means. I have in my hands now a package of pastilles of water of Lourdes, which was sent to my brother by friends. He refused to use them, saying there might be nourishment in them. He would bathe his forehead with the holy water but said he would have nothing to do with the pastilles.'

His demeanour that last weekend in August was calm and his condition stable. Although he didn't sleep much on Sunday night, he was in good form for Mary's visit on Monday morning, 30 August, Day 18.

'I am convinced I will not be released,' he said to his sister, 'and it will be better for my country if I am not released.' There was no regret in his faint voice. There was no fear. It was just a fact that he realised and seemed to accept. When Mary mentioned that so many influential English newspapers were by then evincing sympathy for his protest, he told her: 'If the people of England were sincere, one day's stoppage of work would secure my release.'

That feistiness disappeared on Monday afternoon when he took a turn so bad he was soon listed as critical. Muriel MacSwiney was present for three hours and when she emerged from the prison, journalists noted that she looked pale and wore the troubled visage of a woman suffering under great stress. Gone was the relaxed and bright look of just ten days previous. The strain was starting to tell after she'd endured another tortuous stint during which her husband was conscious but unable to speak, and, apparently, moving ever closer to inevitable death.

Very often, the only sound in the room between them was the hacking cough that visibly pained him as he lay in the bed. The doctor had also come in to remind Mrs MacSwiney again that the Lord Mayor had, in his opinion, passed the point where food would do him any good.

After doing his own usual nightly vigil at the bedside that evening, Father Dominic emerged and confessed he found the mayor considerably weaker and undoubtedly nearing death, Yet, as always, the priest still paid tribute to his courage in the face of the ordeal, telling reporters he continued to show 'indomitable will'.

That spirit manifested itself again on Tuesday morning by which time he'd recovered enough strength to deliver a message of solidarity to his colleagues in Cork Jail, his fellow hunger strikers whose protest was receiving nothing like the extensive coverage of his own plight.

'Greetings to all my comrades in Cork Jail,' said MacSwiney. 'I am with them in spirit, thinking of them always and praying hourly for their welfare.'

There was no shortage of others continuing to take up verbal arms on his behalf. At a meeting of the Labour Party mayors of London boroughs held in Battersea Town Hall, a motion was passed to telegraph Lloyd George in Switzerland to warn him about the possible violent ramifications because of 'the cruel vindictiveness of the policy of his Majesty's Government.' JR Clynes, a Labour MP in Manchester and the son of an Irish immigrant, sent a telegram of his own to Switzerland. 'The release of MacSwiney would be an act of justice and mercy above Court's martial law. His death will add enormously to the dangers which the kingdom is facing.'

None of those quite matches the lyricism of James O'Grady, Labour MP for Leeds South-East and a child of Irish parents, who, in a public letter, lambasted the Welsh Prime Minister on the grounds of ethnic disloyalty.

'You claim to be a Celt! Whenever did a Celt resist an appeal for mercy? If ever he did, then he was a traitor to the race and to the psychology of the race. Lord Mayor MacSwiney is a brother of ours sentenced to two years of imprisonment for a political offence. If your own offences in that direction received the desserts that your opponents of 20 or more recent years declare they deserve, you should be committed to the torture of British prisons for the rest of your natural life.'

In prison, the death watch continued. When MacSwiney awoke on 1 September, Day 20, his brother Sean was by the bedside. He'd been there all night. That was how serious things had become. He was there because it was assumed the end might come at any moment. To pass the time early that morning and to keep him abreast of the news from home, Sean read his brother stories from the *Freeman's Journal*. It seemed to brighten his mood to hear of Ireland. As was now the routine, Muriel, Annie and Mary then came in to do shifts of their own throughout the day. None of the women were heartened by what they saw, all admitting afterwards that he was looking worse and worse.

'I should not be surprised if I were summoned to the prison before the morning,' said Father Dominic at 9 o'clock that night, upon finishing his visit during which he had, as was now usual, administered Holy Communion. 'The Lord Mayor is very much worse than he has been since he came to Brixton, and the ghostly pallor of his face, which tonight I noticed for the first time, gave me a shock. His complexion was naturally sallow; tonight it is deathly pale. He has not slept during the day and he is very restless. The pain in his heart still continues and he cannot bear the weight of the bedclothes over the region of his heart. The numbness in his right arm is extending to his right leg. His right side however is not yet affected. He is still perfectly conscious, but he spoke with greater difficulty than ever – in short painful grasps. His face and head are much cooler than they have been and there is a kind of dewy perspiration on his forehead. These symptoms fill me with alarm.'

On 2 September the prognosis was no better. His arms were being periodically massaged to try to relieve the pain of the neuritis but an air of gloom hung over the room.

'I feel that the end is near,' said Mary. 'He realises he is very low and asked me this morning to read to him from the Devotional Manual, "Certain Thoughts on Death".' Her brother Sean went even further, telling reporters that but for two hours of sleep that he was able to get on Wednesday night, the mayor might have been dead already.

These poignant details were carried in the following day's newspapers alongside one more official reminder that as long as he remained committed to the hunger strike, MacSwiney was doomed to die.

'None of the mercy which some seek to invoke for the Lord Mayor was shown the eighty policemen who have lost their lives in Ireland,' said Hamar Greenwood, Chief-Secretary for Ireland, in a statement from Lucerne, where he had travelled in order to personally brief Lloyd George on the situation.

That the case continued to divide public and political opinion throughout Britain was demonstrated that day by John Hamilton-Gordon, the Marquess of Aberdeen, adding his voice to the chorus urging MacSwiney's release. This was newsworthy because the Marquess had served two stints as Lord-Lieutenant of Ireland and had finished his second sojourn as recently as 1915. Here was a man with intimate knowledge of Irish affairs and British policy in the country.

'To compare his case with that of a criminal designing to escape punishment is not only callous,' wrote Hamilton-Gordon, 'but shows desperate inability to understand the spirit and motives which led this young man to what is in essence an act of self-sacrifice for the sake of a cause in which with all his heart and soul he believes.'

As the verbal jabs continued from each side, Mary MacSwiney kept up the grim task of updating the press about the prisoner's condition while simultaneously squashing growing rumours that he must surely be receiving food by some surreptitious means. Upon leaving Brixton Prison that Friday night, 3 September, Day 22, she described him as 'conscious but sinking fast' before reiterating to reporters that the only sustenance he received, apart from occasional glasses of water, was some medically-prescribed salts given each morning to prevent blood poisoning

Inevitably moved and occasionally inflamed by the daily drip feed of information about his plight, work stoppages had now become commonplace throughout Ireland as the ordinary citizens sought to take what action they could to demonstrate their empathy with their compatriot dying in a London prison. With the workers at Jacob's Biscuit Factory and McCren's Shirts among the 4,000 to have downed tools earlier in the week, more factories, shops and public houses shut down for a time on Saturday, 4 September so staff could attend masses being said in churches across Dublin to offer spiritual comfort to MacSwiney and to his hunger-striking comrades in Cork.

Over 300 employees of the Irish Paper Mill Company in Clondalkin walked in procession to hear Reverend Father Traynor recite the rosary in a nearby church. Afterwards, they marched in unison back to their work stations. In a show of solidarity, The Irish Paper Mill Company announced that it would pay them for the time they took off. These events were not going unnoticed and the British authorities in Dublin were being inundated with demands for information and updates from their concerned colleagues in London.

'The Cork Martyr has filled the stage again today, and "London" shows signs of having got the wind up,' wrote Mark Sturgis, an Under-Secretary at Dublin Castle, in his diary entry for that day. 'I seem to have spent the day with cipher telegrams. The pick of the bunch is LG [Lloyd George] to Bonar Law for transmission to us asking the opinion of (1) the Civil (2) the Military and (3) Police heads if (A) he dies (B) is released … If he dies we expect a big row but think we are quite able to deal with it. If he is let out we do not see how we can ever hold another hunger striker again and must let out the present men in Cork Gaol. The release of MacSwiney would not affect soldiers much either way, but it would take the heart right out of the police … It would convince everybody that that Gov. had been bluffing again and would make our job impossible. I'm sure there could be no excuse for it except the certainty of Peace as a result and that is impossible.'

As the size and frequency of the prayer vigils was worrying the British, MacSwiney himself was struggling anew. When Muriel sat beside him that Saturday afternoon, Day 23, the only time he talked was to complain about how exhausted he felt. The lack of any sustenance was taking such a toll that he was almost unable to converse with his sisters during their visits. In the absence of any meaningful contribution from himself, a war of words continued to rage about him.

On Sunday, 5 September, Day 24, Andrew Bonar Law issued a public statement emphasising the government's intransigence. He declared that as an 'avowed rebel', MacSwiney had been lucky not to have been shot upon capture, a belief that prompted Liam de Róiste to ask: 'Since when has it become the universal practice of civilised nations to immediately shoot on capture an unarmed man?'

Bonar Law also touched again upon the belief that the release of the prisoner would lead to a complete breakdown of the machinery of law and government in Ireland. While acknowledging 'how large a part sentiment plays in all human affairs', he was unequivocal about what the future held.

'The policy of the government has been made clear from the outset, and if the Lord Mayor dies in prison the responsibility will rest in some degree upon those who, by their repeated appeals, have encouraged the belief that the Government should prove insincere in their determination, and the hope that notwithstanding all declaration to the contrary, his misguided action would eventually lead to his release.'

Annie MacSwiney authored the reply from the family, describing Bonar Law's words as 'an insult to freedom, honour, truth and every democratic principle. Eighty per cent of the Irish people have asserted the right to freedom which was so fulsomely lauded in the case of Poland and Czechoslovakia. Do you call the Poles rebels because they are determined to be free? Why then do you call the Irish rebels because they desire likewise? You and the people who elected you are causing the death of Terence MacSwiney and his comrades because they have a living belief in and will die for the ideals you pretend you fought for.'

CHAPTER 4

Labour Pains and Accusations

Dear Madam,

I have your letter and as desired beg to inform you that the balance lying to the credit of the right Honourable Terence MacSwiney at this office is (pounds) 51.12.4 (say fifty-one pounds, twelve shillings and four pence). I enclose a blank cheque which may be required. I should like to take this opportunity of personally expressing my great regret at the circumstances which necessitated your communication.

Letter from the manager of the Munster and Leinster Bank in Cork to Muriel MacSwiney c/o Brixton Prison, 8 September 1920.

On 5 September, Day 24, Father Denys Mathieu came to the gates of the prison, carrying a bottle of holy water from Lourdes that he wished to give to MacSwiney. Just over three years earlier the Benedictine priest had given permission for the prisoner's wedding to be held at a quaint little church in Bromyard, Herefordshire that Mathieu had almost single-handedly built to cater for the area's Catholics. The marriage of Muriel Murphy and MacSwiney, presided over by Father Augustine, was the first to be conducted in St Joseph's and was carried out under the same peculiar circumstances as much of their relationship.

The pair had first met at a party in Tilly Fleischmann's house in Cork at Christmas, 1915, an evening when MacSwiney read poetry and his future wife gave a piano recital. Twelve years her senior, he was the first 'rebel' that the English-educated Muriel, who moved in very different circles, had ever met, and his arrest by the British soon after their first encounter may have added to the glamour surrounding him. Over the course of the following two years, he was in and out of jail so often that they spent as much time corresponding by letter as they did courting in person.

By the time of their nuptials on 8 June 1917, MacSwiney was interned at Bromyard (a raid on his house having yielded offensive documents), a curious sentencing allowed him to live on the High Street in the village but not to travel farther than ten miles from it. Still, special permission had to be granted for him to be married at the nearby church. Before the ceremony, an Irish Volunteers' uniform was smuggled across from Cork so that he could wear it down the aisle. In spite of the warm season, he wore a great coat on his way to the altar. Only upon conclusion of the civil part of the ceremony did he finally throw off the outer garment to reveal the green of the Volunteer. By then, it was too late for any protest from the registrar of the church.

So much had changed since that afternoon just three summers

back. Now Father Mathieu was in London, seeking to reconnect with the Corkman suddenly garnering international headlines with his hunger strike. The French native knew enough of MacSwiney's faith (he used regularly take mass at St Joseph's while interned) to realise that the water from the French shrine would offer spiritual consolation to him in this dark hour. Unfortunately, the Mayor's condition that particular day meant that Mathieu was unable even to get in to visit with him. He passed his gifts on to Mary to deliver.

Having received the sacrament from Father Dominic that morning, MacSwiney weakened over the next few hours. When his wife left his bedside in the afternoon, she was almost too distraught about the deterioration she had witnessed to talk to reporters outside the prison. 'He's dying fast,' she said. 'My husband is lying flat on his back. He is conscious. At long intervals, he is able to utter a disjointed word. There are increasing signs of weakness but he is not in pain.' Then she rushed away, visibly upset.

Inside, Mary MacSwiney remained at her post by her brother for the next few hours. That evening, Father Dominic returned, to discover that apart from weakening significantly since morning, his friend was now experiencing renewed bouts of dizziness as he lay in the bed, his head spinning. At one point that evening, the priest leaned over, his hand damp with holy water and made the Sign of the Cross on MacSwiney's head. This was his final act before leaving each night, anointing him with the blessing: 'That God by the power of His Cross might give fortitude to this mind and strength to his heart and power to his shoulders to bear his cross for the liberty of Ireland.'

As Sunday night became Monday morning, there was little change, and a now familiar routine took place. Fresh food was brought to his bedside, as it had been since he arrived in the prison, in the hope that he might see it and decide to end his fast. Just like all the other days, he shook his head and turned away from the temptation.

'The doctors said: "The food is always there, and he can eat at any time",' said Mary MacSwiney. 'And the curious thing was that they changed the food to meet his condition. At first there was chicken and eggs, and the like. And as he got weaker afterwards they brought him chicken broth, meat essence, milk with brandy, and the things he would naturally get if he would take food. And we were invited to give them to him.'

Of course, his family and friends refused to do that. Not an easy thing to do, especially after he confessed to them that the sights and smells were having a profound effect on his appetite.

'Although some people say that the desire for food disappears after a few days' abstinence, it is not so in Mayor MacSwiney's case,' said Father Dominic, that Monday, 6 September, Day 25. 'He is still hungry but refuses to take anything although it is brought in to him regularly. The Lord Mayor looked pale, drawn and haggard this morning when I administered the usual sacrament. The local rumour that he received the last sacrament today is not true. MacSwiney has intervals of dizziness and is only able to speak in short gasps, owing to difficulty in breathing, and any attempt at continued conversation is impossible.'

By this point, the differences in his condition could be measured from hour to hour. Father Dominic couldn't believe how much MacSwiney's countenance changed between his morning and his night visits that particular day. The availability of this type of nuanced and regularly updated information meant that those interested in his ordeal were also privy to nearly every small detail. And they were, inevitably, moved accordingly.

At a special meeting of Dublin Corporation that Monday night, Lord Mayor Laurence O'Neill tabled the following motion:

'That this council do now adjourn for one week as a protest against the slow murder of the Lord Mayor of Cork, which is being committed by the British Government in Brixton Jail. That the heartfelt sympathies of the citizens of Dublin be tendered to the Lady Mayoress of Cork and the MacSwiney family in these hours of desolation. That to the citizens of Cork we also express our appreciation of their giant-hearted citizen, Lord Mayor Terence MacSwiney and his colleagues in Brixton and Cork Jails.'

On Tuesday morning, 7 September, Day 26, Muriel MacSwiney sat down for an interview with a journalist from the Associated Press. The report noted that she was a slender woman of youthful appearance who spoke with composure and with a rather defiant backward toss of the head. It also detailed how she spent several hours each day in the London offices of the Irish Self-Determination League, writing letters and meeting newspaper correspondents, before heading off to Brixton Prison sometime after noon to begin her daily ritual by her husband's bedside, holding his hand and offering what little consolation she could.

'I am positive he will see his task through,' said the Lady Mayoress. 'Of course it is only his conviction that he is fighting for an ideal that has enabled him to survive. I am fully reconciled to hearing of his death. His battle is mine, for it is one I took on myself when I married him three years ago while he was in England under a deportation order. Our lives since then have been mainly spent in evading my husband's arrest or waiting to be reunited through his release from prison. Thus the role I am now playing is one to which I have been long accustomed.'

At this juncture, press interest was overwhelming and the major English papers were becoming more and more sympathetic to MacSwiney's situation.

'Now the majority of public opinion and of the press in Great Britain is unquestionably for the Lord Mayor's release,' went an editorial in the *Observer*. 'The instinct of this public opinion is unquestionably sound. A Government not guided by it in such a matter must be dangerously out of touch with it. What moves the country is the doubt hanging over the case – the just fear of cruel disproportion between death and the offence.'

That particular sample of coverage hit the streets in Britain on Sunday morning, 5 September. At that time, one thousand miles away, Prime Minister Lloyd George and his entourage of twenty-four were packing their bags and preparing to pull out of Lucerne. Way ahead of schedule, they took the 10.30am train to Zermatt and, while this was assumed to be the first leg of his journey back to London, no details of his exact movements were released. No reason was given for the premature departure or heightened secrecy but plenty were implied.

On 31 August, an employee of the Geneva tramways, named Oeuvray, sent a telegram to Lloyd George warning that he had twenty-four hours to release MacSwiney or else face the consequences. The police arrested the man who then claimed his only intention had been to frighten the Prime Minister into changing his stance on the issue. Other threats were made against his life and, as one report put it, 'the menace of assassination' hanging over the Premier was being taken so seriously that Scotland Yard dispatched a special bodyguard who travelled all the way from London to Switzerland to bolster the safety cordon around the Welshman.

His journey home took two full days, including stops in Riffelalp and Viege. En route, he took time to speak to newspaper correspondents and to make a rather extraordinary offer. After reiterating yet again that the government would not be swayed by hunger strikes, he mentioned that if guarantees could be given that the murder of policemen in Ireland would cease, he felt sure that his government would free MacSwiney and his fasting comrades in Cork Jail.

While some around London were willing to interpret that as a softening of the official position and were even inclined to see it, at the very least, as an olive branch, it was regarded in a very different light by those in the MacSwiney camp.

'It is amazing that your government, having tortured Irish patriots in your prisons for weeks, when they are at the point of death offers to release them if they proclaim themselves murderers and suggests it will kill them if they do not,' said Arthur Griffith, Acting Priomh Aire of Dáil Éireann. 'You English are indeed, as Tolstoi said, the most barbarous of all peoples pretending civilisation.'

'If the government is satisfied that murders are taking place,' said Father Dominic, 'why doesn't it capture the murderers and execute them?'

The less than charitable reading of the offer was inevitable since Lloyd George had wrapped it in a welter of more typically offensive quotes. Apart from reviving, for the benefit of the world's press, the old falsehood that Tomás MacCurtain was murdered by Irish Republicans, and commenting facetiously on the irony of one Celt quarrelling with another, he accused MacSwiney of trying to commit suicide, and warned again that releasing him would destroy the morale of the police and soldiers in Ireland.

'I have watched this case with pain,' said the Prime Minister. 'But pain must not obscure duty. The picture of the British government "doing to death" an ardent patriot in a British jail has no relation to fact … There is no doubt that the organisation in which Mr. MacSwiney held a very important position and took a leading part – that of Brigadier – was actively concerned in the work of murder, by which more than eighty devoted men of the Irish forces, many of them ex-soldiers, have been slain, and twice as many suffered serious injury.

'We have positive proof that the so-called Irish Republican Army and the particular brigade of it to which Mr. MacSwiney was attached, was concerned in these murders and attempts to murder. Papers signed by some of their own commanders have come into the hands of our officials. Either then we must hand the South of Ireland over to something calling itself a republican army, and leave the North of Ireland to fight it out without intervention, or we must protect men who are defending the flag. All I hear makes it clearer to me that this murder conspiracy is organised by a small body of men who are terrorising the large mass of Irishmen.'

Almost as soon as the Prime Minister returned to Downing Street, he received yet another missive from the determined Redmond Howard. In his latest attempt to end the hunger strike, he advocated a 'truce of God' (a temporary cessation of hostilities), and put himself forward to physically take the place of MacSwiney and to serve the remainder of the two-year sentence in Brixton Prison in the Mayor's stead.

'I make this offer in the hope that it might be followed by men of greater standing and reputation than myself whose position would in itself be a guarantee that the more extreme parties would be only too anxious to use their influence in the direction of peace if only they could be convinced of the Government's sincere desire to end the age-long misunderstanding between the two races,' wrote Howard. 'Surely the possibilities of such an occasion and the memory of the sacrifices made by the Irish during the war do not constitute too weak a claim for such a truce of God – if only for one month – when possibly the whole future solidarity of the Empire depends upon it.'

Apart from garnering plenty of press coverage for the man himself, Howard's good intention came to nothing. It was lost in Lloyd George's homecoming, an event that was greeted with a chorus of prominent figures adding their tuppence worth to the conversation about MacSwiney. On 7 September, Sir Donald Maclean, MP for Peebles and South Midlothian, and leader of the Liberal Party, became the latest high-profile politician to speak out in MacSwiney's favour when he declared that there was a remarkable consensus of opinion against allowing him to die. Another Liberal icon, Herbert Asquith, declared along similar lines.

'I think the decision to allow the Lord Mayor of Cork to die in prison a political blunder of the first magnitude,' said the man who'd been prime minister from 1908 to 1916. 'I would gladly intervene if any appeal of mine could lead, even now, to wiser counsels prevailing, but I fear that the latest declarations of Ministers preclude any such hope.'

Behind the walls of the prison, MacSwiney was oblivious to the machinations he was causing in the corridors of power in London and Dublin. After the earlier scares, his condition seemed to have stabilised that week. In his daily reports to the Home Office, Dr Griffiths, the senior medical officer at the prison, who had been away on holidays for the first two weeks of MacSwiney's incarceration, expressed surprise at how well he'd maintained his physical strength to this point. He also spoke of how giddy the prisoner had been one afternoon, and of his own (failed) attempts to persuade him to take some brandy to remedy that state. He blamed the excess of visitors imposing too much on MacSwiney for him incurring a mild high temperature.

'In the course of conversation with him and Mrs MacSwiney yesterday, I told them that circumstances might arise when he became too weak to resist nourishment or he might become unconscious, and that under those circumstances I should take any steps I thought proper as I could not as a doctor stand by and do nothing' wrote Griffiths on 9 September, Day 28. 'They agreed that this would be a proper course, but he added, that when he regained consciousness he would still refuse food. He has referred again to the matter this morning and says that he wants it to be distinctly understood that nothing but release will induce him to take food.'

In these reports, Griffiths cautioned regularly that he expected MacSwiney to suffer a sudden and serious collapse that would end his life sooner rather than later. Perhaps motivated by the fear of having him die on his watch, the doctor was relentless in his efforts to persuade the family to get him to take some sort of food.

'If he would only take a spoonful of milk it would be possible to release him immediately,' said Griffiths in yet another plea to the sisters.

'Of course it would,' replied Annie MacSwiney. 'But if he did so, he would no longer be of any use to Ireland for he would be false to his principles.'

Griffiths countered with a suggestion that the family appeal to the Republican government in Dublin to order him to cease his protest, a directive he felt that a soldier as disciplined as MacSwiney would surely obey. Annie dismissed the very notion but did bring it to the attention of her brother.

'No such order will come from Dáil Éireann,' said the Lord Mayor, 'and if it did, I wouldn't obey it.'

All that week, the British Trade Unions Congress had been meeting down in Portsmouth. After TUC President JH Thomas (Labour Party MP for Derby) had delivered his annual address, Ben Turner spoke and said there had only been one omission from the speech – a call for the release of the Lord Mayor of Cork from Brixton Prison. The audience erupted in enormous and sustained cheers in response to Turner's remark and the TUC duly dispatched the following telegram to Downing Street.

'This Congress, representing six and a half million workers, views with horror, and indignation, the Government's decision to allow the Lord Mayor of Cork to die. We wish to remind the Government that rebellion was first preached by those who are condemning to death others who are fighting for their country. We, in the name of the whole organised Labour movement, will hold the Government responsible for the death of the Lord Mayor of Cork, and remind them that such blind stupidity will render a reconciliation between Ireland and Britain almost impossible.'

It was nothing that hadn't been said before, but coming from such a large constituency these sort of opinions ostensibly carried weight. Obviously buoyed by this statement, Mary MacSwiney headed to Portsmouth on Thursday, 9 September, accompanied by Lieutenant-Commander Joseph Kenworthy, a retired naval officer and Liberal Party MP for Hull. She wanted nothing less than the opportunity to speak to the delegates and to ask them to call a general strike. In rejecting the first request, Thomas nullified the second.

'If any of you think for a moment of the torture that this woman has been through for the past three weeks,' said Thomas of her wish to speak, 'you ought to know quite well that it would be madness to allow anything of the kind. The torture she is going through naturally imposes a strain that has become difficult to bear…'

Even if her desire to spark a national strike was a tad over-ambitious, MacSwiney was less than pleased when Thomas tried to placate her with an offer to dispatch one more stern telegram of protest to Downing Street.

'I did not want to urge direct action,' said Mary later. 'I desired only to have three minutes of plain talk with the representatives of six and a half million working people of England. I was told that if a strike was called tomorrow they would not be able to get half a million to leave work.'

Insult was added to this injury by Thomas's subsequent decision to refuse a request from the floor that the parliamentary committee of the TUC demand to interview Lloyd George about the matter.

'I do not think it is a good thing for our movement to merely invite rebuffs, unless you are going to meet them some way,' said Thomas. 'We have already been personally to the Government and the Parliamentary Committee could have done no more.'

While all this was going on, Edward Troup, a Home Office official, had posited the idea that Thomas himself could be used as an intermediary between the Lord Mayor and the government. Aping the offer Lloyd George had made from Switzerland the previous week, and echoing the 1882 Kilmainham Treaty under which Charles Stewart Parnell promised to uphold law and order upon release from that jail, Troup wanted Thomas to ask MacSwiney to do a deal where he would be released, in return for his pledge to 'do everything in his power publicly and privately to stop the killing of policemen in Ireland'.

Like the TUC's telegram of protest, nothing came of Troup's plan either.

Chastened and depressed by her experience in Portsmouth, Mary returned to the prison and continued her part in the struggle. After seeing her brother again, still in pain, his arms now wrapped in bandages, she informed reporters that he remained as defiant and as alert as ever. 'When I said it was Friday the tenth, Terence said: "It is the beginning of the fifth week of my hunger strike".'

In spite of that sort of occasionally uplifting comment, the official bulletins about his health that were put out by Art O'Brien and the ISDL continued to sound grave. 'Lord Mayor grows weaker, he suffers much pain but his mind is perfectly clear,' was the one issued on the afternoon of Day 29. Later that evening, the tone was equally gloomy: 'Lord Mayor is very, very low…'

Elsewhere that day, a rumour went around London, claiming that Eamon de Valera, from his temporary billet at the Waldorf-Astoria in New York, was about to intervene in the strike. 'Such a thing has never occurred to me,' said de Valera in a statement released to quash the falsehood. 'The rumour circulated in Cork that I would intervene at the last minute is far-fetched. Lord Mayor McSwiney is fighting his own battle and knows what he's doing.'

This wasn't the only story doing the rounds. There was also speculation that were MacSwiney to die, de Valera would return from America, get arrested and begin a hunger strike in the mayor's place. This was not a scenario the Corkman wanted to envisage, and in a conversation with Art O'Brien, he expressed his view that the British government's determination to force feed rendered all future hunger strikes moot.

'He thought their present experience should be the end of the hunger strike as a weapon,' said O'Brien. 'In future those imprisoned by the enemy should be considered as casualties, and they should suffer their term of imprisonment without resistance, unless for some immediate purpose.'

At this stage, the sincerity of the medical reports being issued by the family and the ISDL about the gravity of his condition can be determined by the fact that that very week, the aforementioned Troup began to solicit legal advice about the handling of MacSwiney's body following his death. There is no greater indication of how close the authorities thought he was to the end than Troup's correspondence with Sir AH Dennis, the Treasury Solicitor, regarding this matter.

Having been previously warned by Dublin Castle that, if allowed, the funeral would involve enormous processions and public obsequies, most likely in London, Dublin and Cork, each designed to maximise the propaganda of his passing, Troup was anxious to know if it might be within the law to deliver the body directly to Cork. There, it could be handed over to the family, greatly reducing the potential for symbolism and protest.

'The matter may prove in the course of a day or two one of great political importance,' wrote Troup, his urgency an indication of the growing concern that MacSwiney was fading fast. At the same time, the London Metropolitan Police were also expressing reservations about the public order implications of the funeral beginning in their jurisdiction. Having endured a riot outside the prison in August, the police figured his death might cause even more severe disturbances.

It wasn't just the authorities that were expecting his imminent demise. In an effort to explain to its readers how this man had survived this long without food, the New York Times sought an independent medical opinion about the human metabolism from Guy's Hospital. 'Mayor MacSwiney is entering the danger stage of his fast,' said the unnamed physician. 'Observation of previous cases of the same nature has taught that at the end of four weeks' abstinence from food a man begins to draw on his last reserves of potential energy so that unless the Lord Mayor resumes eating, any day may bring collapse and the end … The fact that the prisoner is taking water fortifies him to a considerable degree.'

On 11 September, Day 30, the extent of the government worry can be gleaned from Lloyd George and Bonar Law summoning Sir George Newman, Chief Medical Officer at the Board of Education and the Ministry of Health, to a meeting. According to Newman's account of their discussions, the politicians were so concerned about the possible implications of MacSwiney's death that they begged him to do everything he medically could to keep the Lord Mayor alive.

Newman would later boast that he kept the prisoner alive for over forty more days. Was this the Quaker physician claiming to have used clandestine means to fortify MacSwiney against his own wishes during that time? Or was Newman merely claiming that by supervising the medical and palliative care given at the prison he ensured the hunger striker lived much longer than most expected?

The authorities were now so baffled by MacSwiney's continued endurance that they firmly believed he was being smuggled food in some way, shape or form. The discovery of an unidentified substance on the floor of his cell on Day 30 prompted a flurry of activity among the prison officers. This find seemed to confirm their suspicions that some sort of stunt was being pulled. Upon forensic examination, the morsel was identified as a piece of soap. Undeterred by this failure, the next step involved examining MacSwiney's faeces in the quest for evidence that he was being sustained. Again, this proved a fruitless search.

'Then began the insinuations in the papers that we were giving him food secretly,' said Mary MacSwiney. 'We never gave him food but we were giving him water. Sometimes he would say give me some water and we would go and get him some water, even when the nurse was in the room. But from the day that this propaganda began that we were feeding him secretly, we could not give him the water; we would let the nurse get him the water. We had to watch like lynxes from beginning to end. Every step held a trap for us. And all that was to counteract the deed that was creating so much sympathy for Ireland all over the world.'

MacSwiney himself was getting more and more irritable at the daily attempts to get him to eat. The same day that the mysterious fleck of soap caused such a stir, he'd launched a broadside at Dr Griffiths after he'd gone through the usual motions of offering to feed him.

'He is very bitter and says that he is being as surely murdered by the Government as if he were shot by bandits at the roadside, and speaks of his wonder at the Medical Association tolerating it,' wrote Dr Griffiths. 'He does not seem to see any point but his own apparently and the effort to argue with him or to persuade him to take food seems useless.'

Griffiths' daily report made no mention of any marked change in his condition, yet the official ISDL bulletins for Day 30 were especially bleak, documenting what they regarded as a serious deterioration. The disparity between the accounts of the doctor and the MacSwineys were an inevitable side-effect of the propaganda war. Each side suspected the other of either downplaying or exaggerating his suffering to promote their own interests.

Upon arrival that particular morning, Mary and Annie testified that they found their brother in an exhausted state. He had slept for just one hour the previous night, was suffering from extreme dizziness and experiencing severe pain in the back and the limbs. His sisters spent four and a half hours by his side, and when they left Annie told reporters: 'He has reached the worst point. Today for the first time he was so weak I could not read to him and when I asked him a question he had to think a while before he could answer. His face has assumed the grey colour of death.'

Muriel took her place for the afternoon shift and witnessed a further decline. Word came from the prison at around three o'clock that he was in a very bad way. The gravity of the situation was such that the authorities, ever worried about the public disorder that might greet his eventual passing, ordered a doubling of the guards at the gates.

'The Lord Mayor is very much worse,' announced the statement from the Irish Self-Determination League that night. 'He seems to have suddenly collapsed and has not spoken all day, but is still conscious.'

Despite most people feeling he was down to his last hours, he survived another night and lived to fight another day with Griffiths.

'Will you take food?' asked the doctor on Sunday morning, 12 September, Day 31.

'I will put it in a nutshell for you,' replied MacSwiney. 'I am here as a matter of duty and my example is a good one for those in Cork.'

The people of Cork remained gripped by his struggle. At a meeting of 200 RIC pensioners in the city the previous day, a resolution was passed urging the Government to release the Lord Mayor of Cork and the other hunger strikers in the city's own jail. Mrs MacSwiney received telegrams of support that weekend from, amongst others, The Demobilised Soldiers of Cork, The Rebel Cork Benevolent Association of San Francisco, and the All-Ireland Conference of Nurses and Midwives. The groundswell of support was building and building.

On 11 September, Dublin had ground to a standstill at 10 o'clock. The tramway service was suspended until midday while its employees attended specially-convened masses for MacSwiney in a dozen churches. It was noted in the newspapers that the Protestant shopkeepers of Dalkey had closed for business as a mark of respect. The members of the National Teachers' Organisation held a mass of their own at the Pro-Cathedral. The following Monday afternoon, the hotel and restaurant branch of the Transport Workers' Union marched through the streets and then filled the same church for a recital of the rosary and the offering of more prayers on his behalf.

England was not immune to the protests either. South London witnessed a rally of its own that weekend, and an estimated 10,000 people turned up for a pro-MacSwiney demonstration in Glasgow. Grist to the mill at both those demonstrations was the fact that the *Observer* had given its now weekly sermon on the subject.

This particular editorial lambasted the government's policies in Ireland and blamed the Prime Minister and his colleagues for creating a situation it described as 'this monstrous chaos'. Apart from announcing that MacSwiney should have been released as a matter of statesmanship in order to take the higher ground, an act which might have caused the murders of policemen to cease, the paper offered a succinct appraisal of the damage the ongoing protest was doing to Britain.

'The Lord Mayor of Cork is no longer a mere man, but a symbol, fixing the attention of mankind. His release in the well-judged manner we have suggested would have caused him to be forgotten in a few days. By his death, he will be remembered for ever. For weeks he has been allowed to make himself a magnificent instrument of British propaganda. His case excites more interest and emotion in the United States than the Presidential election. Every enemy we have rejoices that Brixton Gaol, at Government expense, has been made to our own detriment the theatre of this tragic and vivid film.'

CHAPTER 5

Wild Geese Chases

Distinguished Sir,
Our organisation, consisting of eight thousand members
engaged in the humble profession of commercial employees,
wishes to make its voice heard by you, in order to express the
concern of all Catalonia for the heroic, sublime and now
tragic gesture of the Lord Mayor of Cork. If there is still time,
we, who are also inspired by an ideal, most earnestly request
you to grant the freedom of the Lord Mayor of Cork. This
remarkable man, who from his prison displayed day after day
his unbending will to sacrifice his life on behalf of his ideal of
nationhood, a man who possesses such firm spiritual courage
and who has attained such admirable sublimity...
Letter from CADCI, a Catalan Trade Union in
Barcelona, to Lloyd George, 1 September 1920.

On the morning of 23 August, Day 11, a Broadway actress named Eileen Curran, accompanied by her friends, Helen Crowe and Helen Merriam, arrived outside the British Consulate at 44 Whitehall Street in New York. Bent on launching a protest vigil, Miss Curran had adapted the words of a well-known English ballad called 'Trelawney', and printed them on a placard two and a half feet long by three feet wide. It read:

'And shall MacSwiney die?

And shall MacSwiney die?

There's twenty million Irishmen

Who'll know the reason why.'

Carrying that banner aloft, she began marching up and down the street outside the consulate. Behind her in this brief parade, Miss Crowe was waving a placard of her own, asking the pertinent question: 'Are two Mayors of Cork to be murdered in six months to sustain British rule in Ireland?' Soon, the trio was joined in this demonstration by half a dozen more women, some of them carrying signs, including one detailing the murder of Tomás MacCurtain. For a time, a crowd of a couple of hundred onlookers gathered to see what the fuss was all about. Police officers came upon the scene as well but there was no hint of disorder to the proceedings.

Three thousand miles from where MacSwiney's health continued to falter, his cause was being advertised and explained on the streets of Manhattan. More significant yet, this picket garnered plenty of New York newsprint because the hunger strike had become a staple of the headlines there, where it would remain a front page regular over the next two months.

When reporters asked who exactly was behind these protests, Dr Gertrude B Kelly, a Waterford native, a surgeon, and a well-known figure in the Irish Republican movement in Manhattan, answered: 'American women'. Their nationality counted for little on the second day of their picket when somebody in the US

Navy office, located in the same building as the British Consulate, dumped a bucket of water on the ladies from on high.

At around the same time as the naval miscreant was dousing one set of the distaff protesters, another delegation from the group, which went by the official title 'the American Women's Pickets for the Enforcement of America's War Aims', was in Washington for a sit-down with Secretary of State Bainbridge Colby. They urged Colby to use his influence with the British government to try to effect MacSwiney's release. When he replied that he could guarantee nothing but would take that request under advisement, the women answered: 'Taking the matter under advisement would be regarded by half a million American women as an evasion equivalent to positive negation.'

Following the meeting with Colby, the women dispatched identical telegrams to Governor James Cox, Senator Warren Harding and Parley Christensen, the respective presidential candidates from the Democratic, Republican and Farmer-Labour Parties. Brief and to the point, they asked the nominees 'if the principle of self-determination for which we went to war is a reason for deporting a man from his own country and murdering him in prison.'

All of these worthy gestures were merely a preamble to the seismic events of 27 August. The SS *Baltic* was the White Star liner from which Archbishop Mannix had been hastily removed by British soldiers off the coast of Ireland earlier in the summer. Reluctant to allow the outspoken nationalist prelate to land in Cork for fear he'd foment further rebellion there, Downing Street succeeded in angering Irish Catholics even more. With the return of the *Baltic* into New York harbour, these ladies recognised a unique opportunity to garner more publicity for their cause. Even before the ship came into sight of its berth at Pier 59 that day, the pickets began milling around the docks, asking longshoremen to down tools and to refuse to unload its cargo.

They were asking the workers to walk out on two counts: Revenge for Mannix and justice for MacSwiney. Their dual mandate was evident from the placards they carried and the sheets of paper they distributed outlining the ill-treatment of the bishop and the plight of the mayor in faraway Brixton. Arriving on the waterfront just in time to coincide with lunch break, they beseeched every employee they met: 'Quit your jobs now, and we will tie up every British ship in this port.'

'Will you stand back and see MacSwiney killed by the British Premier,' shouted one of the protesters. 'Will you see the Mayor of Cork suffer in jail?'

'No, no, no!' replied her fellow travellers.

Once the *Baltic* had docked and disgorged its passengers, the demonstrators infiltrated Pier 59 itself in an almost comical scene.

'Where do you think you are going?' asked the customs guard at the gate.

'Oh,' replied one of the women, 'we just want to get a peep at the big ships.'

Before the security men could respond, the women, already heading up a phalanx of over 100 longshoremen, were on their way through. They occupied a space in between the *Baltic* and another vessel, the *Olympic*. One of the ladies then clambered onto the back of a truck to deliver an impassioned speech, appealing to those working the ship to walk off the job and join the protest. By some estimates, around 100 coal stokers immediately did just that. They were soon joined by twice that number of longshoremen.

Between first and second generation emigrants, the docks were such an Irish stronghold in New York then that workers were often divided up into gangs along the lines of county allegiances. Most who worked there were avid members of the Ancient Order of Hibernians, committed supporters of the physical force brand of nationalism, and generous contributors to the myriad collections for Irish causes that were taken up on a regular basis. Even so, it was impressive that 500 or so of them were that quick to give up a day's pay in a job where work wasn't always guaranteed, in order to row in behind what the papers would dub 'The Irish Patriotic Strike'.

And it wasn't just the Irish who were moved by the pleas. At the Cunard and Red Star piers, several hundred more joined the throng. The most notable addition was the arrival, as noted by the following day's *New York Times*, of '100 negro longshoremen who were employed in loading the steamer *Norman Monarch*.' For nearly three-quarters of a century, the Irish and the African-Americans had been at loggerheads along the docks, their relationship a potent brew of strike-breaking, territorial squabbles and racial tension that occasionally turned deadly.

The willingness of black dockers to throw in their lot with a protest organised by people with whom they'd had so much trouble sums up the impact the MacSwiney case was having in America. This type of ecumenism was, however, just in keeping with the mood of the day. At the Anchor Line facility, a similar story unfolded as dozens of workers left the liner *Calabria* and two freighters moored alongside. Having started with a group of well-intentioned women on 19th Street in Chelsea, the cavalcade mushroomed into the thousands en route to 44th Street where two more freighters, one bearing the Union Jack, the other the French tricolour, were soon embroiled in this impromptu industrial action.

'Few if any developments in the entire history of the New York waterfront could equal, or explain, this extraordinary event and the convergence of class, nationalist and racial slogans it generated,' wrote Bruce Nelson. 'In this case, "British" coal passers, many of them wearing small American flags on their coats, stopped work in support of the "Irish Republic" and black longshoremen shouted "Free Africa" as they joined the strike.'

Although it appeared organic and spontaneous, and was reported as such by the papers the next day, the entire production had been meticulously organised over the previous week. Helen Golden, another actress and veteran of the Whitehall Street protest, had planned the whole affair with the help of leading Irish Republicans in the city. They'd kept their intentions so clandestine that most of the women turned up that Friday morning unsure of what exactly they'd be doing at the piers.

'Well, we did it,' said Eileen Curran. 'We're trying to show the English that American women of Irish birth can keep them busier than they've ever been in their lives. Let them release MacSwiney and then we'll begin a new effort to compel them to let Archbishop Mannix into Ireland.'

Emboldened by the success of the venture, the group immediately cabled a message to Lloyd George: 'The sound of death in the throat of Terence MacSwiney is the death knell of your adventure in Ireland. We hear the bells tolling. The people are gathering. Oil your tanks, polish up your guns.'

As the clock in Brixton Prison ticked into the late evening of MacSwiney's fifteenth night without food, New York's waterfront thrummed to the sound of his cause. With over 2000 men having departed their posts, and every British ship on the North River paralysed by the stoppage, James Lynch, an organiser with the Marine Firemen, Oilers and Watertenders Union, told reporters that men working every British ship from Galveston, Texas in the south, to Portland, Oregon in the west would be asked to do likewise. If that ambition proved to be a tad optimistic, over the next couple of weeks smaller strikes broke out, amongst other places, across the river in Hoboken, New Jersey and up the coast in Boston. For a couple of weeks, the protest seriously hampered traffic and slowed down loading and unloading of ships in New York.

On the night of 27 August, however, the symbolic success of the day itself was all that mattered when 3500 people shoehorned into the Lexington Opera House for a meeting called to bring 'the facts of the MacSwiney case' to the American public. With a couple of thousand more standing outside for the duration of the gathering, the tone for the evening was set by the arrival on specially-chartered buses of some of the crewmen from the *Baltic*. The sight of the coalies marching onto the stage almost brought the roof off the building and fired up the crowd for three and a half hours of speeches from a stellar line-up, including a quartet of TDs in Harry Boland, Patrick McCartan, Liam Mellows and Eamon de Valera.

Aside from the events on the docks, the talk of the theatre that night was how the *New York Times* had waded into the fray with an editorial critical of the hunger strike in particular and the Irish in general.

'The whole case is epitomised in the determination of the Mayor of Cork to starve himself to death in an English prison. His suicide – for such it would be – would make him at once a martyr and a hero in Irish eyes. And Ireland has ever craved heroes and martyrs. She would rather have a long roll of them than the largest degree of self-government possible within the empire. But the English government cannot, without ceasing to be a government, allow convicted criminals to go free simply because they will not eat. And there, in little, we have the entire Irish difficulty. Ireland makes impossible demands.'

During a speech some reckoned to be the most emotional of his eighteen-month stint in America, de Valera addressed the *Times'* characterisation of suicide.

'If I were in MacSwiney's place, I would like to have someone speak for me,' he said. 'MacSwiney will die if he does not get his liberty. If MacSwiney dies in an English prison, 100,000 Irishmen are ready to do the same thing. They tell us it is a suicide. But he dies like a soldier and his death is at the hands of the enemy. He is offering his life just as would a soldier on the battlefield. England may do what she will with MacSwiney's body, but MacSwiney's spirit will triumph over that brute force and make Ireland's cause victorious. MacSwiney doesn't want to die, as no sane man looking on the sweetness of life does but he is making a sacrifice for the greatest principle in the world – liberty.'

On this and many other occasions during this episode, de Valera also sought to explain the Corkman's motivation by invoking the memory of Patrick Henry, an icon of the American Revolution, who delivered the famous 'Give me liberty or give me death' speech urging action against the British forces in 1775.

'He [MacSwiney] is acting as a faithful soldier of the Irish Republic, daring death for his country's sake. The British and pro-British press is preparing the way to make it appear that his death will be suicide. The *New York Times* has already taken up the British cry. Yet I have no doubt that the editor who penned the lines deprecating MacSwiney's action would write columns proclaiming the nobility of the sentiment "Give me liberty or give me death". Why not apply to MacSwiney the standard by which you measure Patrick Henry?'

Word of de Valera's eloquent efforts on his behalf reached MacSwiney in his bed, from where he dictated a message that was cabled to New York by Father Dominic: 'Greeting. Lord Mayor expresses deep gratitude on behalf of self and comrades. Your generous tribute will sustain them in carrying on their struggle to the end. They put their trust in God and are satisfied that if they die the recognition of the Irish Republic will be advanced near to victory. God Bless and guard you in your noble work.'

How quickly the hunger strike had captured the imagination of Americans can be gleaned in many different ways. The constant reports from the prison and its environs had become such a fixture in the press that on 1 September the *New York Times'* London correspondent could tell its readers as per its daily update: 'His relatives seem a little more anxious than they did, Mrs. MacSwiney not paying her customary visit tonight.'

In New York that same night, 5000 packed Ebling's Casino on the corner of 156th Street in the Bronx for another demonstration called to protest MacSwiney's continued incarceration and to demand his release. 'If MacSwiney dies,' shouted James Connolly, one of the featured speakers, 'King George will!'

On 4 September, the American Commission on Irish Independence, the body which had fought for Irish representation at the Versailles Treaty Negotiations the previous year, was a little more diplomatic, requesting that Senator Harding and Governor Cox add their voices to the chorus of Americans protesting against 'the inhuman treatment of the Lord Mayor of Cork'. Within twenty-four hours, the mayors of Boston and New York had sent telegrams to Lloyd George, both pointing out that allowing MacSwiney to die would be against the principle of America's war aims.

'As Mayor of New York, the largest city in the United States, and speaking for its citizens, I respectfully urge you not to disgrace our war aims by further imprisonment of Lord Mayor MacSwiney whose heroic fortitude in representing even unto death the opinions of the citizens who elected him has won the admiration of all the peoples who believe in rule of the people by the people,' wrote John F Hylan.

Over the course of the next week, the City Commissioners of Hoboken, New Jersey cabled both the prime minister and King George V, requesting the mayor's release, and the Hindustan Gadar Party of San Francisco (the American branch of the Indian independence movement) expressed 'its deep indignation and protest against the inhuman, barbarous and deliberate plan of slow murder of Mayor MacSwiney of Cork.' The California State Council of the Friends of Irish Freedom announced its ambition to organise nothing less than a boycott of English goods sold in the United States.

Accounts of all these various demands, protestations and meetings were filtering back to the MacSwiney family in London. Upon leaving the prison on 6 September, Day 25, Muriel told reporters: 'My husband is worse than he was yesterday. He was able to talk to me for a few minutes. You can hardly imagine that he could be so bad. Our only hope now is in America, and for the American financiers to withdraw their money from English securities. Apparently, Labour in England can do nothing for us.'

Against the background of so many varying expressions of support from the United States, little wonder Mrs MacSwiney felt that country was her husband's last best hope. The next day, she gave an interview to the Associated Press in which she made a point of thanking 'the many sympathisers with Ireland's cause in America'. Apart from acknowledging those who had inundated her with letters and telegrams since her arrival in London, she also cited the New York dock strike as evidence of how America was the one nation with the economic power to get England's attention and to force it to act.

With that in mind, she authored two cablegrams to the White House that week:.

To President Wilson, Washington

You, sir, enunciated the principle of self-determination for all nations. My husband Terence MacSwiney, Lord Mayor of Cork lies dying in an English prison because he upholds the fight for, and is prepared to sacrifice his life for, that principle. Tried by a foreign court which he does not recognise in his native land, and forcibly cast into jail, his only possible weapon of protest is his refusal to take food. I ask you to use your influence with the English government to prevent the perpetration of an outrage on civilisation.

To Mrs. Wilson, White House, Washington

I have just cabled your husband, asking his intervention for one who is dying to uphold the principles for which America entered the European war. I ask you in the name of humanity to support that request. My husband, the Lord Mayor of Cork, is dying because he will not acknowledge England's right to imprison Irishmen. His death may be a matter of hours...

While those entreaties elicited no response from a White House where, unbeknownst to the American people, a stroke had turned Wilson into a bystander for the last year of his presidency, the US State Department did offer a rather curt reply to a request from Peter MacSwiney, his New York-based brother, that they intervene.

'I beg to inform you that from precedent established in cases of this kind,' went the telegram, 'the Department finds it is not in a position to make protests to the British authorities against the arrest and imprisonment of one, who like your brother, is not a citizen of the United States.'

Still, there was no shortage of those willing to append their name to the MacSwiney cause. At the final session of the first United Negro Improvement Association convention in Harlem,

Marcus Garvey, the famed black nationalist who thought Irish republicans offered a great example to his own cause, told his followers he'd sent a telegram to Father Dominic to deliver to the Lord Mayor. It read: 'Convey to McSwiney [*sic*] sympathy of 400,000,000 Negroes.'

It wasn't just Americans being moved by the growing spectacle of a man fasting to death. The mayors of Montreal and Quebec made representations to the British government advocating his release. In Mercedes, Argentina, the Irish expatriate community held a lively meeting protesting the 'inhuman treatment' and pledging support to MacSwiney. In Melbourne, the South Australian Labour Congress passed a resolution protesting his imprisonment and urging immediate release 'in the interests of humanity and justice'.

Nearer home, a joint meeting of the Manchester & Salford Labour Party and Manchester & Salford Trades Council on 26 August passed a resolution demanding an immediate release 'in the interests of humanity and peace' and put on record their disgust at the government's treatment of the prisoner. Twenty-four hours later, a disparate gathering of Mancunians, including local politicians, clergymen, trade unionists, Irish nationalists and representatives of various women's groups met at Merchants Restaurant and put their names to a telegram pleading for King George V to use his royal prerogative.

Two days earlier, on 24 August, Arthur Griffith, acting-president of the First Dáil since de Valera had departed for America the previous summer, wrote a letter to heads of state all over the world. Apart from briefing them about the circumstances of the arrest, arraignment and deportation to London, he reminded them about 'the declarations made by the heads of the Allied and neutral States when the Burgomaster of Brussels [the mayor of the Belgian city was held captive by the Germans for much of World War I] was treated with a lesser indignity and harshness.'

Some were more amenable to this cry for help than others. On 26 August, George Gavan Duffy, a member of the Dáil for south County Dublin, and its envoy to Paris, went public in the French press with a follow-up letter he'd written to Premier Alexandre Millerand. In it, he asked that the French government pressure its English counterparts to release MacSwiney, since France, in his opinion, had saved the British Empire through its immense sacrifices in the war. Duffy's plea attracted attention, though not all of it was of a type he'd envisaged.

'About 8.30 p.m. on the 31st Aug, a messenger came to the Grand Hotel from Millerand,' wrote Duffy. 'M.[ichael] M.[MacWhite – Irish *chef de mission* in Paris] was present. The messenger speaking with extraordinary trepidation, told me he was instructed by the Premier to request me to leave France by the following day. I asked if this was definite. He said that it was absolutely definite and that a formal order of expulsion would be issued at once if I did not submit … There was no doubt then (and there is no doubt now as a result of special enquiries) that the sole cause was my appeal to Millerand and its publication (together with the immense and sympathetic publicity given to this and the Lord Mayor's case and to Ireland generally in the French press).'

Duffy wasn't exaggerating about the favourable coverage being afforded the hunger strike by the majority of the French newspapers. Apart from lengthy daily updates, replete with colourful descriptions of the scenes inside and outside the jail, MacSwiney had also elicited plenty of editorial comments.

'Has not every human being the world over heard the cry of pain from Ireland on her knees praying around the bed of agony of the Lord Mayor of Cork,' wrote *La Libre Parole*. 'This monstrous affair is only a cold, political assassination slowly drawn out which revolts the imagination and the heart of all those who have any degree of sympathy for England.'

'Over in Brixton in a cold and lonely cell a man is agonising,' wrote *Le Carnet de la Semaine*. 'His crime is to have dreamed of liberty… That no voice has been raised in Paris, Rome, Washington or Moscow is what surpasses the understanding of any sane and sensible man.'

'There is a man dying for the liberty of Ireland …' said *Le Merle Blanc*. 'Is it because Lloyd George is able to keep your feet cold this winter that you have allowed him to commit this abomination? Is it, I ask, a question of coal?'

While the forensic level of interest in the case around France can be gauged by reports that one Parisian theatre actually issued updates about MacSwiney's condition in between acts each night, not every press outlet was sympathetic. A *Paris-Midi* correspondent, writing under the pen-name 'Diplomate', authored a critical piece in which he accused Sinn Féin of establishing a regime of terrorism, and contended that the British government was doing their utmost to prevent Ireland falling into a bloody civil war.

But, with so many other journalists on MacSwiney's side, Duffy's expulsion drew more positive attention to the case than even the publication of the original letter. Unofficially informed that he could remain in France were he to give an undertaking not to spread any more 'anti-British propaganda', he refused that offer and caught a train to Brussels. Belgium had taken notice of events in London, too. In the 'Monthly Review of Revolutionary Movements in Foreign Countries', British government agents warned that 'the case of the dying Lord Mayor of Cork was exciting an evanescent interest in Flemish Circles.'

Earlier that year, James Joyce had moved to Paris and, according to his biographer Richard Ellman, the hunger strike was the only episode during the Irish War of Independence that captured the imagination of the exiled genius. This may have been down to the frequent speculation that MacSwiney was a distant relative of his or could just have been a by-product of the massive publicity the protest was receiving in the French capital.

Whatever the motivation, on 27 August, barely a week after MacSwiney's arrival in London, Joyce sent a postcard from Paris to his brother Stanislaus in Trieste. On it, he'd written a poem entitled 'The Right Heart in the Wrong Place', in which he drew parallels between Mac Swiney's situation, with only 'black famine' for his supper, and his own run-ins with English officialdom, and in particular Horace J Rumbold, London's man in Switzerland.

The growing international curiosity about what was happening in Brixton was, at least in part, down to the convenient location of the jail where the British government had decided to billet MacSwiney.

'By taking him to London, he was in the spot where newspaper reporters from all quarters of the world are,' said Mary

MacSwiney. 'And the result was that the reasons for the hunger strike were heralded all over the world, and did more good for Ireland than anything that has happened for a hundred and fifty years ... England was very surprised at the great wave of sympathy beginning to go throughout the whole world, and then she began to try to counter that propaganda in every way she could. The papers began to say that the doctors were feeding him; that they were giving him proteids in his medicine. I called the doctors' attention to it and they pooh-poohed it and said: "Who cares what the newspapers say? Who pays any attention to it?"'

A lot of people were paying attention. The extent of the coverage began to figure in the reports sent back by both British newspaper correspondents and British consulates abroad. They could not help but be concerned given that, in so many countries, the majority of papers tended to side with the prisoner rather than his jailers.

'Yesterday he was unknown outside Ireland,' wrote Madrid's *El Sol* in a profile of MacSwiney. 'Today the whole world is familiar with his name. Lloyd George's government will not call a truce so great is their haste to continue the martyrdom of Ireland. As the memory of this man will live long in the history of England, it is right that we should know something of him.'

The posterity line was also taken by *Giornale d'Italia*: 'Lord Mayor MacSwiney will be canonised in the course of centuries, when Englishmen will join in his glorification, just as recently they joined in the apotheosis of Joan of Arc.'

Another Italian, Benito Mussolini, described the hunger strike as '*Uno stoicismso superbo*'.

While Italians were as au fait with the daily updates of the hunger strike as most other Europeans, the government there didn't react like their French counterparts when Irish envoy Sean T O'Kelly publicly petitioned Signor Giolitti, the Premier of Italy.

'Your Excellency, I take the liberty of calling your attention to a matter about which it would seem impossible that you, your government and the Italian people can remain indifferent. I refer to the case of the Lord Mayor of Cork, who at the moment is awaiting death in an English prison for his patriotic principles. I beseech you to add your powerful voice and that of your government and people to the voices of the whole civilized world when, in the name of humanity, it demands that this man is saved.'

In the Vatican, Pope Benedict XV received telegrams, letters and missives from Irish bishops and clergymen regarding MacSwiney and the larger situation in Ireland. On 3 September, Day 22, it was reported in the London papers that following mass that morning, the pontiff stayed behind in the chapel to pray for the dying mayor.

'About this time Father Augustine OFM was in the Church of St Francis in Assisi when a Frenchman who was speaking to him found that he came from Cork,' wrote Moirin Chavasse. '"Cork! he exclaimed. "Did you know the Lord Mayor of Cork?" Father Augustine replied he knew him well and the Frenchman in excess of homage fell on his knees and kissed the ground at his feet.'

If there was no doubt four weeks into the strike that the world had sat up and taken notice, there were constant attempts to amplify the interest and to seek out the assistance of other nations. On Monday, 13 September, a letter, signed by the

MacSwiney family, was delivered to every foreign embassy and legation in London. Once more outlining the details of the case, it offered a sketch of the background situation in Ireland, and appealed to the governments of Europe and America to do what they could to prevent this "flagrant violation of all principles of liberty".

'If the present tragedy is allowed to proceed, we are confronted with the unparalleled crime of two Lord Mayors of the same city being murdered within six months of each other by a supposedly civilised government. We are of the opinion that this is a grave concern for all governments. Owing to the very close relations existing between modern nations, a government outrage in one country reacts in another. It is clear to us that if the crimes now perpetrated in Ireland in the name of the English Government are tolerated, the foundations of the governments of all nations will be imperiled. We ask you to lay this letter before your government ...'

CHAPTER 6

Forty Days and Forty Nights

What good is it to live a long life when we amend that life so little? Indeed, a long life does not always benefit us, but on the contrary, frequently adds to our guilt. Would that in this world we had lived well throughout one single day. Many count up the years they have spent in religion but find their lives made little holier. If it is so terrifying to die, it is nevertheless possible that to live longer is more dangerous. Blessed is he who keeps the moment of death ever before his eyes and prepares for it every day.
Thomas à Kempis, *The Imitation of Christ*, Chapter 23, Book 1.

More than five hundred years before Terence MacSwiney became Lord Mayor of Cork, a German-born monk named Thomas à Kempis sat down in the monastery of Mount St Agnes, near Zwolle in the Netherlands, and wrote a book called *The Imitation of Christ*. First published in 1418 as a manual of devotion for monastics, ascetics and mystics, it would become one of the most influential texts in all of Christianity, sought out ever since by those trying to find solace in spirituality and guidance as to how to live a life closer to God.

Befitting somebody with such a profound faith and such a contemplative streak, MacSwiney owned a well-thumbed copy of *Imitation*, replete with notes handwritten into the margins and his favourite passages underlined. Too weak now to be able to focus on a book, he found comfort in having his sisters read aloud from his own copy or having Father Dominic recite from the Irish-language edition he always carried in his soutane. He insisted that each reading begin with selections from Chapter 23, Book 1, the section titled 'Thoughts on Death'. He found consolation in paragraphs like:

'See, then, dearly beloved, the great danger from which you can free yourself and the great fear from which you can be saved, if only you will always be wary and mindful of death. Try to live now in such a manner that at the moment of death you may be glad rather than fearful. Learn to die to the world now, that then you may begin to live with Christ. Learn to spurn all things now, that then you may freely go to Him. Chastise your body in penance now, that then you may have the confidence born of certainty.'

A man stoic enough at this time to seek out meditations on the nature of death knew the end was coming. On 14 September, Day 33, MacSwiney did what many people do when they believe the clock is about to run out. He spoke to his wife, Muriel, about the funeral arrangements. During the long hours of silence lying there in the bed, he had obviously composed a picture in his head of how it should look and sound.

'I want it to be a simple ceremonial, with Catholic rites of course,' he whispered as she leaned over, better to hear his fading voice. 'And let the funeral orations be spoken in the Irish language.'

Still, the authorities weren't giving up on him just yet. That same day, one of the nurses, carrying out orders given her by the doctor, beseeched him one more time to take some of the food available and to end the protest. He wasn't receptive to the idea.

'Do you think I'm going to give way after my long hunger strike?' he asked. All of the staff in the jail had seen enough of his resilience to realise by then that here was a man not for turning. Beyond the walls of the prison, however, the efforts to take the matter out of his hands continued.

That morning, 14 September, the Standing Committee of the Irish Peace Conference sent another telegram to Lloyd George. Coming three weeks after its first plea, this constituted 'a final appeal to you to release the Lord Mayor of Cork and other hunger strikers on the grounds of humanity, as it daily becomes more clear that is an indispensible condition in the present circumstances to the possible success of any movement towards an Irish peace.'

The sincerity of this request can be gleaned from the diverse make-up of the signatories.

Apart from Anglo-Irish stalwarts like Sir Horace Plunkett, Sir Nugent Everard (Lord-Lieutenant of Meath), and the Cork industrialist Sir Stanley Harrington, there were prominent military names too. Major-General Wanless O'Gowan was a distinguished veteran of the Battles of Ypres and the Somme while Major-General William Bernard Hickie had a history of exceptional service with the British Army, stretching from the Boer

War right through until 1918. This was hardly a selection of men with axes to grind against the London administration, and not the type of characters whose objectivity in this matter could be easily questioned.

Elsewhere in Dublin that same afternoon, the ninth annual conference of the Association of Municipal Authorities met at City Hall, elected MacSwiney, in absentia, as its new president, and then adjourned the meeting in sympathy with his suffering. One more gesture of solidarity that garnered positive column inches, but little else. In search of greater impact, Mary MacSwiney sent out yet another letter, this time for the American journalists in London to print in their newspapers back home.

'Can the American people not force their government to act in the name of humanity and civilisation?' she asked. 'If England does not release at once the Lord Mayor of Cork and his comrades, let America see to it that the money England owes America is called in, and let American investors, individuals and companies withdraw their support from English investments. We do not ask you to go war with England; we do ask you to act at once before it is too late by exercising economic pressure.'

The call for an Anglo-American economic war was made as the British cabinet met to consider the ongoing deterioration in Irish affairs and, in particular, the MacSwiney case. At the conclusion of the session, it was declared that the government's position regarding all the hunger strikers remained unchanged. Any prisoner refusing food would be allowed to die. The unwavering public stance came amid reports in The *Times* of London that back-channel negotiations were making the chances of peace in Ireland a more and more realistic possibility.

'An important message from our Irish Correspondent rein-forces the case for mercy upon the Lord Mayor of Cork by a new and concrete argument,' wrote the *Times*. 'It appears that during the past three weeks negotiations have progressed between some of the most trusted leaders of moderate opinion in Ireland and influential men in the Republican movement. The very exis-tence of these negotiations has been secret; but the urgency of the situation is now held to justify their disclosure, and we are told that, if the Lord Mayor of Cork dies, the last hope of settle-ment on the basis proposed will disappear... Knowledge of the difficulties which must beset the labours of Irishmen of goodwill in the present condition of their country, and certainty of the embarrassment which the death of Alderman MacSwiney must bring upon them, have weighed with us more than any other considerations in impressing upon the Government the folly of their present course.'

There was a new urgency to the whole thing now, prompted by what turned out to be the erroneous presumption that his death had to be imminent. That sort of gloomy thinking was inevitable given the grim news emerging each day from the prison. On Day 34, Muriel reported that his eyes had suddenly become very dull, and he was suffering severe headaches and pain all over his body. By now, he was so sore he had been placed upon an air mattress to try to offer him some relief from the tor-ment of the bed.

Twenty-fours later, his wife found him 'extremely weak and very nearly worn out' as Day 35 passed with the usual roster of visitors. During Annie's stint by the bedside in the morning, he'd slept for a couple of hours. When she got up to leave at

1pm, he woke suddenly and called her back to sit some more. His principal complaint to her was the severity of the headache that just wouldn't go away. Father Dominic ended his shift eight hours later with a bulletin that the mayor remained conscious and his condition largely unchanged.

Three thousand miles away that very day, a horse-drawn carriage, laden with dynamite, exploded on Wall Street, killing thirty-eight and wounding over 400 people. Although eventually blamed on Italian anarchists, one of the many callers who tried to claim responsibility for the carnage in the immediate aftermath was a man declaring that the attack had been carried out by Irish Republicans as a tribute to MacSwiney.

In Dublin on 17 September, Day 36, he was on the minds of his colleagues when the members of Dáil Éireann came together for the first time since the hunger strike began. JJ Walsh (Cork City) proposed and Padraic Ó Maille (Connemara) seconded a resolution that was unanimously passed, before an order was given to immediately send a copy to Brixton Prison. The wording read:

'Dáil Éireann, assembled in full session in Dublin, records its appreciation of the loyalty and devotion of the Deputy for Mid-Cork and Chief Magistrate of Cork City. To him and to the sufferers in Cork Jail it sends, on behalf of the people of Ireland, assurance of sympathy and admiration. In that assurance the duly elected representatives of the people of Ireland are confident, all the civilised nations of the world join.'

That day, the MacSwiney family told the press they had witnessed a serious collapse during the afternoon and described him as 'very low' that evening. However, in his update for the Home

Office, Dr Griffiths described him as unchanged, apart from the gradual day-to-day deterioration that was a consequence of going without food for so long. The difference between the two accounts of that single day prefaced future problems.

In his official daily communiqué about the mayor to the Home Office the next evening, 18 September, Day 37, Griffiths wrote that he 'found him sitting up in bed being washed. He seems able to take a helpful part in the proceeding himself. The nurse informed me last night that he had been talking a good deal to his friends and reading the newspaper.' Obviously, this painted a very different picture of the scene outlined by the family who described him as 'weak but still conscious' although somewhat refreshed by two uninterrupted hours of sleep.

The stark contrast between the two reports took on added significance forty-eight hours later when a remarkably similar update to that of Dr Griffiths' was printed in the *Evening News* of London. Apart from carrying telling, intimate details, such as his temperature (97) and pulse (78), it described a patient on the way back from the brink rather than on the way out.

'In the afternoon, he was able to sit up in bed and be washed,' wrote the *Evening News*. 'He seemed to have sufficient strength to assist in the procedure. He was able to talk a good deal and read newspapers with interest.'

This portrait of the prisoner as an almost hale and hearty soul was far removed from that of a skeletal man ebbing away in a prostrate position, on what was looking like becoming his death bed. Predictably, the image of him sitting up reading the newspaper coverage of his own demise angered those who had spent so many days in vigil, watching him struggle to summon the energy to articulate even the shortest sentences. Not to mention their reaction to throwaway remarks in the article claiming that MacSwiney, like some uncooperative witness, was 'well but sulky and disinclined to answer questions'.

After consultation with Art O'Brien, the family released a statement, announcing that no more information would be given to the English press. As a result of what they regarded as an ongoing campaign of misrepresentation against the mayor, and repeated efforts to spread falsehoods about those close to him, they had no choice but to withdraw all cooperation from English newspapers.

'At the commencement of the struggle in Brixton Prison, most of the organs of the English Press [then apparently not subject to any particular Government control or instruction on this subject] treated the matter fairly, or as fairly as could be expected, in their columns. As the interest of the public in England was stirred by the reports in the Press, and demonstrations were taking place nightly in front of Brixton Prison, the English Government got apprehensive, and at a certain stage, the Chief Commissioner of Police issued a note to the members of the Newspapers Proprietors' Association asking them, should certain information come to their knowledge, to withhold it from publication. Therefore statements given to the Press by the relatives and friends of the Lord Mayor were, in the case of many of the English papers, distorted from their proper meaning, and in many instances, absolutely false reports were given, words and statements being attributed to the relatives and friends which they had never used or made ...'

Aside from alleging that the level of nefarious government

interference had risen in accordance with the level of interest in the case all over the world, the family accused the Home Office and Edward Shortt of deliberately misleading the public and of playing a part in the *Evening News* report that had offended them so much.

'… the Evening News for 20th September gave figures from an "Authoritative Source" which are only available for publication to the Home Office. This same report also suggested that the health bulletins issued by the friends and relatives of the Lord Mayor were not true. The report further contained statements in reference to the Lord Mayor which were false and misleading. A letter sent to the Evening News, controverting these statements and challenging him to produce his "authoritative source" and asking for the same prominence to be given to this letter as to the original report, was not published.'

In response to what they saw as newspapers allowing themselves to be used as the heavy artillery in a government misinformation campaign, the MacSwiney family and everybody in their circle chose to stop doing interviews with English journalists or news agencies, and to refuse them access to the daily bulletins regarding the mayor's condition. This ban would not apply to representatives of foreign newspapers or agencies who remained in good standing.

'In arriving at this decision, the relatives have taken into account that some organs of the English Press have resisted the attempts of their Government to make them the instruments of this despicable campaign. In order however, to make it still more clear that this struggle is one, not between individuals, but between the two nations of Ireland and England, they deem it advisable to break relations with the English Press organisations as a whole. The torture, agony and slow murder of the Lord Mayor affects the honour of the nation to which the English Press belongs and just as the Chief Commissioner of Police issued an instruction to the members of the English Newspapers Proprietors' Association to suppress certain news, so now the relatives of the Lord Mayor leave it with the members of that Association to protect the honour of their nation and to deal with the case of the Lord Mayor on those grounds.'

The allegation that the government had asked the Newspapers Proprietors' Association to withhold information about MacSwiney's condition and thereby manipulate their daily updates about the prisoner was quickly denied. The Home Office and the NPA immediately refuted charges that they had been complicit in trying to offer misleading reports about his status. While nurses who tended to MacSwiney were questioned as to the source of the newspaper information and warned about making statements in print, his brother Sean sought to explain that the family had never intended getting embroiled in a propaganda war.

'We did not court publicity when my brother entered this strike,' he said. 'We really were amazed at the world's interest in his case. However, when such interest was aroused we saw it as a means of calling the world's attention to Ireland. The family is sincerely grateful for the manifestations of sympathy which have reached us. We have played fair with the public which was so kind to us. We have not attempted to hide any angle of this case.'

By now, an all-out public relations contest had broken out. At the same time that it was facing down accusations of manipulating the English press, the Home Office had to answer allegations in American news outlets claiming that MacSwiney wasn't being properly looked after by the Brixton authorities.

'There is no foundation for the statement in American papers regarding the treatment accorded the Lord Mayor of Cork. He has from the first been allowed the privileges granted to political prisoners and has never been required to wear prison clothing. Since he has, by his refusal of food, reduced himself to a state of weakness, he remains in bed in a large room in the hospital and enjoys the best medical attention. He is nursed by two trained women nurses, one of whom is constantly with him day and night, and everything possible has been done for his comfort. Excellent food suitable to his enfeebled condition is kept constantly by his bedside, and his nurses have done their best to induce him to partake of it.'

As was now the custom, the family responded almost immediately to this. Mary MacSwiney made the counter-argument, reminding the British and, by extension, the wider world, that the issue here was less about a prisoner's rights and more about a government's right to hold him in the first place.

'The Home Office is simply trying to draw a red herring across the track of the real question at issue. The present protest of the Lord Mayor is not directed against the kind or degree of treatment meted out to him, the protest is against the act of imprisoning him. It is a declaration before the world that Ireland denies England's right to set up its house within the Irish Republic or to arrest and imprison citizens of the Republic. The circumstances of the Lord Mayor's arrest form the first open blow at Municipal Authority in Ireland. He was treated with the utmost indignity on his own official premises; his private room was raided and municipal documents seized. He was then tried and condemned by an alien court for having under his control a police cipher, of which he and he alone, as Lord Mayor of the City was entitled to have the control.'

Amid the ongoing welter of name-calling, accusations and counter-accusations, MacSwiney's condition remained perilous yet stable enough to prompt renewed and more persistent discussions about his amazing longevity. The *Sunday Times* broached the issue on 19 September, Day 38, with a provocative headline: 'Who is feeding MacSwiney?' It was a question perfectly pitched to appeal to those who believed this man couldn't possibly be surviving without some sort of sustenance this far into his sixth week of fasting.

'Everybody is asking who is feeding him,' wrote the *Sunday Times*. 'There is no doubt at all that the government is not giving him food, or any of the prison officials. It is suggested that his visitors, priests and relatives are getting him sufficient food to keep him alive.'

When the question was put directly to the Home Office, it replied: 'If he is [getting food], we do not know it.'

The *Times*' article went on to compare his case with a storied episode involving Dr Henry S Tanner. Back in 1880, Tanner had gone without food for forty days at Clarendon Hall in New York City to prove the therapeutic benefits such a periodic deprivation might have on the human body. He'd earlier claimed to have undergone a forty-four day fast in 1877 and the Clarendon escapade was set up as a way for him to finally silence his doubters.

Predictably, those watching MacSwiney fade before their eyes were incensed at his protest being compared with a medical stunt.

'No nourishment or food is being given to the Lord Mayor,' said Art O'Brien in a statement.

His chaplain placed the accusation that he had to be receiving some sort of rations, by whatever clandestine means, in a wider context.

'Statements, at various times, in the British Press, alleged that the Lord Mayor was taking food, was able to be up, and such like,' said Father Dominic. 'These were all absolutely false. The Lord Mayor never had any food from the evening of his illegal arrest until he became unconscious. Casual visitors, as myself did too, sometimes saw him look pretty well, and they unthinkingly reported that he was much better than they expected to find him, and so on. Such thoughtless persons were unaware that this was due to the system, in its search for food, coming on some nutritious portion of itself.'

That Sunday night, MacSwiney and Dr Griffiths had a serious argument when the mayor complained that the medicine being administered to him tasted a little too sweet. Even in such a weakened state, he had the wherewithal to suspect sugar might have been added to the substance by the authorities. When the doctor dismissed the very notion of such a thing, he grew agitated, raising his voice as best he could and denouncing the way in which Griffiths and the nurses were constantly on at him to take food.

'He is becoming sulky and unpleasant in his manner and beginning to resent very strongly being offered food by the nurse or my asking if he will have some,' wrote Griffiths.

On Monday, 20 September, Day 39, the prisoner was visited and thoroughly examined again by the Medical Commissioner of British Prisons. Afterwards, MacSwiney (or, one suspects, Art O'Brien working on his behalf) released the same statement he'd issued upon his first examination by the commissioner exactly one month earlier.

'He [the Medical Commissioner] confirmed the report of the prison MD Dr Higson, and informed me that my health was in a very serious condition. He impressed upon me the gravity of my state and then read a document from you, warning me that I would not be released and the consequences of my refusing to take food would rest with myself. Nevertheless, the consequences will rest with you. My undertaking on the day of my alleged court martial that I would be free alive or dead within a month will be fulfilled. It appears from your communication that my release is to be in death. In that event, the British government can boast of having killed two Lord Mayors of the same city, within six months – an achievement without parallel in the history of oppression. Knowing the revolution of opinion that will be thereby caused throughout the civilised world and the consequent accession of support to Ireland in her hour of trial, I am reconciled to a premature grave.'

As might have been expected from somebody able to sign off on as strident a response as that, he was described in the family reports for that day as conscious, able to talk at irregular intervals but still obviously weak. Muriel MacSwiney told reporters she was convinced only the righteousness of his cause was keeping her husband alive at this point.

Despite the fractious state of relations with the English press, there were still plenty willing to see righteousness in his actions. That morning, the *Manchester Guardian* carried a letter in which a reader compared the treatment of MacSwiney by the British government to the way the Germans had handled the case of Edith Cavell during World War 1. A nurse who helped over 200 Allied troops escape from occupied Belgium, Cavell was court-martialed and executed for her role in saving the lives of so many of her compatriots.

'Edith Cavell became an English martyr and many feel that her story carries with it a large part of what they love and prize most in English tradition,' wrote RA Sampson of Edinburgh. 'Now change the name and the details, and has not our Government done exactly the same thing with Terence MacSwiney that the German Government did with Edith Cavell?'

This then was the background story as the 40th day of his fast approached. For a devout Catholic, here was a significant milestone. Indeed, inside Dublin Castle, there was even misguided speculation that surviving past the biblical fast of Jesus Christ would alienate the plain people of Ireland who'd regard such a thing as somehow sinful.

'With lots of the peasants, MacSwiney lost favour when he had fasted more than 40 days,' wrote Mark Sturgis. 'They regarded the beating of Our Lord's record as a blasphemous presumption.'

To mark the arrival of the fortieth day, MacSwiney prepared a statement for release to the international press in order to reach as many of the Diaspora as possible around the world. Apart from giving thanks on behalf of himself and the hunger strikers in Cork Jail for the mass cards, prayers and spiritual support coming to them from Irish people everywhere, he also sought to place their fasting (and by extension their struggle) in a religious context.

'Tomorrow I shall have completed forty days without tasting food, and though lying here helpless, my faculties are as clear as ever. I attribute this to the spiritual strength I receive from my daily communion, bringing me bodily strength, assisted by a world of masses and prayers. My comrades, who are fasting two days longer than I, are clearly sustained in this manner. I believe God has directly intervened to stay the tragedy for a while for a divine purpose of his own. It is incredible that the people of England will allow this callous, cold-blooded murder to be pushed to the end. I think God is giving them their last chance to pause and consider. But if their determination is to go on, our resolution was prepared from the beginning and we are prepared to die...We feel singularly privileged in being made the instruments of God for evoking such a world-wide expression of admiration and support for the cause of Irish independence, and the recognition of the Irish Republic, and if we are to die, we are called to even the greater privilege and happiness of entering the devoted company of those who died for Ireland...'

In reality, the fortieth day was overshadowed somewhat by bloody events back home in Ireland. On 20 September, Day 39, eighteen-year-old Kevin Barry was arrested following an IRA attack on the British Army in Dublin during which two soldiers were killed. That same day, the RIC retaliated for an assault on two of their officers by sacking the north county Dublin town of Balbriggan. Seamus Lawless and Sean Gibbons were killed while in police custody, and fifty-four houses and a hosiery factory were burned down. Inevitably, the escalation in violence was much bigger news than the now depressingly familiar reports from the prison.

So, Day 40 passed in the same way as so many of the others before it. MacSwiney slept fitfully during the night and was in a weakened condition come morning. Muriel spent hours by his bedside and said afterwards he looked to be in great pain and hadn't spoken all day long. Indeed, the doctors considered him so frail that they advised his wife and sisters to try not to speak to him or to excite him unduly. The night bulletin, issued by the Irish Self-Determination League on the family's behalf, described no great change in his overall condition, conceding only that he was slightly brighter than earlier.

In some updates that appeared in the next day's papers, those details were accompanied by a statement from an unnamed Home Office official. Asked whether MacSwiney was being fed, he replied: 'Not that we know of, but you must remember his relatives have free access to him.'

For the first time, the government went public with their belief that the family was smuggling sustenance to the prisoner.

CHAPTER 7

God and the Gun

Corkmen in Dublin extend sincere sympathy to you and family.
If Terry dies, we shall have vengeance.
Telegram received by Mrs MacSwiney, 11 September.

On the day he accompanied the Lady Mayoress to Brixton Prison for the first time, Art O'Brien gave an interview in which he warned about the potentially larger ramifications of allowing the hunger strikes in London and Cork to continue until the first fatality.

'If any of the Irish political prisoners die, the Irish people the world over will hold it to be an act of murder on the part of the English government,' said O'Brien. 'The situation is viewed with extreme gravity by the leaders of the Irish movement in London who anticipate very serious consequences if the suggested Cabinet decision is persisted in.'

A standard-issue quote for public consumption, there was an ominous ring to it because, behind the scenes, O'Brien had been, from early on, working with Michael Collins on plans for reprisals. Apart from being the public face of the Irish Self-

Determination League in Britain, and the Dáil envoy in London, O'Brien was also a key figure in the IRB, the Gaelic League, Sinn Féin, and just about every English-based group with any affiliation, cultural, paramilitary or political, to Ireland. This allowed him easy access to many different parts of society, a facility he exploited to the full during the hunger strike.

As the major domo of the Irish community in London then, O'Brien was the man with whom Collins regularly corresponded from the moment MacSwiney transferred to Brixton. Apart from sharing details about the mayor's condition in their letters, the pair also discussed elaborate schemes ranging from an escape plan to retaliatory military action.

'Men have gone across last night, and three others went across this morning,' wrote Collins on 26 August, alerting O'Brien to the arrival of personnel who would be available to assist in any attempt to liberate the prisoner. 'You will get our people together – that is to say – yourself, and mobilise every possible bit of assistance that can be secured in London. One man who accompanies the Corkmen is already known to you, and to —— [Name blanked out in the records]. He will be their guide.'

O'Brien replied with a memo detailing the arrival of Murray (presumably Fred of the Cork IRA), assuring Collins that the preliminary arrangements were being made. Obviously, the frailty of MacSwiney's condition meant that any scheme to break him out of jail had a very limited shelf-life. A man in such a weakened state could die in the attempt to get him from the prison bed to a safe house.

Whether it was the time factor or the danger of moving a sick individual, those involved may also have quickly realised that

As a travelling teacher in County Cork, Terence MacSwiney cycled from school to school.

Above: Volunteers training at Coosan Camp, Athlone, 1915.
(l to r): William Mullins, Richard Mulcahy, Sean Lester, unknown, Donal Barrett, Terence MacSwiney, John Griffin, Liam Langley, Pierce McCan, Austin Stack.

Left: Three of the MacSwiney sisters. Annie and Mary would be key players in the drama; Peg (Margaret), was by then a nun in North Carolina.

Right: Peter MacSwiney, who had emigrated to New York, became one of the regular roster of visitors at his brother's bedside during the last weeks of his hunger strike, along with their younger brother, Sean, below.

Left: Annie MacSwiney and her older sister, Mary (Máire), below, founded Scoil Íte in Cork. Both staunch Republicans, Mary was also a founder member of Cumann na mBan.

Mary (Máire) MacSwiney.

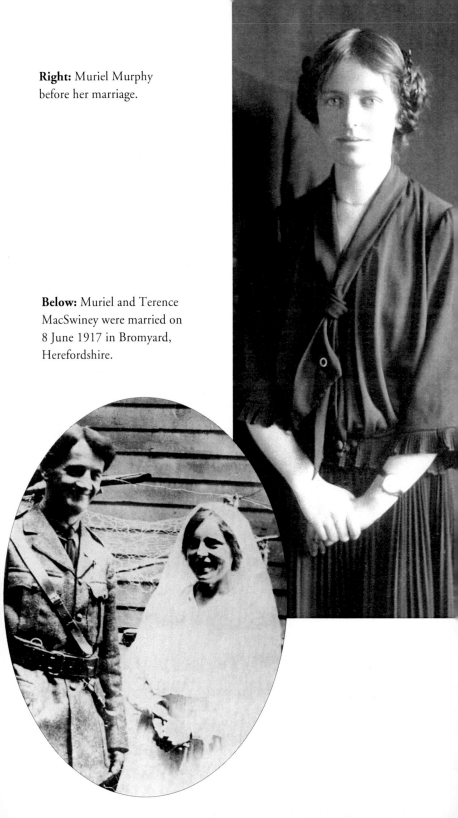

Right: Muriel Murphy before her marriage.

Below: Muriel and Terence MacSwiney were married on 8 June 1917 in Bromyard, Herefordshire.

Terence and Muriel
MacSwiney with their
baby daughter, Máire.

Inset: Annie, Terence, Mary,
and Muriel holding Máire.

Above: Terence MacSwiney at Rochestown
Capuchin College with Fr Bonaventure, Br Aidan,
Fr Colman and Fr Francis.

Right: Lord Mayor Tomás MacCurtain, who was
assassinated on 20 March 1920.

Below: Sean McDermot and Herbert Moore Pim visit
the Volunteer Hall, Cork, 1915. Tomás MacCurtain is
second from left, front row, beside McDermot and Pim
(bearded). Donal O'Callaghan, who succeeded
MacSwiney as Lord Mayor, is fourth from left, middle.

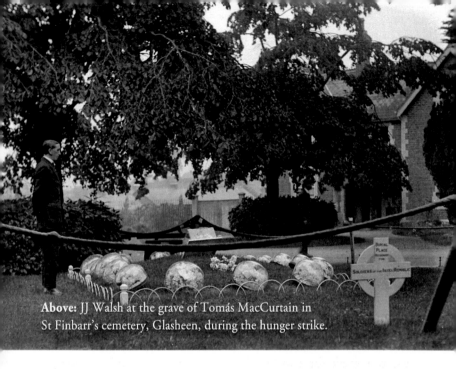

Above: JJ Walsh at the grave of Tomás MacCurtain in St Finbarr's cemetery, Glasheen, during the hunger strike.

Below: MacSwiney's letter to his comrade, Cathal Brugha, written in Brixton Prison on 30 September 1920. 'Ah, Cathal, the pain of Easter Week is properly dead at last.'

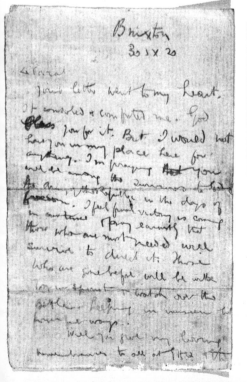

springing him from prison might also negate all of the positive publicity he was generating for the cause around the world. In the midst of exchanges regarding the arrival of clandestine agents from Ireland, and private updates about MacSwiney's health that were for Collins's eyes only, O'Brien also reminded him about the urgent need to maximise the propaganda potential available from the strike.

'I was very much alarmed at his appearance,' wrote O'Brien on 4 September, Day 23. 'What impressed me most, however, was the great contrast between his practically lifeless body and the mind so thoroughly alive and alert, as shown by the expression in his eyes and face. I only stayed with him two minutes. He was too weak for conversation. One thing he said however, which was of note is: "In another week, this will be finished one way or another." It seems extraordinary that he should have hoped of lasting another week. This is, of course, for your own information.'

Over the course of the previous year, IRA units, some dormant since the aftermath of the Easter Rising in 1916, had been forming and reforming all around Great Britain, an obvious and inevitable reaction to the deteriorating situation in Ireland. While some were ramshackle groups of exiles and patriotic children of the Diaspora, more were highly-organised and determined to strike some sort of expatriate blow in the War of Independence.

It's not a huge leap to conclude, too, that certain individuals were attracted to the movement anew by the furore surrounding the MacSwiney case, with the London and Liverpool branches both recording significant increases in numbers recruited by the end of 1920. Similarly, the birth of a Tyneside unit in September of that year has to be viewed in the context of feelings running especially high among the Irish in the north-east of England about the way things were transpiring in the English capital.

'As Terence MacSwiney's ordeal set off riots in Brixton, it also spurred The GHQ staff in Dublin into action – or at least into considering action,' wrote Peter Hart. 'Their first idea was to take hostages, to be exchanged for MacSwiney's release. In early September, Michael Collins told Art O'Brien to "go ahead with finding that place for a hostage". A week later, O'Brien wrote back about the "apartments". As MacSwiney's condition worsened, this became an assassination plot: Lloyd George's death in exchange for MacSwiney's. The rest of the Cabinet were soon included as well. Gunmen were sent from Dublin and Cork to prepare several elaborate plans; some stayed for months.'

Just two years had passed since Cathal Brugha, then IRA Chief of Staff, had arrived in London to supervise a proposed slew of political assassinations. Back then, some of the more prominent targets in the upper echelons of English society had even been issued bodyguards, and large cordons had been put in place at locations around Westminster and Whitehall to stave off any Irish attempt at blowing up symbolic institutions. This time around, the scheme was along similar lines.

'While MacSwiney was dying, it was decided to kill an English minister by way of reprisal,' wrote Frank O'Connor in his account of the plan. 'A young Volunteer officer in the country threw up his position and volunteered for the job, He received Pounds [sterling]100 to support himself and his men in London while they took their bearings. Finally, it was decided to kill a

certain minister at a function in Oxford. The men were inter-
cepted in Oxford itself by messengers sent out by Collins to stop
them. The young officer returned to Dublin.'

Collins seems to have realised the potential negative publicity
that might accrue from any high-profile assassination attempts.
At a time when events in Brixton Prison had commanded the
attention of newspapers all over the world, so many of whom
openly sympathised with MacSwiney's plight, killing a government minister or Lloyd George himself could have turned a lot
of those who were leaning towards the cause away from it.

As was already evidenced by the way in which security had
been cranked up around the Prime Minister on his way back
from Switzerland in early September, the British were well aware
of the possibility of serious and violent reprisals. They were also
smart enough to deduce that the longer the strike went on, the
less the chances of some sort of overt military action being taken.

'The English press is swinging a bit Governmentwards about
holding McS. [MacSwiney] and that if he dies and there is any
attempt to attack "Statesmen" in England they'll lose much sympathy,' wrote Mark Sturgis at Dublin Castle in his diary for 8
September, Day 27. 'Personally I should regard it as less of a
tragedy than the gunning of us here but probably I am preju-
diced.'

Police districts around Ireland received letters warning of the
fall-out should MacSwiney perish.

'If Lord Mayor dies, Resign: if wise – OC Cork,' went one
message.

'Resign. Revenge for Mayor of Cork,' went another.

The whole situation was even more complicated by Collins

becoming embroiled in broader political machinations.

In August, Collins gave an interview to Carl Ackerman, an American journalist whose work was syndicated in several newspapers in the US, and a British spy. Ackerman was reporting his information-gathering in Ireland directly to Sir Basil Thomson in Scotland Yard. Although Collins gave him typically feisty declarations of Ireland's intent to fight to the death, Ackerman wrote a private summation of the conversation for Thomson in which he asserted that, off the record, the most wanted man in Dublin hadn't closed the door to peace or negotiations based on Ireland getting her own courts, police and administration.

According to the journalist, Lloyd George preferred to act on the public perception that Collins had slapped the British government in the face with his demands rather than the off the record perception that he might be up for negotiating.

'The Premier intended to test the Sinn Féin organisation by a much more severe "third degree",' wrote Ackerman. 'His starvation campaign might be worth a game of political chess. Feelers were put out to see whether Sinn Féin would "listen to reason" if Mr MacSwiney were released. One of the Lord Mayor's nearest relatives herself wrote a confidential note to Mr [Richard] Mulcahy [IRA Chief of Staff and best man at MacSwiney's wedding] asking him to call off the hunger strike. This note was duly photographed by Scotland Yard before it reached Mr Mulcahy, without any Irish man or woman suspecting it. Scotland Yard agents had the habit of obtaining such confidential letters quite frequently. But Mulcahy and Collins, who alone had the power to issue orders to Irish Volunteers, could not be reached by the pleas of relatives and they were immune from social and political pressure because of their methods of living … While Mr Lloyd George and others moved their pawns in the game of chess for Mr MacSwiney's life, Collins and Mulcahy refused to play…'

While there is no question that Ackerman had more than one lengthy meeting with Collins, his version of events regarding the family and efforts to call off the hunger strike is contradicted by the testimony of those directly involved. Other bit-part players in the drama also offer up competing accounts of what happened.

Corkman Sean Murphy claimed that when he dropped into the Irish Self-Determination League offices in London in early September, he saw a written note from Michael Collins that was a direct order, telling MacSwiney: 'I now order you to give up the strike as you will be ten times a greater asset to the movement alive than dead.'

Here is how Murphy recalled the incident in an interview with Moirin Chavasse three decades later.

'When I got to Art O'Brien's office, there were present Art O'Brien, Sean McGrath, Mary MacSwiney, Fred Cronin of Cork … and to the best of my recollection Peter MacSwiney and a Dublin Volunteer dispatch carrier. Michael Collins' letter was in his own handwriting, and was handed to me and my comment was the same as all in the room with the exception of Miss MacSwiney. We were unanimous he should carry out Michael Collins' order. Miss MacSwiney would have "no surrender" and she was very emphatic that she would beat the British Government. She stated she would interview Commander Kenworthy that night in the House of Commons and get him to accompany her to a Labour Congress that was then sitting, to the best of my memory in Brighton, the following day, and get them to declare a General Strike …'

Murphy's account of that incident is uncorroborated and contains errors. The Congress he referred to took place in Portsmouth and, at that time, Peter MacSwiney was still in New York. This version of events is also fiercely contradicted by, amongst others, Florence O'Donoghue, Intelligence officer of the Cork No.1 Brigade of the IRA. According to Murphy's testimony, Collins had information that the British were determined to allow MacSwiney die in prison and so, to his mind, continuing the tactic to that end was pointless.

Whatever the validity of Murphy's memory, the nearest thing to a violent reprisal on MacSwiney's behalf – aside from the prison gate riots – came on 25 September, Day 44, when the Metropolitan Police arrested a man named Kelly Symington in his flat near Brixton Prison. Having discovered four rifles and various items of Sinn Féin paraphernalia, they charged Symington with sedition and possessing weapons, and immediately the security barriers around the prison were bolstered anew.

Apart from the shock of discovering arms so close to the jail, the extra measures were motivated by MacSwiney's continuing deterioration. With each passing day, it was assumed that the end drew ever nearer and the authorities feared that, when it came, his death would bring the possibility of violent demonstrations to the gate. The presence of forty officers now patrolling the perimeter at all times bore witness to how seriously they took all these threats.

Bishop Peter Amigo was a native of Gibraltar who, during sixteen years in charge of the diocese of Southwark in London, gained such a reputation for having an outsized social conscience that he was known as 'Friend of the Poor'. An outspoken Catholic prelate, unafraid of jousting with his own immediate superior, Cardinal Francis Bourne of Westminster, the head of the church in England, Amigo was never likely to remain a dispassionate observer while a hunger strike was taking place in a prison in his own bailiwick. Inevitably then, he became a loquacious and tenacious campaigner on MacSwiney's behalf.

'As Bishop of many Irish priests and people in the large Catholic Diocese of Southwark, I ask clemency for Cork's Lord Mayor who is dying in my Diocese,' wrote Amigo, in a telegram to the Prime Minister on 5 September, Day 24. 'Resentment will be very bitter if he is allowed to die.'

In and around this time, he also petitioned Sir Hamar Greenwood, Chief Secretary for Ireland, Sir Edward Troup at the Home Office, and Andrew Bonar Law. When all these entreaties failed to impact, he sent a second missive to Lloyd George, accusing him of placing MacSwiney in an impossible position and ruining all future chances of ever properly answering the Irish question.

'... the dying man has no power whatever to stop the awful murders in Ireland while Irish people say that the outrages are being committed by soldiers and police which could be prevented by the Government. If the Lord Mayor dies, in all probability the young people will keep quiet though greatly exasperated, but the good name of England will be much affected thenceforth throughout the whole world. Once more as a Catholic bishop I ask for mercy and I beg you not to make it impossible to bring about a solution of the Irish difficulty.'

This was a courageous stance for Amigo to take and one that often brought him into conflict with his own parishioners. Unlike Cardinal Bourne, whose mother, Ellen, was a Dubliner, the bishop had no Irish blood in his family. His affection for the country and its cause emanated completely from the early years of his career spent ministering to the immigrant poor in East London. Thereafter, he became friendly with several Irish bishops and priests throughout England, and began to regard his own government's policies in Ireland to be misguided and costly.

'The Irish can be won, but never driven,' he speculated in a letter written to Downing Street two full years before MacSwiney arrived at Brixton Prison. It was inevitable then that this character would do his utmost to assist the mayor. Apart from allowing Fr Dominic leave to serve mass to the prisoner, Amigo was in regular contact with the rest of the family. On their behalf, he tried and failed to get the hierarchy of the Catholic Church in England to issue a joint statement condemning the government's behaviour. From early September, he had told Mary MacSwiney that his cathedral would be available for a funeral if it came to that.

'We need not however begin to arrange yet,' he wrote. 'It may be that the miracle in which your sister [Annie] believes, may yet take place. Let us go on praying.'

His personal involvement and passionate commitment were in marked contrast to the contribution of Bourne. A much more conservative character, the cardinal appeared loath to comment in public about the dispute even after receiving a desperate plea from Mary MacSwiney.

'Your Eminence knows that my brother, the Lord Mayor of Cork, already has lived through forty-seven days of fasting for the principles of justice and freedom,' she wrote. 'Those who know how overworked he was at the time of his arrest did not expect him to live a week under the ordeal. Those of us who have been watching him through all these weary days have come to the inevitable conclusion that he has been supernaturally sustained in his struggles. When the forces of the spirit are sustained in such a fight against the forces of injustice and tyranny we naturally expect to find your Eminence on the side of the spirit. I therefore ask you plainly to call together your Bishops in England to condemn the action of your Government in their attitude toward my brother and his comrades in the Cork jail, and in the name of Christianity to demand their instant release. Even yet it may not be too late.'

While Bourne's reluctance to engage may have had something to do with the cardinal being good friends with Lloyd George, he did make some effort in private on MacSwiney's behalf. In a telegram to the Home Secretary, Bourne mentioned that he was coming under increased pressure to ask the government to show clemency and that he would personally support any such decision. This was a token gesture especially measured against Amigo's repeated entreaties to various higher powers, and even more so in the context of the importance of his religion to MacSwiney himself.

'Daily he received with edifying devotion Holy Communion, to which he attributed all his strength,' said Father Dominic.

'Frequently, by permission of the Bishop of Southwark, I said Holy Mass at his bedside. He often spoke of how helpful his religion had been to him. He spoke in loving admiration of Tomás [MacCurtain], and Eoghan Roe [the legendary Ulster chieftain who had fought for an independent Catholic Ireland in the 17th century], and of the magnificent combination in them of the qualities of a soldier and a Catholic.'

Aside from allowing the visiting priest from Cork to say mass, the Bishop of Southwark's role in the entire spectacle was impressive, too, given that his comments often attracted trenchant letters of criticism from his own flock. More than one of them wanted to know how the bishop could support a man who was, in their mind, effectively trying to commit suicide in jail. Not to mention the moral dubiety of allowing him to receive Holy Communion on a daily basis.

'Even if those who think that the Lord Mayor of Cork is committing suicide were actually right, most of them would acknowledge that he is in good faith,' wrote Amigo by way of explanation to one correspondent. 'Just as no sincere Protestant should be disturbed by a priest on his death bed, so other well-meaning people must be left to their faith. The Confessor judges the particular case and feels justified … My own opinion is that the Confessor is perfectly right in Mr. MacSwiney's case, but I wait till feelings do not run so high before answering your questions whether hunger strikes are lawful when national interests are concerned …'

From early on this was an aspect of the protest that had provoked much debate in ecclesiastic circles. Was MacSwiney committing a sin by killing himself, or was this, as Amigo asserted, a much more complex and difficult to decipher conundrum? Given the mayor's deep faith and his abiding love of Catholic ritual, it was just as well this particular discussion took place, not in the prison but in the pages of newspapers and religious publications. Even in the unlikely environs of church newspapers, it was a topic that inspired passionate argument and provoked vicious comment.

This particular facet of the protest had been kick-started by Father Bernard Vaughan. A renowned Jesuit preacher, Vaughan originally made his name working with the poor in Manchester and London, then travelled England and all over the world, sermonizing about the evils besetting modern society, the spectre of socialism, and, amongst other things, the dangers of giving women the vote. On 4 September, the *Tablet*, a weekly newspaper for English Catholics, published his take on giving sacraments to a hunger striker apparently bent on dying for his cause.

'Personally, from my reading of theology, moral and dogmatic, I should not feel entitled to administer the rites of the church to any one, no matter what his nationality, who was deliberately dying through a hunger strike,' said Vaughan. 'But I am free to admit that other theologians, far more learned than I am would reverse my verdict on the subject. Some moralists there are who deny that hunger striking cannot be justified, others have drawn a distinction between objective truth and subjective error. But as you are asking for my personal view of the subject, I give it for what it is worth, without comment on any one who may differ from me.'

Although the preacher was simply addressing ethical questions that had long been a feature of hunger strikes involving

Christians, his comments sparked a conflagration of statements and counter-arguments that spilled over from the pages of the Catholic newspapers and magazines into the mainstream press. It reopened a discussion about the morality of the practice that had started when James Connolly became the first Irish nationalist to hunger strike in 1913, gained momentum as Eamon de Valera and others fasted after the Easter Rising, and intensified following the death by forced-feeding of Thomas Ashe in 1917.

The responses to Vaughan's opinion varied from the personal ...

'I would remind your reverence that were it not for the sacrifices in the past, made by men of the race and type of Terence MacSwiney, for the faith which you profess and preach, Father Bernard Vaughan would have little business in England as a priest,' wrote Sean Harvey, an Irishman living in London in a letter to Vaughan. 'I suppose you know something about the special English legislation dealing with Jesuits.'

... to the more profound.

'As I write these lines, there lie men and boys, fired with all the old chivalry and idealistic self-sacrifice of medieval monks and friars, dying because, in assertion of a great spiritual principle, they make their last protest against an unchristian and barbarous tyranny,' wrote Professor Alfred O'Rahilly, registrar of UCC and such a devout Catholic that he would be ordained a priest after the death of his wife. 'They refuse to concur in the crime against our country by taking prison-offered food ... Before the astonished gaze of a world materialistic, dull, brutal, they symbolise and incarnate all that is noble and spiritual and earthly in the soul of man.'

John Vaughan, Bernard's brother and the assistant bishop of

Salford, waded into the fray to defend his sibling and to take issue with Father PJ Gannon who'd written a lengthy treatise on the subject for the academic journal, *Studies*. Amid the acrimony and the attempts to settle what was really an intractable argument (was he intentionally trying to die or merely trying to effect his own release?) the history of the hunger strike as a political weapon was touched on. Everything from its presence in the Brehon Laws (the act of achieving justice through starvation) to Saint Eusebius's refusal to take food from his Arian captors back in the 4th century was cited.

'So many discussions have been raised on the subject I may tell you that I do not consider the act of the Lord Mayor as that of a suicide, and I cannot conceive how any priest could refuse him the sacraments on that ground,' said Archbishop Mannix in an interview with the French newspaper *La Libéré* in which he gave his tuppence worth. The support of high-profile figures like Mannix and Bishop Cohalan in Cork, and the constant presence by MacSwiney's bed of a religious in Father Dominic, led many to conclude that the majority of the Catholic Church was on his side.

'Practically the entire church has pronounced against the theory of suicide,' wrote Ricardo Baeza in the Madrid newspaper *El Sol*. 'In every Catholic church in the United Kingdom, masses have been offered for Terence MacSwiney. The Holy Father prays for him in the Vatican and nobody would refuse him burial in consecrated ground.'

The truth was a little more complicated than the way the Spanish journalist perceived it. The imprimatur of Pope Benedict XV, known as the Pope of Peace for his efforts during World War I, had been desperately sought but wasn't forthcoming. An expression of support from the Pontiff would have silenced those questioning the morality of the fast, and would also have ratcheted up the pressure on the English government to bring the ordeal to a non-fatal conclusion. Inevitably then, the Vatican, a city with a standing population of Irish clerics, became the location for much intrigue once the hunger strike began.

On one side was the English Cardinal Francis Gasquet. Although then in charge of the revision of the Vulgate, the early fifth century Latin edition of the Bible, Gasquet happened to be in London for the duration of the hunger strike. While there, he met on four separate occasions with Lloyd George. Given that during World War I, Gasquet and his secretary Dom Philip Langdon had sent crucial information about the Central Powers' activity in Rome back to Downing Street, the cardinal's relationship with George led the Irish at the Vatican to conclude that he was a paid agent of the British government.

Against that background, it was hardly surprising that the MacSwiney supporters in the Papal State believed that, in collusion with Cardinal Merry del Val (whose brother Alfonso was Spanish ambassador to Britain at the time), Gasquet and Langdon were orchestrating a move to get the Pope to condemn the hunger strike as a suicide. It's alleged that Gasquet wrote to Cardinal Gasparri, Secretary of State in the Vatican, from London, explaining that a condemnation from the Pontiff would help offset the damage being done to the church in England by MacSwiney.

Obviously, a critical statement from on high, most especially one accusing MacSwiney of trying to kill himself, would have affected a devout Catholic such as the mayor and would most likely have divided some of his supporters too. Whether or not the perceived English machinations were having an impact, it only took one Irish cleric overhearing an English priest boasting about a forthcoming condemnation from the Congregation of the Holy Office (the church body formerly known as the Inquisition, which ultimately adjudicates on all matters of faith) to prompt a counter-movement.

Immediately, Monsignor Michael Curran, vice-president of the Irish College in the city, went to Monsignor Caretti, then Consultor to the Holy Office, and made the case that surely they would need to hear the Irish side of this argument before making any pronouncements on the affair. The case for the defence of MacSwiney was put forward by Father Peter Magennis, Superior-General of the Carmelites and a committed nationalist. Monsignor Lottini, Assessor of the Holy Office, was also reported to have delivered a very pro-MacSwiney opinion directly to the Holy Father himself.

Amid all the speculation – and Reuters reported that the Vatican was inundated with messages for and against MacSwiney – the mayor's family received word from an Irish churchman who'd had a forty-minute audience with Pope Benedict, half of which was supposedly devoted to a discussion of the hunger strikes in Brixton and in Cork. This cleric informed the family that the Pope did not regard what the strikers were doing as 'committing suicide' because the motive alone determines whether such self-destruction is justifiable. According to this admittedly second-hand report, the Vatican believed that MacSwiney and his colleagues were dying because their deaths would be the consequences of the only course their consciences in the circumstances permitted them to take.

All of these conflicting reports, positive and negative signs, eventually counted for naught. Despite the politicking by both Irish and English interests in Rome, the morality of hunger striking until death remained a theological matter, and that trumped all the nationalist posturing. Ultimately, Pope Benedict XV did what is normally done with an ecclesiastical dispute of this nature. He left the matter of resolving it to the Holy Office, knowing full well that MacSwiney's protest would end (in death or release) long before a Congregation that normally took years to make a decision would deliver any sort of verdict.

'You may be sure that if the Lord Mayor of Cork is not dead when a decision in this case will be given,' said Archbishop Ceretti to Cardinal Gasquet, 'then he will never die!'

CHAPTER 8

Doctors Differ, Patient Refuses to Die

We grieve with you in the tension of your long agony. The silent masses now dumb at the outrage on humanity being committed by the British government cannot storm your husband's prison. They will not, however, forget. They now see in its nakedness, the hypocrisy of the plea which that government recently called on the millions of the noble-minded of the world to assist it and they will yet rock that Bastille of the subject nations – the British Empire. Please tell your noble husband and have conveyed to his comrades suffering with him the heartfelt gratitude of the Irish nation and the Irish race and may God give you all his consolation.

Letter from Eamon de Valera in New York to Muriel MacSwiney, 26 September.

Five days after the Cork City Corps of the Irish Volunteers had been born amid violent and chaotic scenes at Cork City Hall on 14 December 1913, 150 of those who had enrolled at the inaugural meeting turned up for their first proper assembly at An Dún in Queen Street. Among those who gathered at the venue to begin the attempt to 'secure and maintain the rights and liberties common to the whole people of Ireland' were Tomás MacCurtain, Sean O'Hegarty and Terence MacSwiney. This was the rather cramped place where, under the baton of Bill Goodwin, a former sergeant in the British Army, the new recruits, a disparate group of idealists, dreamers and serious activists, underwent their first military drills and training.

Nearly seven years down the line, MacSwiney lay on his hospital bed in Brixton, and if those first stuttering moments of his involvement in the pan-nationalist movement seemed far, far away, they remained close at heart. On 24 September, Day 43, he dictated a letter to his friend O'Hegarty, a final farewell poignantly imbued with a remembrance of times they had shared and could still recall with fondness.

'A last line in case I don't return – I want to bid you God speed for the future and it sends me back to the past. Do you remember the first drill in the Dun under Goodwin when we took the floor eight strong. I was in the first square, and I think you were. We had many vicissitudes together since and much good work for the Republic. How happy it is to recall the wonderful progress. I pray, Sean, you may be spared long enough to carry on the good work – to come safely through the battle and live in the hour of victory. I am very weary and must stop. Goodbye Sean. God bless you and give you a long life under the Republic.'

As might have been deduced from the gloomy tone of the last line, he had suffered a setback the previous day. After her visit, Mary described him as weak and prostrate, a word that was beginning to crop up again and again in dispatches. What better way to describe a man stretched on a bed, waiting to die, than prostrate?

'His cheeks and temples are sunken and his body is badly ema-ciated,' said Father Dominic on 23 September, Day, 42, in an update he laced with another vigorous defence of the allegations that reports of his suffering were being exaggerated for the bene-fit of the press. 'He has had an almost continual headache for ten days but his mind is always clear. The league's reports of his extremely weakened condition are not overdrawn. It is not true that the prisoner daily reads the newspapers. He reads for a few minutes at a time but the paper is always held for him by a nurse. It is also incorrect to say that MacSwiney shaves himself. He is shaved every two or three days by a warder.'

As if to prove the veracity of his own argument, the priest also told reporters that MacSwiney's burial place had already been organised. When the time came, he would be interred alongside his friend and predecessor Tomás MacCurtain, in the part of St Finbarr's Cemetery in Glasheen, Cork, allotted to 'the victims of the English'.

'I am having him [MacSwiney] sprayed freely with eau de cologne about the head and face,' wrote Dr Griffiths in his diary for that day. 'And no doubt the absorption by the mouth of the spirit vapour is having a good effect.'

24 September, Day 43 saw a slight amelioration in his symp-toms. The headache wasn't as severe as it had been for much of the previous week, and he managed a few hours of uninterrupted sleep. An increasingly rare boon. For all that, he remained extremely weak and, in terms of conversation, was only able to muster up a few words to the relatives continuing their daily vigil by his side. Still, that he was alive at all by this point was extraor-dinary in itself, a fact that drew comment from different quarters

in the space of a few days.

'The prolongation of life seems to be absolutely wonderful – in fact, nothing short of miraculous,' wrote Michael Collins to Art O'Brien on 25 September, Day 44.

'I find him to be a veritable miracle,' said Archbishop Mannix to journalists outside the jail on 27 September, Day 46. 'To me it is a miracle.' This was not just a pithy quote delivered for the benefit of promoting the cause in the press. In private correspondence, the archbishop confessed to being absolutely astounded at how little his condition had changed in the three weeks since his last visit.

That sort of good copy was valuable because the propaganda war had intensified even more. This was in part because the scale of newspaper coverage had begun to shrink. After the initial burst of drama and the almost daily expectations of imminent death, the whole affair had gone on so long now that less and less column inches were devoted to the subject because, really, there was very little new to add. Even allowing for the occasional spectacular contradiction between the doctor's reports and those of the family, the bulletins generally began to blend into each other.

'The doctor says he finds him very much weaker,' declared the ISDL memo for 26 September, Day 45. 'His reserve of strength is so slight he is unable to stand the exertion of being read to.'

'He is very much exhausted,' went the report for Day 46, 'but still conscious.' Even if those snippets were augmented by the odd stirring quote – Mary declared him 'unrelenting as ever' on 27 September, Day 46 – there was precious little variety to the drip feed of information coming from the prison. There could hardly be during such a long, torturous process as waiting for a man to succumb to starvation.

In the background though, the authorities continued to believe that something other than willpower was keeping him alive and so strong this long. On 25 September, Day 44, Griffiths speculated almost plaintively in his memo: 'I wonder how much longer it is going to be until the end.'

Yet, the doctor continued to foster suspicions that something nefarious was afoot, penning another report to the Home Office in which he voiced his concern that the communion wafer being delivered each morning had to contain something much, much more restorative than the Body of Christ.

'I have made another enquiry about the tablet which the day nurse states that Father Dominic administers each morning,' wrote Griffiths. 'I was anxious to get a specimen of the solution in which the tablet is dissolved but she [the nurse] says that it is impossible as the priest puts the tablet into a teaspoonful of water and the patient drinks it out of the spoon.'

The squeezing of space in the newspapers didn't affect the enthusiasm of the family for wanting to disprove the type of conspiracy theories that were flourishinig. Motivated by the recurring and (to them) hurtful allegations that he was being surreptitiously fed, somehow, by someone, the sisters took drastic action. Without even informing Muriel of their plan, they decided to steal some of the medicine by his bedside in order to take it away to be independently analysed.

Capitalising on a rare moment when no nurses or doctors were present in the room, Mary took an empty perfume bottle from her handbag and poured a sample of the medicine into it.

Careful to take enough for the laboratory to be able to work with, she didn't take too much in case of arousing suspicion among the prison staff. The tests conclusively showed that the liquid was exactly the type of 'purgative medicine' the prison doctors claimed it was. There were no foreign bodies present in it to indicate that some curious form of nourishment was being given against the prisoner's will.

The chemists did find it odd that there were traces of alcohol in the medicine, at least until it was explained to them that the sisters had smuggled it out in an empty perfume bottle. Now satisfied that there was nothing sinister being administered through his meds, the family then decided to try to prove this in a more public and objective way. They enlisted the services of Sir Norman Moore, president of the Royal College of Physicians, and somebody described by newspapers of the time as the leading pathological and anatomical expert in Great Britain.

Following an examination on 25 September, Day 44, Moore announced that, in his medical opinion, MacSwiney could still recover fully from the ordeal if he was to stop immediately. Beyond that, however, he couldn't hazard a guess at how much longer he could survive without food.

'I cannot predict how long MacSwiney will live,' said Moore afterwards. 'He is astonishingly active mentally and the whole case is almost incredible, bordering on the miraculous. Of course you cannot compare this to previous fasting records, which have never been carried to the extremity as this.'

In private, Moore had given the family an even more upbeat prognosis: 'I cannot understand how he lives,' said Moore to Mary MacSwiney. 'Despite his long abstinence from food he does not appear to be a dying man. In fact I do not consider him in immediate danger of death.'

As a public relations manoeuvre, involving Moore was a clever initiative. Here was a stalwart of the British medical establishment, a trusted figure in English society, and a physician of national renown whose objectivity and independence regarding the patient could hardly be questioned. Moore wasn't apparently aware that the MacSwiney family had called on his services as part of their grand scheme to silence the naysayers with scientific proof that the mayor was not being fed.

'We got the most eminent doctor that we could,' said Mary MacSwiney. 'We did not tell him anything about the analysis, needless to say. We told him to examine the medicine, that we wanted to be satisfied that the doctors were not putting any proteids in the medicine they were giving my brother. We asked that the doctor go there for another reason. There was a rumour that my brother, being on the point of death, was to be moved to a nursing home; that the authorities were afraid to have him die in prison, and wanted him to be moved outside. We wanted independent medical testimony that he was not able to be moved. They gave us that permission.

'I think their idea was that that they wanted to represent to the outside world that they wished to be as nice as they possibly could to us and they did not want to refuse us anything they could possibly grant. Our purpose in having the doctor was to make a public statement that my brother was not getting any food in his medicine. We knew from the analysis but we wanted a specialist to make the statement. The doctor [Moore] making the examination was very nervous indeed when he went in, but on coming out the first thing he said to all of us was: "The Lord Mayor does not want to die. He has no intention of committing suicide".'

'Of course we knew he did not want to die. What he wanted was freedom. The doctor came away from his interview with my brother evidently with a very high opinion of his character and principles. And I told him straight out that we wanted the assurance that the doctors were not feeding him secretly, and he gave us that assurance and said we might trust the doctors because they were all honourable men. And of course we had obtained our object as far as the papers were concerned; and from that day on there was not a hint in any of the English papers that the doctors were feeding him secretly.'

While Mary was correct in her assertion about the immediate value of Moore's testimony, she greatly overstated its impact. Speculation regarding allegations of mysterious feeding methods would continue and only mushroomed the longer the strike went on. She also seems not to have known that Moore was also reporting back to the authorities. Indeed, at one point, the Home Office asked him to meet with Mary and Annie to beseech them to intercede with their brother and to ask him to give up the strike. A conversation that didn't go too well.

'If I live to be as old as Methuselah,' said Mary, 'he will not take food!'

In his own account of this conversation, Moore didn't sugarcoat the vehemence of the women's response to his plea.

'They [the sisters] seem more determined, if possible, than he was,' concluded the doctor.

From statements like that came the inference that MacSwiney

was somehow sticking to his guns out of fear of offending his sisters, and in particular Mary. Eight years his senior and almost a mother figure to him, she was regarded by many, including Bishop Daniel Cohalan, as the most hardcore nationalist in the family and the one driving the entire production.

'Because of her public posture, Mary was thought by many to be rigid and unfeeling, a stereo-typical spinster schoolteacher of the early twentieth century,' wrote Charlotte Fallon, her biographer. 'These accusers pictured her with shoulders set, speaking through pinched lips, prodding Terence to do his duty, maintain his fast and be a hero for Ireland. If it had not been for her stern admonishments, some believed, Terence would have forsaken his fast. When she refused to have him force-fed, some believed her heartless and callous whereas, in reality, she would have loved to have ended her brother's suffering as she had always sought to mitigate any of his pain as they were growing up. She had too much respect for his commitment to do so, however. Her brother's wishes would not be countermanded because as long as he was conscious and in control of his faculties, no amount of pressure would change his mind.'

In an effort to end the protest, prison officials were bringing pressure to bear on every member of the family at different times and often unbeknownst to each other. When alone in his bed, the Lord Mayor was told repeatedly how difficult it was for his wife and sisters to witness his suffering and was constantly asked to call a halt to the strike in order to stop causing his loved ones so much pain and anguish. The women, meanwhile, were regularly pleaded with to get him to eat and to stop such a talented and noble man dying such a wasteful death.

'Doctors, my wife and sisters are with me in this,' said MacSwiney one day when the cajoling became too much. 'They would not ask me to stop. They would think me a coward if I did.'

Mary MacSwiney was present for that declaration but even still the doctor on duty wouldn't relent. Later that afternoon, he approached her and claimed that the mayor had confessed he was anxious to give up the fight but was afraid to do so lest his family think him cowardly and disown him after. A rather preposterous gambit under the circumstances.

'Of course, my brother did not say that,' said Mary. 'He told us afterwards what he had said. And he told us over and over again how much we strengthened and supported him because we were with him.'

Fair or not, the characterisation of Mary as the architect of the affair, and the woman who refused to yield is probably in some measure down to her subsequent role as a vehement and vocal opponent of the Anglo-Irish Treaty. In a famously lengthy and hardline speech during the bitter Dáil debate on that matter, she gave a performance that cemented her public image forever as a woman unwilling to compromise.

In a similar vein, Muriel was, rightly or wrongly, judged in certain quarters to be the weak link in the family chain. While she may have originally gained this reputation due to an animosity between herself and Mary that predated the hunger strike and seems to have been there since her marriage to Terence, she also embarked on at least one solo run to endeavour to get the whole thing called off.

'She made occasional trips back to Ireland,' wrote Francis J

Costello. 'One of them involved a visit to Alderman Tom Kelly, Lord Mayor of Dublin, with a personal plea that he issue a statement, asking her husband to end his protest. Kelly appears to have drafted such a statement and submitted it to the *Irish Independent*, but after a visit by Mary MacSwiney, he withdrew the letter.'

For all their differences in personality and troubled personal relationship, the two women offered remarkably similar summations of the doctors they witnessed treating the mayor each day.

'We never had anything like scenes because I do not give people the opportunity to do that, to have a fight or anything like scenes,' said Muriel of her attitude to those tending to her husband. 'We were always very civil to each other. But the head doctor [Dr Griffiths] thought it was utter foolishness for a man to refuse to eat when he always had food before him. Being an Englishman, he could not understand why a man should die for a principle. But the subordinate doctor [Dr Higson], I must say, was more sympathetic. He never urged me to get my husband to take food after that one time when he told me what it would mean for our children, which I think from an English doctor's point of view, I did not mind him putting before me. He did not say much more to me after that but the other ones did.'

Higson had been the doctor on duty when MacSwiney first arrived in Brixton because Dr Griffiths, the more senior man, was away at the time. There's no question which one the entire family preferred.

'Dr Griffiths was a very capable man, and the willing tool – I say it deliberately – the willing tool of the Home Office in everything they did,' said Mary MacSwiney. 'Dr Higson was a very human man whose attitude showed that he sympathised with my brother, but he was helpless. One day in talking with him and he was pointing out his helplessness, I told him one position he might take although I knew he would not. He could have come out and condemned his government and resigned his position for its inhumanity. Of course he would not do it. That would be asking an Englishman to be heroic. Of Dr Higson, I have nothing to say but good. He made our time at Brixton as comfortable as he could, and I do not blame him for anything that happened. His only fault was that his courage was not equal to his heart.'

Perhaps the person best equipped to judge the efficacy and humanity of the medical staff was Fr Dominic. Nobody spent quite as much time by the bedside as he did, a privilege that gave him an overview of the way in which his friend was being looked after and an insight into the way they regarded his cause.

'While the doctors and nurses did all they could for him yet the nurses were merely mechanical ones, and the doctors though forced to admire his heroic fortitude and extraordinary will-power were unsympathetic and even hostile as far as the hunger-strike was concerned,' said Fr Dominic. 'They looked on it, or pretended to look on it, as a foolish game. They were frequently a cause of distress to the Lord Mayor by their lecturing him on the foolishness of his act, and by placing before him the sorrow he would inflict on his wife and family, as well as endeavouring to show how useful he would be alive and strong after two years to work for Ireland. No-one, they used to urge, can see any use or benefit coming from your present act.'

The doctors were blind then to the way in which his plight

had caused the world to pay attention, first to him and then to the Irish situation in general. Nobody was more aware of his worth in this regard than Art O'Brien.

'If MacSwiney were to capitulate now, it would do Ireland more harm than his past action has accomplished for the good of the cause,' wrote O'Brien on 27 September, Day 46, in a bald assessment of the mayor's value to the larger struggle. 'He will not give in.'

Twenty-four hours later, on Day 47, MacSwiney himself didn't sound so sanguine. At one point during Mary's visit he complained of terrible pain in his right arm and then confessed to her: 'I am quite used up.' In their bulletin that night, the ISDL told reporters that there was very little change to report and that he was 'still in an extremely weak condition'. Having recorded his pulse at 48 beats per minute, Dr. Griffiths delivered a missive to the Home Office with an account of his status that day which was similar to the ISDL's apart from one striking detail.

'He complains of tingling pains in his right shoulder and arm and of general weariness,' wrote Griffiths. 'He seems depressed and sullen this morning. He is able to move his limbs and body apparently without much difficulty in the bed. His skin is firm and elastic but some of his large muscles have become very wasted and flabby. He was reading a book when I went into the ward this morning … His face is becoming thinner and his aspect more anxious. On the whole, there is little to note except the slight, gradual physical deterioration.'

The image of him with a book in hand jarred with what the family knew to be the reality of his situation. By this point, he could barely focus while they read to him his favourite passages from *The Imitation of Christ*. And while the Home Office report for 29 September, Day 48, mentioned how the change from day to day was so slight as to be almost imperceptible, it also admitted 'his emaciated face and weakened voice tell the tale of gradual deterioration'.

In the latest sign that those around him believed MacSwiney could go at any point, plans were put in place at this point to bring Albert Power to the prison for a visit so that the finest Irish sculptor of his time could begin work on a posthumous death mask. If that was a macabre and artistic piece of propaganda planning by Art O'Brien, events in Ireland had taken a more violent and darker turn.

During the seventh week of the hunger strike, there had been a failed attempt to assassinate Major General Strickland, commander of the British forces in Munster, an attempt to shoot Tomás MacCurtain's widow in her own front garden, and a bomb attack on Cash's department store in Cork that was followed by a gun battle between Republicans and troops on Patrick Street. Elsewhere, the Black and Tans had burned the towns of Kilkee and Trim, and dragged the mutilated body of a Volunteer through the streets of Ballaghaderreen, County Roscommon in reprisal for the deaths of two RIC men in an earlier ambush at Frenchpark.

While MacSwiney's battle to stay alive was inevitably dwarfed in terms of Irish and English newspaper coverage by this escalation of violence back home, he remained a cause célèbre in the foreign press. That so many of the overseas correspondents were sympathetic to his cause continued to bother Downing Street.

The government was unhappy at the way in which their prisoner was being portrayed. Spanish newspapers carried daily updates on his condition and occasional larger features, explaining the wider political and military situation in Ireland, replete with gushing prose.

'It may be given to him to see in the brightness to which every day brings him nearer, the Ireland of tomorrow in whose soil his ashes will be sown,' wrote Madrid's *El Sol*. 'Terence MacSwiney is dying and when he dies, an impassable abyss will have opened between the two islands. There are spirits which work more actively from the realms of shadows than any living agitator.'

In France, the socialist Parisian daily *L'Oeuvre* was equally fervent.

'The death of MacSwiney risks making the Irish Sea an impassable abyss,' wrote Gustave Tery, its most famous crusading journalist. 'If England does not give in, she is opposed to a nation that is equally determined and the result will be that the British Empire will be shaken to its foundations.'

On the other side of the Atlantic, where de Valera continued to put the hunger strike to maximum use as a propaganda tool, the *New York Times* carried a report of MacSwiney's name being invoked at the annual mass of the Veteran Guard of the 69th Regiment, the 'Fighting Irish' of the US Army. Before a congregation of 500 soldiers past and present, Father James A Dunnigan delivered a sermon in which the mayor was the star turn.

'Terence MacSwiney, in the prime of his life, and in the full vigour of his manhood, is sacrificing all that is near and dear to him in life – love of wife, love of child, love of home and love of all that life holds out to him. Yes, he is sacrificing life itself on the altar of Ireland's liberty. Just so surely as the death of martyrs was the seed of the Catholic Church, just so surely would the death of Terence MacSwiney and his fellow heroes sow the seeds of the Irish Republic.'

Elsewhere in New York, one of the female picketers still protesting regularly outside the British Consulate on Whitehall Street bore aloft a banner with a rather lengthy message that carried the implied threat of a forthcoming assassination attempt: 'George Bernard Shaw says "I would not be in Lloyd George's shoes for a good deal." MacSwiney is near death. Lloyd George's shoes may soon be empty!'

Violence was on the minds of the Irish Diaspora in Argentina too. There, British agents discovered that an expatriate organisation called Circulo Irlandez (Irish Circle) was plotting to try to blow up the Edifico Britanico in Buenos Aires if MacSwiney died. A building occupied by the British Legation, the Royal Wheat Commission, the Royal Mail, and a host of other British business and political interests, it was chosen as the most obvious symbol of Empire.

As all this tumult was taking place in his name all over the world, MacSwiney continued to ebb away. Following an examination on 29 September, Day 48, the doctor concluded that the prisoner was near the end of the reserve of fat stored by the body. One more troubling milestone. Still defiant however, he refused an offer to take aspirin to alleviate the pain being caused by pins and needles in his limbs. It may have been that he was suspicious that they were trying to slip something more substantial than pain medication to him. This was inevitable given that the atmosphere of paranoia (perhaps justifiable) continued to fester.

Witness the latest family salvo in the ongoing war with the British newspapers:

'The relatives of the Lord Mayor of Cork wish – in view of the campaign of misrepresentation undertaken by the English government and supported by the English press – to state emphatically that they have not, at any time, supplied, nor are they now supplying food or nourishment in any shape or form to the Lord Mayor, and that, even had they supplied any food or nourishment the Lord Mayor would not have accepted it, as his determination not to take any nourishment, except on his unconditional release, remains unshaken. They have further the very best reasons for knowing that no food or nourishment has been administered to him at any time by the prison officials or anyone else. He has not been massaged either with oil or alcohol, nor has any attempt been made to introduce nourishment into his system by any form of external application.'

CHAPTER 9

'The Play's the thing...'

KING: ... He has chosen death:
Refusing to eat or drink, that he may bring
Disgrace upon me; for there is a custom,
An old and foolish custom, that if a man
Be wronged, or think that he is wronged, and starve
Upon another's threshold till he die,
The Common People, for all time to come,
Will raise a heavy cry against that threshold,
Even though it be the King's.
The King's Threshold, a play by WB Yeats (1904).

In the summer of 1920, WB Yeats was living in Oxford where, like so many others around the country, he consumed the daily newspaper reports of the terrible drama taking place in Brixton. Sixteen years earlier, he'd written a play about a poet in ancient Ireland, named Seanchan, going on hunger strike to protest the king's refusal to allow him to sit on the council of the state among the other 'Makers of the Law'. Yeats's own artistic sensibility had been stimulated afresh by the non-fictional plight of the Corkman in London, and on 26

September, Day 45, he wrote a letter to Lennox Robinson, the playwright and manager of the Abbey Theatre in Dublin, to apprise him of this fact.

'If I can make a few hours leisure I will examine *The King's Threshold* which I think of partly rewriting. The Mayor of Cork may make it tragically appropriate.'

The next day, he wrote to Lady Gregory on the same subject.

'If I feel I can do it, I will give it the tragic ending it has always needed and make some other changes. Events this autumn may make it very appropriate.'

Obviously still fascinated by the theory and the actuality of the hunger strike, Yeats again put pen to paper on 29 September, Day 48. This time, he wanted to mention to Robinson the possibility of the Abbey staging *The Revolutionist*, a play of MacSwiney's which it had been considering for production before his protest began.

In all of the events since his arrest on 12 August, here was a part of MacSwiney's identity that had been largely subsumed by the miasma of political and personal recriminations. Although trained as an accountant, he was, at heart, a writer. A member of the Cork Literary Society and the Gaelic League, he was a founder of the Cork Dramatic Society and dabbled in poetry, political journalism (his contributions to *Irish Freedom* would be anthologised in the book *Principles of Freedom*), and playwriting. Before his life, and those of so many of his contemporaries, had been hijacked by their involvement in the struggle for independence, his most fervent wish was to make a career from the written word.

In a 1913 letter to his sister Margaret, a nun then living in

Asheville, North Carolina, he pondered moving to America to improve his literary prospects. Whatever he lacked, it certainly wasn't application or work ethic. Between his debut 'The Last Warriors of Coole' in 1907 and 'The Revolutionist' seven years later, he wrote six plays in all. While some of his output received better notices than others, each touched on overt political themes reflecting the troubled Ireland of the time, and every line evinced a man desperately trying to improve and to hone his craft. It had been ever thus.

To train himself to write for the theatre, he read everything from Aristotle's *Poetics* to GE Lessing's 'Laocoon: The Limits of Poetry and Painting'. He devoured the works of European icons like Molière, Harold Ibsen and Maurice Maeterlinck. Always, he studied these classic texts with an eye to enhancing his own ability. Even though he didn't find much to admire in the milieu of George Bernard Shaw, he was smart enough to realise that there were technical lessons in that canon too for a neophyte like himself to acquire.

The same constant desire for self-improvement was why he often turned up to Cork Dramatic Society rehearsals even when the play they were putting on wasn't his own. How better to learn about the stage than by immersing himself in every aspect of it?

'He practised literature for the sake of Ireland – never to become famous or to make money,' wrote Daniel Corkery, his friend, co-conspirator in the Cork Dramatic Society, and somebody who would go on to achieve the literary recognition of which MacSwiney once dreamt. 'One idea had him constantly in its grip – the freedom of Ireland; and with him freedom meant just freedom and nothing else: he was always a Separatist.'

In *The Revolutionist*, his most substantial and ambitious undertaking, there is much of MacSwiney himself evident in Hugh O'Neill, the central character, a nationalist in an Ireland that has gained a measure of Home Rule. Unhappy that the country has settled for something less than full self-government, O'Neill refuses to give up on the idea of full independence and, like MacSwiney with his own ill-fated publication *Fianna Fáil*, establishes a newspaper to promulgate his beliefs. In the final, poignant scenes of the play, O'Neill ends up literally working himself to death for the cause and his penultimate speech took on an eerie tone given the situation in which the author ultimately found himself.

'Tell them nothing matters if they don't give in – nothing – nothing – the last moment – that's the important time – the grip then ...What's the good of being alive if we give in?'

Six years after first being published, MacSwiney's meteoric rise to fame had the doyens of the Abbey Theatre, prompted by the influence of Yeats, suddenly reconsidering 'The Revolutionist' for production. There is no word on whether this bit of potentially good news ever penetrated the walls of Brixton Prison where, by now, the playwright was involved in writing of a very different kind.

As September drew to a close, there was a sense of a man almost tying up loose ends, trying to get his affairs in order while he still had his faculties about him. As the daily recipient of letters, notes and cards from home and abroad, he embarked on a burst of activity, dictating replies to correspondents in Cork and Dublin. In many of these his mood is that of somebody bidding farewell to those with whom he has toiled for so long.

On 30 September, Day 49, he wrote a reply to his good friend Cathal Brugha, the Minister of Defence in the Dáil government, and veteran of the Easter Rising.

'Your letter went to my heart. It consoled and comforted me. God bless you for it. But I would not have you in my place for anything. I'm praying that you will be among the survivors to lead the army of the Republic in the days of freedom. I feel final victory is coming in our time and pray earnestly that those who are most needed will survive to direct it. Those who are gone before will be with you in spirit to watch over the battle helping in unseen but powerful ways.

Will you give my loving remembrances to all at GHQ, and the officers and men of the Dublin Brigade of whom we are so proud and to the organisation as a whole. Its work goes on splendidly. Remember me specially to Mick C, Dick McKee, Diarmuid, Rory O'Connor, Gearoid, Austin – too many names come before me. But don't forget Leo Henderson. I'm sending a line to Dick M – too tired to go on.

Whatever I suffer here is more than repaid for by the fruit already reaped and if I die I know the fruit will exceed the cost a thousandfold. The thought makes me happy and I thank God for it.

Ah Cathal, the pain of Easter Week is properly dead at last.

I wish I could say all that's in my heart to thank you for your beautiful letters. God guard and preserve you for the future. God bless you again and again and God give you and yours long years of happiness under the victorious Republic.

With all a comrade's love, God bless you.'

The Easter Week reference was the most significant element of the letter, a telling allusion to the fact that MacSwiney, Tomás MacCurtain and the rest of the Cork Volunteers hadn't participated in the 1916 Rising. Over three days that weekend in 1916, the leadership in Cork had received seven conflicting messages from Dublin, each new set of chaos-inducing instructions appeared to contradict and countermand the last orders. For MacSwiney, the confusion that led to himself and his comrades, men who'd spent more than two years training for just this moment, sitting on their hands while their colleagues were being killed 160 miles away, depressed him greatly.

Cork's failure to rise on that occasion was the subject of two independent investigations by the Volunteer executive and the Supreme Council of the IRB, both of which exonerated MacSwiney and MacCurtain for the comedy of inertia. Still, the farce had such a lingering effect on the pair that some speculated they may have even suffered from survivors' guilt. At one point during the debacle that Easter, MacSwiney could be seen in the Volunteer Hall in Sheares Street, striding up and down the floor, trying to alleviate his frustration by reading consoling passages from a book. That same edition of Kempis's *The Imitation of Christ* was by his bedside now, as he finally struck a very different kind of blow for Ireland.

Towards the end of 30 September, Day 49, MacSwiney had fallen asleep briefly but awoke shortly before midnight. He lay there, wide awake, as the clock ticked past 12, marking the arrival of his fiftieth morning without food, another milestone. For the remainder of that night sleep proved elusive and every waking moment was hallmarked by severe pain in his arms and back. The official bulletin described him as 'much weaker'. Upon arriving for her first visit in two days, Muriel was shocked at how 'wasted' he now appeared, his ribs protruding even more and the beating of his heart clearly visible beneath the covering sheet. In the space of forty-eight hours, he had, by her reckoning, slipped significantly.

'His sufferings no pen could write,' said Father Dominic. 'Try and conceive the pain you suffer in your shoulders and back and in your knees, the stiff numbing pain in the calves of your legs, the agony in your heels, instep and ankle if you remain a quarter of an hour outstretched on your back. What a relief to bend your knees, and draw them up towards your body. But even this little relief our heroic soldier could not have; for the flesh had wasted from his knee joints and the weight of the clothes on them was insupportable.'

Following his visit with the mayor on 25 September, Sir Norman Moore had departed London for the best part of a week. Whether this was by accident or design is not known. Upon his return to the city on 1 October, Day 50, Moore found his name back in the news when Mary MacSwiney, still on the counter attack over the continuing allegations about food being slipped to her brother, went public about the physician's unwitting role as dupe in her strategy to prove that he remained without nourishment of any kind.

'We wanted someone who was entirely free from the Home Office or other Governmental connections to make a thorough, impartial examination. Sir Norman was recommended as one of the best authorities available,' said Mary. 'He made an analysis of all medicines administered to my brother from time to time to allay severe headaches and other local pains. He inspected oils and other preparations used in massaging his limbs to prevent bed sores and other skin troubles and made a minute examination of his heart and lungs. The physician questioned the prisoner, his nurses and attendants, and at the conclusion of the examination, said it was certain my brother was not receiving nourishment in any form ... He expressed the belief that either of three things would be most likely to bring death eventually – a clot of blood on the brain or heart, due to sluggish circulation; rupture of the lung, due to its weakened state since his severe attack of pleurisy several years ago, or heart failure during sleep, when his vitality is at its lowest. That's what Sir Norman said, but somehow I do not believe there will be any cause. We have every faith that my brother is destined to live.'

Day 50 was a typically productive shift for Mary MacSwiney. Apart from firing the latest salvo in the ongoing public relations war, she sent letters to Cardinal Bourne, and to Randall Davidson, Archbishop of Canterbury and head of the Church of England, asking both clerics to marshal the bishops in their respective religions to condemn the government and to demand that her brother be released. Audacious requests that would go unanswered.

The next morning, 2 October, Day 51, yet one more attempt was made to persuade the prisoner to take food. The doctor on duty effected what he called 'a final appeal' to MacSwiney, informing him that he was going to sink faster from that point on and surely die. That prospect didn't move the mayor any.

'My mind is made up,' he whispered in a scarcely audible voice betraying the weakness of his condition. 'My decision is irrevocable.'

It was becoming more and more irrevocable. After seeing him that day, his sister Annie painted a disturbing picture of a man reduced to mere skin and bone. She told reporters that her brother, who once weighed in at around the 10 stone 10 lbs mark, was now down to 5 stone 10 lbs, and starting to resemble a skeleton in the bed.

'I don't know how to describe him,' said Geraldine Neeson, Muriel's friend and bridesmaid who had smuggled the Irish Volunteer uniform over to MacSwiney for his wedding, after she made her first and only visit. 'He looked shrunken in the bed. But his face hadn't changed much except it was pale. He spoke quite lucidly but in a very low whisper and every movement of course was agony. The weight of the bed clothes, everything was terrible for him. I had my little chat with him, told him things. Then as I was leaving, he called me back and that effort alone must have been bad and he said to me, "Geraldine I know you have a big trouble at the moment and I pray for you every day."'

Despite his physical disintegration before their very eyes, the mind remained surprisingly active, capable and engaged. On 4 October, Day 53, he dictated a message to his constituents in mid-Cork wherein he mentioned his enduring affection for that part of the county down around his beloved Ballingeary, and also expressed the hope that, if the time came to fill his vacant seat in the Dáil, the person they chose would have certain qualities.

'If I may not return, and my place has to be filled, I trust the rule of having an Irish-speaking representative will be maintained. In any event, I shall always be with you in spirit watching over your work and over all the places I loved.'

That a man whose daily toil was now a struggle merely to survive had the future of the Irish language on his mind sums up what the native tongue meant to him and how alert he remained under these trying circumstances.

While the issuing of these statements was a huge effort, depleting his shallow reserves of energy and often taking an age to dictate, others thought differently about his condition. That very morning, the *Daily Mail* described a scene inside the jail in which, among other things, it claimed: 'The Lord Mayor's hand was steady enough to shave himself and he reads his daily newspaper with interest.'

This was the latest of these canards put out to discredit him and to insinuate into the public mind that, some way, somehow, he must be getting sustained with food. It contained the kind of detail designed to have people thinking that all the disturbing reports of an emaciated stick figure, lying prone in a bed, were exaggerations and fabrications designed to appeal to people's emotions. So opened one more front in the propaganda war.

The ISDL retaliated by issuing a bulletin detailing how the helpless MacSwiney was shaved by a male orderly between 7 and 9 each morning, using a safety razor. Furthermore, he'd deteriorated so much that his family no longer even read the papers to him – as they once had – because it was too tiring for him. Instead, they offered a précis of the news of the day just to keep him up to date with the outside world. The picture painted was of somebody dying a slow and painful death, a world removed from the *Mail*'s mischievous image of him hale and hearty, shaving before then thumbing through the London dailies at his leisure.

'During all the time he kept as still as possible,' said Fr Dominic. 'This he did with a view to preserve his life and conserve his strength as long as he could. Though prepared to die and quite willing to offer his life for his country and his principles, yet he was not anxious to die. He was anxious to live to see our flag saluted by the nations of the earth; but if his life was necessary to hasten the day of its accomplishment, he was quite willing to offer his life. But every ounce of value he could get out of his earthly existence he was determined to get, to use it for Ireland's benefit.'

In truth, he was at that time much the same as he'd been for the past six weeks or so. 'No appreciable change,' wrote Father Dominic in a telegram on 5 October to Donal O'Callaghan, the Deputy Lord Mayor of Cork. O'Callaghan's response touched on the slow and sapping pace of the hunger strikes in Cork and Brixton prisons.

'The position here with regard to the [eleven] men continues unchanged, the particular men vary from day to day but in no great danger,' wrote O'Callaghan, the man who ran City Hall in MacSwiney's absence. 'Personally I have long since come to believe that this state of affairs is to continue indefinitely and that we will find ourselves old men, with the Channel running between, sending one another periodical messages, such as "situation unchanged", or, as you vary it today, "no appreciable change". Some of the men here seem to suffer somewhat more than they used to. Does Toirdhealbhach [one of a number of spellings of Terence in the Irish language] suffer much? Please remember me to him. Best wishes to yourself and the other watchers at Brixton.'

MacSwiney's high-profile office and the decision to move him to London had turned his strike into an international cause célèbre that overshadowed, in terms of publicity and newspaper coverage, the exact same sacrifice being made by his comrades in Cork prison. While too often their suffering was a mere footnote in reports, a paragraph at the end of the daily Brixton update, the eleven in Cork were always uppermost in the mayor's thoughts. He would regularly speak to Father Dominic about these men, obsessing, for instance, over the fact that Joseph Kenny had a wife and children waiting for him, and so much to lose in this fight. The same day on which his chaplain communicated with O'Callaghan, MacSwiney dictated a lengthy and quite extraordinary letter to the Cork hunger strikers that was part prayer, part call to arms.

'On your 56th day I greet you. I ask you to join with me in the following prayer for our people suffering such persecution in the present crisis: "O my God, I offer my pain for Ireland. She is on the rack. O my God, Thou knowest how many times our enemies have put her there to break her spirit but by Thy mercy they have always failed. I offer my sufferings here for our martyred people beseeching Thee, O my God, to grant them the nerve and strength and grace to withstand the present terror in Ireland, not only for two months but for two years if needs be; that by Thy all powerful aid, the persecution may end in our time and Ireland arise at last triumphant. Thy power, O God, is Ireland's resurrection. If we are to die in prison, it is Thy will, accept our willing sacrifice for our people. May we in dying bring glory to Thy Name, and honour to our country that has always been faithful to Thee. We rely on Thy mercy to sustain us in the last moment for the constancy of our martyred people and the redemption of our country. God save Ireland! God save, Bless and Guard the Irish Republic to live and flourish and be a model government of truth and justice to all nations. May the liberty of the Irish people shine with Thy Glory, O my God, forever and ever. Amen."

'Comrades, if we twelve go in glorious succession to the grave, the name of Ireland will flash in the tongue and flame through the world and be a sign of hope through all time to every people struggling to be free. Let that thought inspire us, and let our dying prayer be an exhortation to each other and to our people that everyone be prepared to sacrifice everything and God will at last redeem our country.'

While MacSwiney was waxing spiritual to his compeers back home, in a way that demonstrated the depth of his faith and how he viewed what he was doing as a quasi-religious sacrifice, the *London Evening News* made one more inquiry at the Home Office, asking for further clarification that the Lord Mayor of Cork was not being fed. The Home Office assured the paper that he wasn't receiving sustenance of any kind, bolstering this assertion with an assurance: 'Government agents are always in attendance at the prisoner's bedside.' The officials also mentioned that suitable food for a prisoner in his condition continued to be placed by his bedside each evening, just in case he felt like giving up.

'We always have food on the side of the bed for him to have,' said Dr Griffiths. 'There was always all sorts of nourishment left on the bedside, and, if necessary, remedies.'

The constant supply of food gave birth to one of the more

outlandish conspiracy theories about how MacSwiney was enduring.

'One of the latest [rumours] is that he is being fed with "vapourised beef" with which the atmosphere of his room is impregnated, and which, therefore, he cannot help inhaling,' speculated the *Daily Telegraph* on 6 October, before going on to offer yet one more possible explanation for his survival. 'Another suggestion is that Roman Catholic enthusiasts are administering secret nourishment, so that a "miracle" may be proclaimed to the ignorant peasantry in Ireland.'

Griffiths' report for 6 October, Day 55, noted a slight rise in MacSwiney's pulse. This bump was put down to his excitement at seeing his brother Peter arrive at the prison. Then working in a shoe factory in New York, where he had been receiving almost daily telegrams updating him about events in Brixton, Peter MacSwiney came directly from the pier at Southampton to south London. It took him a while to gain entry at the gate, however. A special dispensation had to be secured from the Deputy Governor before he was finally allowed up to spend time by the bedside of a sibling he hadn't seen since emigrating some years earlier.

Afterwards, Peter gave a graphic and animated account of his visit to reporters.

'I hurried over here hoping I would arrive in England in time to attend my brother's funeral, and I marvel at the fact that he is still living, though there is no doubt that the end is near. Even the Government doctors say my brother is dying. He himself is reconciled to that fate. He expects death before many days. His faith would not permit him to face death with a lie on his lips ...

I cannot find words to describe the scene inside or to express my contempt for the government responsible for what is taking place. So weak was my brother that he could not even shake hands with me, and it was only by bending my ear close to his mouth that I could catch the few whispered words he was able to utter. I was able to tell him that his prison tortures had roused the feeling of the United States, from the Great Lakes to the Gulf, and from the Atlantic to the Pacific. I told him also that mass meetings of protest were being held in every state in the union, and that the newspapers were every day displaying the keenest interest in the situation in Brixton.'

Peter also informed his brother that the family portrait of himself, Muriel and Máire was being constantly printed in newspapers all across America, hoping that this nugget of information about the extent of international interest in his protest might lift his spirits. He also didn't spare the rod when it came to those responsible for him being in Brixton...

'Here is a man dying for the ideals for which millions of men lost their lives in France -156,000 American lives were lost for the purposes for which America entered the war and these men had apparently died in vain.'

Or the British Labour Party for failing to do more on his behalf ...

'If it was a question of Englishmen being deprived of their beer, there would be a down tools policy and victory inside a week, but where it is a matter of the sacrifice of lives, British Labour remained inactive.'

The brother now joined the roster of visitors, and the passage of weeks had changed the mood inexorably around the bedside.

The mayor now preferred to have one or more of them around at all times, whether for fear of the doctors attempting some forced feeding or just out of a desire for company as he reached a lower and lower ebb.

'After a bit, he did not like to be there without some one of us,' said Muriel MacSwiney. 'Of course we were afraid that he would die at any moment. Nothing but his faith kept him alive. There is no doubt about that. He did not like to be left alone, so one of us would go in the morning and another at noon, and another in the evening, and like that. My husband was perfectly peaceful and happy. I do not think I could have gone on like that if I had not seen him every day because he absolutely radiated peace.'

Several times a day he would urge them when they left the prison to go out and treat themselves, to head up to London and to find the best cup of tea in the city and to sip it with lots of cream. Now and again, he'd jokingly apologise to visitors that he couldn't offer them anything to eat and drink. In more serious moments, though, he recognised the agony it was for his family and friends to witness him disintegrating before their eyes.

'And he often said to us individually,' said Mary MacSwiney, 'that he knew that our part in the suffering was ever so much harder than his, because it is always harder to see one you love suffer than to suffer yourself.'

On the same day that Peter landed from New York, Muriel, Mary and Annie wrote an open letter to Governor Cox and Senator Harding, the Democratic and Republican candidates in the forthcoming United States presidential election. Or, as the MacSwiney women put it, the men vying to 'be called to fill the most important position in the politics of the world'. Invoking the contribution Irish people had made to America's own fight for freedom from England and its subsequent rise to greatness as an independent nation, they demanded a response from the 'future president of the Great Republic of the United States' to the prevailing conditions in Ireland.

'Ireland is the victim of England's unbridled tyranny and terrorism, today, and twenty-five million Irish, throughout the world, would like to hear from him who may be America's president, what he is prepared to do against the foreign forces of brutality and inhumanity in Ireland. The Lord Mayor of Cork, in Brixton Gaol, and his eleven comrades in Cork Gaol, are dying because they will not give up their ideals. Other hundreds in Ireland are being murdered and having their homes burned over their heads, because they dare to oppose the foreign oppressors of their country. Give now, through your press, some message of hope to the Irish population of the world, that the inhumanity practiced by England on Irish prisoners, and on Ireland, cannot continue, with the tacit consent of the other free nations of the world.'

No such message was forthcoming.

CHAPTER 10

From a Whisper to a Scream

I visited Brixton Prison and spent three hours with the Misses Anne and Mary MacSwiney, sisters of Lord Mayor MacSwiney. The prison was surrounded with soldiers on horse and afoot, as if a storm or assault were threatened. One of the Lord Mayor's relatives took his picture with the camera of my niece Sheila King. The picture shows terrible emaciation. The teeth protrude, the temples are hollow, the eyes are sunken, but for all that, the holy majesty of the man suffuses a holy calm over his face.

Father James H Cotter, New York, 13 October.

On 7 October, Day 56, a small box of flowers arrived in the prison mail. With a Dublin postmark, the package had been sent from Ireland by the mother and sisters of the late Sean Gibbons who had been bayoneted to death in the Sack of Balbriggan back on 9 September. The accompanying note was brief yet poignant.

'Please give these flowers to Lord Mayor MacSwiney. They were sown by the late, murdered Sean Gibbons RIP, and were plucked from his garden today. As one of Ireland's martyrs, he is praying in Heaven today for "The Mayor and the boys", and for the success of Ireland's freedom.'

Next morning came a telegram from Cork, a reply to the prayer MacSwiney had sent the hunger strikers there earlier in the week.

'Your comrades in Cork Jail greet you on this your 57th day. Realising that yours is the harder fight made in the midst of the enemy, we pay homage to your inflexible will. Sustained in our struggle by the will of God, and fortified by your example and our confidence in one another, we await with calmness the issue, prepared for death if need be, in the cause of the Republic. We gladly join with you in your prayer committing our people and our cause to the mercy of God.'

If the tone of both those deliveries might have been expected, given their senders, MacSwiney also received correspondence from unlikely quarters.

'We want to send the message,' wrote the pupils of Bedales School in Hampshire, England, a progressive institution that styled itself as a humane alternative to the authoritarian regimes of late-Victorian boarding schools, in their expression of support, 'to show that some people still admire great courage and are not wholly insensible to the sufferings of the Irish people.'

'I'm only 12 years old and I don't know much about politics,' wrote Elsie Phillips from New York, 'but I think the English are brutes.'

Not all the packages and notes were inspirational or supportive. A vial of strychnine was sent in one morning with a rather blunt message attached, asking that it be used to: 'Finish off the brute'.

'Religious friends had been sending him religious emblems from all parts of the world and we had been getting roses and flowers and things like that in little parcels,' said Mary MacSwiney. 'And up to that time we had been taking them upstairs and opening them at his bedside. The day this [poison] came, we had taken this little parcel up and opened it and glanced at it before we showed it to him, and my sister, who had it in her hand, tried to hide it away. But he noticed it and wanted to know what it was. It was impossible to hide it so we showed it to him. And he laughed and he said: "Surely you do not think I would mind a thing like that."'

As he sat by the bedside on Friday, 8 October, Day 57, Art O'Brien felt that no such poisoning would be required because the end looked like it was drawing perilously near. Making his first visit in a while, O'Brien became genuinely distressed at the condition of the man lying before him. The conversation between the pair was punctuated by very long silences as the Lord Mayor struggled to articulate his responses, and to allay the dizziness that had become a constant side-effect of him trying to get words out of his mouth.

Heart complications were detected by the doctors, and every visitor that day encountered a wheezing, struggling man, gasping for air every time he tried to speak. By the time Father Dominic arrived in the late evening, the Mayor took an age to speak, but when he did, he perfectly summed up the direness of his own situation.

'I feel very weak,' he said. 'I have had a bad day.'

Saturday, 9 October marked the dawn of Day 58 but only the number on the calendar had changed, everything else remained the same. The family now recognised and acknowledged that in the previous forty-eight hours he had weakened considerably. Mary sent a telegram back to Cork to bring those at home up to date, and she didn't sugar-coat the message.

'Terry very weak this morning. Seems to have lost much within the last two days. Peter thinks he won't last the day out, but he has not been watching him so long. We don't feel unease about today but there is certainly a great change. Pray hard. He may rally.'

Art O'Brien followed up on his visit of the previous day, this time spending time by the bedside trying to assuage MacSwiney's concerns about the logistics of how his wife, sisters and brothers were being accommodated in London. He also witnessed a cameo with Annie MacSwiney that he later recounted in one of his regular letters to Michael Collins.

'He also made it clear as the life seeped out of him to his sister Annie that it was as a soldier he wished to be remembered first and foremost,' wrote O'Brien. 'At one stage towards the end of the ordeal, he asked her to write down precisely the time in which they spoke and to read it back to him as proof that he was a soldier dying for the ideal of a Republic.'

The militaristic side of his life had been showcased in the *Daily Mail* earlier that week via publication of a document (allegedly found in MacSwiney's desk on the night of his arrest) that proved his involvement in a plot to make grenades. In following up the story, the *Irish Independent* asked the pertinent question as to why this same letter had never been part of the charges against the mayor during his trial.

That he was a commandant in the IRA didn't affect his support among ordinary English people unduly. There was more proof of this at a massive 'Hands-off Ireland!' protest held in Trafalgar Square on Sunday, 10 October, Day 59. While his name was being invoked aloud there, MacSwiney was just a few miles south of the demonstration, struggling. He was experiencing less pain in his limbs than previously, no heart trouble at all but remained stricken by that overwhelming, draining fatigue. Conversation was kept to a minimum, even though Muriel visited twice in the space of hours, because it was believed the effort to speak was bringing on bouts of dizziness and making him weaker.

'I am quite played out,' he confessed to Father Dominic that evening.

Apart from detailing this reduced state of the man himself, that night's bulletin also took to task the continuing newspaper allegations that he was secretly snacking away.

'The paragraphs which have appeared during the week in some of the baser English press, stating that the Lord Mayor was taking food are deliberate falsehoods,' went the ISDL statement. 'No nourishment whatever had been taken by the Lord Mayor, nor would he take any, except that he was unconditionally released.'

The most notable event on 11 October, Day 60, took place in St Paul's Cathedral. A man smashed the glass in the frame of William Holman Hunt's painting 'The Light of the World' that hung in the historic London church. When police were called, the vandal claimed he'd attacked a picture supposed to denote salvation coming to a sinful world as a protest against the continued imprisonment of the Lord Mayor of Cork.

In the prison, that day passed like so many others now, cocooned in an eerie silence that hung around the bed. Very few words were exchanged between MacSwiney and his visitors. When he did speak, it was increasingly more difficult to discern what he was trying to say. There was no question now that he had gotten seriously worse, and rather quickly too. Late that night, he told Father Dominic he felt a 'weariness' unlike anything he'd felt before and that this was causing him to doze off periodically.

Day 61, 12 October, yielded the latest miraculous improvement of sorts and MacSwiney spent hours summoning up the strength to dictate a long letter, addressed to Deputy Lord Mayor O'Callaghan, and to his colleagues in Cork Corporation. Evidently aware of how 'critical' his condition was, he described it as 'a last greeting and farewell'. Yet he somehow found the wherewithal to articulate a lengthy missive that reads like a thoughtful memo to his putative successor and a goodbye note to those who worked with and for him in his role as mayor of the city.

'I wish you to convey an expression of my goodwill and esteem to our colleagues generally on the Council trusting that if at any time I seemed severe on any of them in Council that they will understand it was only in the discharge of my duty as Chairman and that at all times I was anxious that there should be complete co-operation between us all for the good of our City and the Freedom of our Country that I was anxious they should serve as we were eager to serve. I unite all now in one common blessing.'

Beyond the lack of punctuation, it's an extraordinary note: a man on the brink of death, two months without any sustenance, taking the time to express regret to the denizens of, among other local bodies, the Harbour Board and the Lunatic Asylum Committee, for his absence from so many crucial meetings. He even goes on to name-check individuals who had made his brief tenure as Lord Mayor that bit easier. Indeed, he admits to Messrs. Hegarty, McCarthy, Galvin, Delaney, and Ireton that their assistance was invaluable because 'I was quite a novice ... I am glad to feel that our relations were at all times cordial and am certain that the kindly feeling I entertained towards them was reciprocated.'

MacSwiney goes on to ask O'Callaghan to convey his gratitude to all the rest of the staff and to the workmen of the Corporation, each one of whom he hoped to regard as a personal friend. Still he was not done. After all the thank-yous and best wishes, he still summoned the energy to revisit one of his favourite hobby horses, requesting that the use of the Irish language in public business not be overlooked and that there would be no more 'non-Irish speaking mayors in Cork'.

This was also the day that Ramsay McDonald, the prominent Labour Party politician who had lost his seat in the 1918 British General Election, returned to London following a visit to the Republic of Georgia. He brought more heartening news of the impact the hunger strike was having abroad.

'England's treatment of Ireland is doing immense harm to British influence in the Near East,' he reported. 'At Tbilisi, I found that the case of the Lord Mayor of Cork was a general subject of conversation.'

The newspaper coverage on Day 61 wasn't all as positive as that. The *London Evening News* hit the streets with a story that claimed: 'Lord Mayor MacSwiney's remarkably fit condition is due to his partaking of grape juice and the juices of other fruits, and frequently of spirits and wine'. If that wasn't enough, they also mentioned that the doctors reckoned he could last another month yet. Against this background then, it's not surprising to read the diary entry of Field Marshal Sir Henry Wilson, the Longford-born Chief of the British Imperial General Staff, for that date.

'JT Davies [Private Secretary to Lloyd George] read me out yesterday's [Home Office] report on MacSwiney, the Lord Mayor of Cork, by the Home Office doctor. He said that he and another doctor had walked suddenly into the cell and had seen MacSwiney munching something and swallowing it. Later on the nurse found some substance in the basin after he had washed his teeth and this has been to the analyst. The other doctor said that if he had been called to a case such as he found in MacSwiney, he would have ordered gentle exercise.'

That this kind of falsehood was doing the rounds of the upper echelons of the British establishment even after two months of MacSwiney's hunger strike sums up how successful the government was at discrediting him among their own people, and how many influential figures believed he couldn't possibly be surviving without food. Certainly, this was also the line being posited by British agents. That week's intelligence briefing to the cabinet contained a paragraph reporting a secondhand conversation with a member of the Irish Self-Determination League that offered the following on the hunger strike.

'He [the ISDL informer] said that MacSwiney is being fed but that he does not get enough to keep him alive for long and they hope the government will release him just before his death. They realise that everyone in England has lost interest in MacSwiney and look upon him as a fraud, and the only reason for maintaining the hunger strike is that it is benefitting the Sinn Féin cause abroad.'

Not all the foreign coverage was positive. On 13 October, Day 62, the *New York Herald* published testimony from a dozen prominent New York doctors, each one offering the opinion that MacSwiney had to be receiving food. They based their long-distance diagnoses on the medical fact that it would be impossible for a man of his build to go sixty days without nourishment. A sensationalist daily with a history of anti-Catholic and anti-Irish bias, the *Herald*'s story was immediately picked up on by the English press.

Art O'Brien led the counter-offensive, writing a letter to Mr Stuart, editor of the *Herald*, calling into question the ability of a dozen doctors in a different country to diagnose a patient three thousand miles away, on whom they had never even set eyes.

'One marvels that men of scientific training should venture to give such emphatic opinions, without taking the elementary precaution of making an inquiry. What would be thought of any one of those doctors if they treated their patients in such a manner? It would seem that the oft-repeated statements of the relatives of the Lord Mayor of Cork, and also, I may say, of the English Home Office, to the effect that the Lord Mayor is not getting and has not had any form of nourishment, are both equally without result. One can understand that the ordinary public, without knowledge and without easy access to knowledge, should be doubtful about anything which is not a common incident in their daily lives, but one cannot forgive those who have had the advantage of scientific training, when they jump to conclusions in the same ignorant manner as the uneducated public.'

O'Brien broadened out his attack, opening fire on doctors in London who were not involved in the case yet freely gave quotes to newspapers about MacSwiney's condition and the circumstances of his going without food. He also lambasted physicians in general for not being more interested in and fascinated by the scientific and anatomical wonder that was the strike.

'What a commentary on the results of what is known as modern education that those, who are looked to by the multitude to have knowledge of and to cure the human body, should stand aside scoffing, when the most carefully-prepared experiment in a subject of great physiological interest (i.e. the maintaining of the human body without nutriment) is being carried out? For such indeed is the proper explanation of what is happening at Brixton. In none of the known cases of fasting or hunger-striking has the same minute care been taken to prevent the waste of tissue, as is being taken today by the English Government in Brixton Gaol.

'Were the British Government a scientific society and had Terence MacSwiney offered himself for such an experiment, one could have given admiration to both parties. What is to be thought of a so-called civilised government that will forcibly carry out such an experiment on a man, whom they held as a helpless prisoner by main force? And what is to be thought of the medical profession, who, knowing that such an experiment is being carried out, will merely stand aside and scoff?'

He finished this vituperative and often bizarre letter by citing the fact that Sir Norman Moore had independently examined the mayor. Even though the President of the College of Physicians was refusing to talk to the press, O'Brien was sure that the esteemed doctor would share private patient information with his medical colleagues if they would only go to the trouble of contacting him. This, he advised, all doctors should do before commenting further.

The previous week O'Brien had reacted in similar fashion when Dr Angus MacPherson, Assistant Medical Secretary of the British Medical Association, had questioned the validity of the hunger strike. Indeed, following correspondence between the pair on that occasion, O'Brien told MacPherson that the family was willing to pass him daily information so that he could make a study of the effects of depriving the body of nutrition for such an incredible amount of time. MacPherson declined the invitation but was politic enough to declare that he had 'the greatest respect for anyone making a sacrifice for a cause or principle of justice in which he or she is convinced'.

That sacrifice continued to take an ever greater toll. Since the passing of the 60-day mark, there had been more signs of a further and significant deterioration. On 12 October, Day 61, MacSwiney complained of being unable to see properly, a darkness coming down over his eyes and depriving him of vision. One of the doctors also wrote that the prisoner was losing his sharpness of mind and getting mixed up very easily. While the official bulletin subsequently described the mayor as having reached the lowest point yet the following day, he rallied over the next twenty-four hours and, under the circumstances, on

14 October, Day 63, was described as 'fairly easy'.

The relative calm on view that particular morning led those maintaining vigil to surmise that the most worrisome bouts were often followed by periods of comparative quiet. By now, every visitor was careful to ration attempts at conversation, aware of the debilitating effect the mere effort of responding was having. Still, some things remained at the front of his mind. As Father Dominic readied to leave shortly after 10 o'clock on the night of 14 October, MacSwiney asked, in the low, stuttering whisper that was now his normal voice: 'How are the gallant fellows in Cork?'

The eleven hunger strikers at home were struggling much the same as he was. Fading, wasting away, barely holding on. Even if the international press may not have found their plight quite as interesting, MacSwiney never lost his sense of solidarity with his suffering colleagues.

As for Cork itself, well, Cork had problems of its own. Four lorry-loads of British soldiers had raided the City Hall at noon on 14 October, their first visit since the fateful night of 12 August, rounding up every person in the building and searching all offices. John Eager, a clerk in the Highways Department, was arrested for possessing a ticket for the raffle of a revolver.

The next morning, trouble came to the new Ford automobile tractor plant on the Cork docks. During the early shift that day, notices were posted up advising workers that they were forbidden from leaving the premises in order to attend masses being said all over town for the hunger strikers. Every employee was warned that by doing so they risked dismissal and/or having money docked from their wages. At around 11.30am, the vast majority of the workforce walked out the gates and headed to church, just like so many other employees all over the city and county. Upon their return, nearly two hours later, these thousand or so men discovered that the gates had been locked.

During the stand-off that ensued, JJ Walsh, TD for Cork City, went inside to remonstrate with Edward Grace, the American-born managing director of the facility, who told him that the plan was to hire an entire new workforce to replace those who'd left. After some negotiation, Grace rowed back from that idea and declared that all employees would be allowed to return to their jobs on Monday morning. In return, Walsh gave an assurance about the future discipline of the staff and then told reporters that the main issue had been the shortness of notice involved. Grace had told him that if he'd merely been consulted in advance, he'd have been amenable to the idea.

While the Ford workers were risking their livelihoods to pray on his behalf, MacSwiney's own battle to stay alive went on throughout 15 October, Day 64, when, to those who'd been watching him closely, he appeared weaker and closer to death than ever.

'My brother is confident that his case will receive the consideration of parliament soon after that body convenes next Tuesday,' said Annie MacSwiney upon leaving the prison that day. 'It is his hope through Parliamentary action that he will obtain his release. This I believe has kept him alive in the last few days. His mind is clear but his whispers are scarcely audible. The emaciation which has been most marked in his legs and arms is now giving his face an unnatural appearance. Personally I don't think he can hold out much longer.'

On 16 October, Day 65, Winston Churchill addressed a meeting at the King's Theatre in Dundee, Scotland. In a wide-ranging attack on Ireland during which he questioned whether those waging 'terrorism' in the country were real Irishmen at all, and then asserted that the United Kingdom had the resources to rescue the people there from their horrible fate, he saved special mention for the events at Brixton Prison.

'It was during the silly season that the Lord Mayor announced his determination to starve himself to death. If the Government had given way, the whole administration of criminal justice would be broken down.' He paused here to allow the hearty chorus of 'hear, hears' to waft around the hall before continuing.

'The Lord Mayor did not want to die, and the Government did not want him to die but Alderman MacSwiney had many friends in Ireland who wished he would die. After six weeks fasting, the Lord Mayor is still alive.' He paused again, as gales of laughter broke out among his audience. 'Personally, I hope he will survive to see the dawn of a brighter day in Ireland.'

Churchill's figures were incorrect. It had been more than nine weeks now, not six. On this, MacSwiney's 65th day without food, he appeared mentally sharper than previously but, as the ISDL bulletin put it, remained in a condition of 'infinite weakness'. Yet, he was still capable of defiant grandiloquence even under this duress.

'I am content,' said MacSwiney. 'If I die, I will have died for Ireland. It is wonderful to think that I am privileged to give myself for my country. I harbour no vengeance and hold no grievances. Whatever happens is for the best.'

Elsewhere in London that same day, Muriel MacSwiney sat

down to do an interview with Forbes W Fairbairn, a London correspondent for the Universal Service, whose work appeared regularly in several American newspapers. In yet another attempt to advertise her husband's imprisonment in the US press, Muriel delivered a tour de force. Fairbairn was so impressed with her performance under such appalling stress and strain that he described her as 'A perfect Titan of courage and patience'. He also elicited a stunning first-person account of what she had experienced over the previous two months, watching her husband fade in front of her eyes. It is reproduced here in full:

'Terence is the sole occupant of a large, airy prison infirmary, in which there are six beds. His is in the corner opposite the fireplace. On each side wall are several crucifixes that have been sent to him by his friends. There are no other decorations. The two doors are closely barred. The large windows are barred, but there is plenty of light. The room is kept at a high temperature by hot-water pipes and a fireplace.

Terence wears pyjamas and bed-slippers. He has an ordinary mattress. An air mattress had been tried but it was less comfortable than the regular one. His head rests on a pillow and is only slightly raised from the bed. The bedclothes are of the lightest texture but are warm.

The best care is taken of him. He has a bath in bed three times a day, 10 o'clock, 1.30 and 5. He is shaved by an expert barber three times each week. His hair is cut once a week.

The doctor visits him three times each day, taking his temperature, his pulse and using a stethoscope to learn the condition of his heart and lungs. A nurse is in constant attendance. There is a glass-topped nightstand at his bedside on which is water and nourishment suitable to his condition should he care to break his fast.

The report that he is being fed by us or by the Government is absolutely false. It is simply propaganda from the British press. One of his family or Father Dominic is always at his bedside. The vigil is unceasing. His only nourishment – infinitesimal – is the transparent wafer of unleavened bread, not bigger than a halfpenny piece, given him in communion each morning by Fr. Dominic. That is all, except water, of which he drinks a lot. If it were not for the water he would have been dead long ago.

He lies motionless all the time, except when he is lifted for a bath. His body is simply a skeleton. His skin is tightly drawn and parchment like. This morning when I saw him his face was pure white, like marble. The sallowness had gone. His cheeks were sunken. The skin had shrunk back, baring his teeth. His body is absolutely dead, except for his eyes, lips and hands. His eyes and hands are the most wonderful.

The eyes are always bright. The hands are thin and wasted but not so much as his body. He is unable to lift his arms. His fingers jerk back and forth convulsively from nervousness. The slightest touch on any part of his body gives him an exquisite pain. When he wants his bed-clothing moved he signals for assistance with his eyes. It hurts him to touch the cloth with his fingertips. If it wasn't for his eyes and fingers one might think he was dead. Once in a while he moves his head sideways but that for him is a great effort. When he wants water the messages come with his eyes.

His brain is wonderfully clear. He speaks but seldom, but is able to hear clearly. Nearly all of the words he utters are for me. I have to place my ear close to his lips to hear them. Even then I am not always so successful. The slightest effort to speak is so painful that sometimes when I visit him not a word is uttered. Sometimes, he rallies and is able to talk for a minute or so. This is very exhausting.

His main thoughts are for Máire, our two-year old daughter. He has not seen her for nearly three months. When he talks it is chiefly about her. He wants her near him but won't let me bring her in. "I would give everything to see her," he tells me, "but I am afraid the strain on her would be too great. She might not get over seeing me in this condition. It is better if I have to die that she remembers me as she last saw me in Cork."

He loves her heart and soul and she loves him. She is just old enough to know him well. She calls him Daddy. He has her nurse write us daily telling all about her. I read the letter to him.

But as much as he loves Máire and me, he loves Ireland more. I am glad that he is the man that he is. I wouldn't have married him had he been otherwise. I do not think I would even be a good friend unless he was an Irishman, for Irish freedom first, last and all the time. He is just the man I thought him. I rejoice in his fight as much as it hurts me. I love him more and more every day.

Terence hardly ever mentions Ireland. I know and the whole world now knows his views. He is dying for his ideals and his country. Naturally, he shows the greatest interest in Irish affairs, but I tell him only what I think best, so as not to tire him. He is satisfied that he is making the supreme effort for his country. He knows that every day he lives he is vindicating the rights of Irishmen.

Nothing England can do can hurt him now. He knows who is

responsible for his imprisonment and his present condition. He rejoices that he has the opportunity of demonstrating his patriotism to the world. I rejoice with him, and though I love him with all the love woman ever had for a man, I would not have him change one whit.

He always felt that he would die for Ireland. He was a pioneer in the cause at Cork when the people all around him opposed his beliefs. His life has always been in danger. He thought that he would be killed in the rebellion but came safely through. Now he is going through this torture, but gladly, because it is for Ireland. If he dies I will go back to my mother with my baby.

He knows that every day he lives adds just so much to the cause of freedom. If he dies, it will be the greatest blow to British tyranny in Ireland that has ever been struck. Letters from his friends and supporters say the Irish people consider his sacrifice of greater importance and power than the rebellion. I know the Irish people all over the world are with him in the greatest sacrifice a man can make.

He often asks me if the strain is not too great for me to bear. It is a great strain, but I will bear it gladly. He is most cheerful when I am by his side and my visits to him are a comfort to me. It is terrible but I will bear up for his sake. I would not do anything to change his determination.

He cannot read anything. He cannot sit up in bed. He lies motionless all the time. His eyes are closed, except when he is spoken to or when he is looking at a crucifix on the wall. It is his dominant spiritual will that is keeping him alive. That and nothing else. He has been schooled to develop his will during the long fight for Irish freedom. None of us – he included – ever expected that he would live as long as this. I remember his words when he was sentenced. He said: "I will be released within a month, either by death or by the British Government".'

Sixty-one days had now passed since he'd made that statement at his court-martial in Cork.

CHAPTER 11

Forcing the Issue

Terence MacSwiney's hunger strike in an English prison was coming to an end. The result was inevitable; we hoped he would not be released when his body was almost used up. Feeling at home seemed to have sent impulses abroad to the European press; it seemed the most important event that had occurred in Ireland ... He had become a symbol of part of a new nation; disciplined, hard, clear, unsentimental, uncompromising, a conscious using of vigour to build up strength.
Ernie O'Malley, *On Another Man's Wound.*

At 9.45pm on Sunday, 17 October, Michael Fitzgerald died in Cork Gaol after 68 days on hunger strike. Although the fast of Fitzgerald and his ten colleagues predated MacSwiney's and their suffering received much less international recognition, their protest was subject to much the same sort of innuendo and speculation regarding its extraordinary longevity. While many in their hometown believed it was the efficacy and holistic nature of the nursing they received from nuns in the prison that kept them alive, the British authorities and others reckoned them to be receiving some sort of food by some unexplained and never-discovered means.

The first of them to go passed away in a cell the walls of which he and his fellow prisoners had decorated with holy medals, statues of Our Lady, and a photograph of Terence MacSwiney. Having been detained on a charge of murdering Private Jones when the Cork No. 2 Brigade of the IRA ambushed a contingent of British soldiers on the way to church in Fermoy on 7 September 1919, Fitzgerald was never properly tried. Due to the lack of people willing to serve as jurors, he had been in custody without trial for over a year.

'Not tears but joy for our comrade who was ready to meet his God and die for his country,' dictated MacSwiney in a message conveyed to the prisoners in Cork via the office of the Deputy Lord Mayor. 'He has joined the Immortals and will be remembered forever. We do not know who is the second to step on the path of immortality, but by offering unreserved sacrifice we are safeguarding the destinies of Ireland. I join with my comrades in Cork in sending heartfelt sympathy to all the relatives of our revered, fallen colleague.'

Another telegram was sent by Father Dominic directly to Michael Fitzgerald's father.

'On behalf of the Lord Mayor and myself, I tender heartiest and most deep-felt sympathy for the loss you have sustained on the death of your noble son. We know you will be supported in this hour by the immeasurable service of the sacrifice for Ireland. God bless and strengthen you.'

Before that grim news had reached Brixton, MacSwiney's 66th day passed without incident. All things being relative to his recent travails, he looked better than at any time in the previous week. Still obviously weakening by the hour and suffering from a minor cold, he was nevertheless more alert and his mind keener than it had been for some time. He slept peacefully for part of the day, and in the afternoon spoke to relatives with something approaching fluency.

He was quieter on 18 October, Day 67. When he did finally start to speak that Monday morning, it was, inevitably, about the fate of Fitzgerald. He asked his family to pray with him for his deceased colleague and for those still maintaining their own fast in Cork. Following the first of his daily examinations, the good medical news was that the cold remained confined to his head and throat and hadn't yet threatened his vulnerable lungs. The bad news was that the doctors had diagnosed the first signs of scurvy.

Doctors Griffiths and Higson, the usual attending physicians, were accompanied that afternoon by a specialist, Dr Beddard (who had previously visited with Dr Norman Moore). It was Beddard who informed the family that, unless action was taken, the scurvy would develop further and cause serious pain before long. He asked Mary MacSwiney if she could persuade her brother to take lime or orange juice to stave off the onset of scurvy.

'I assure you Miss MacSwiney that your brother will not die in peace if he gets scurvy,' said Beddard. 'He will die with the most terrible tortures. And you had better urge him to take lime juice now.'

'It would be a terrible thing to die with tortures,' replied Mary. 'The matter is in God's hands and we can only ask that He does not let him suffer too much.'

'God has nothing to do with it,' said Beddard, growing more and more agitated. 'The case is in our hands – your hands and my hands. And we shall see that he will have to take lime juice!'

MacSwiney himself was warned by the doctors that as soon as he lapsed into unconsciousness, the physicians would feel compelled, as per their professional oaths, to do all they could to save his life. This would entail feeding him while he was unconscious and unable to object to the procedure. As soon as this scenario (initially mentioned as far back as his first week in Brixton) was put to him, the mayor responded with the now expected note of defiance.

'In his present state of extreme weakness, the Lord Mayor naturally feels such action of feeding him would only prolong his torture,' went the statement from the ISDL that night. 'He wishes it known however that he is perfectly happy. If there is any attempt to feed him while he is unconscious, he will recommence the hunger strike as soon as revived, and whether life or death for him and his comrades is the outcome of the present struggle, they have won their battle, and evacuation of Ireland by the enemy will follow soon.'

More than once during the previous two months, Father Dominic had asked him whether he still had any desire for food. On this particular day, he told his friend: 'I'd give a thousand pounds for a cup of tea.'

In America on 19 October, Day 68, several hundred students at the University of Illinois in Urbana fasted all day long in sympathy with MacSwiney. Nearer home, a meeting of Irish bishops in Maynooth that day culminated in a controversial pastoral letter, which reproved all crime being carried out in the country but pointedly denounced a British policy in Ireland that was characterised by terrorism, partiality and failure. The situation in Brixton was on the minds of the episcopate too.

'... even more cruel and no less fatal to all hope of peace between the two countries is the prolonged imprisonment of the Lord Mayor of Cork, and the other hunger strikers, who make little account of their lives if they can do Ireland a service, in the affliction in which a foreign domination has sunk her.'

In the House of Commons that same plight was simultaneously being regarded in a very different light. Horatio Bottomley, Independent MP for Hackney South, raised the matter with a question to the Home Secretary.

MR. BOTTOMLEY (by Private Notice): Is it true as reported in the Press, that Alderman MacSwiney, Lord Mayor of Cork, now undergoing a sentence of two years' imprisonment in Brixton Gaol, has been on hunger strike for 68 days and is now in a critical condition and, if so, whether, having regard to the suffering he must have endured and to the possible good effect which such action might have upon the present situation in Ireland, he (the Home Secretary) will advise His Majesty to exercise his prerogative of mercy and order the release of the prisoner?

MR SHORTT: The statements in the first part of the question are substantially correct. I cannot advise His Majesty in the way suggested.

Resounding cheers greeted this response from Shortt. When they died down, Bottomley tried again.

MR BOTTOMLEY: So far as the prison authorities are concerned there has been no form of feeding whatever?

MR SHORTT: Not on the part of the prison authorities.

During this brief exchange, voices from the floor had questioned the credibility of the hunger strike and accused Father Dominic of passing food to the prisoner. When Shortt stated that he had nothing more to add on the subject, Josiah Jones, Liberal Party MP for Llanelli and ally of Lloyd George, shouted: 'He has been fed on Coalition soup.'

There was laughter in the house at that quip, so much laughter indeed that a member on the Labour benches beseeched his colleagues to show some respect. Not too many obeyed that instruction and, from the Distinguished Visitors Gallery, a group of turbanned Indian gentlemen looked on bemused at the spectacle of Members of Parliament guffawing about a man dying on hunger strike in an English prison.

Across London, the mood was growing ever darker. That morning, MacSwiney and Dr Griffiths had got into an altercation about lime juice. The mayor felt the doctor had been a little too forceful in suggesting that he drink the stuff, alleging that a threat had even been made to force him to swallow it. A threat he responded to by declaring he'd give up swallowing completely to prevent such action being taken.

Eventually, he demanded and received an audience with Captain Charles Haynes, governor of the prison. This didn't satisfy him either because afterwards he was even more distressed and frantic. Upon arriving in the corridor outside his room at lunchtime, Annie MacSwiney was quickly brought up to speed by her brother Peter.

'When I went in I found him very different from the previous day,' wrote Annie. 'His eyes looked excited and he was evidently very disturbed mentally. He began to speak at once ... The result on Terry was fatal. All Tuesday morning and afternoon, he was quite unlike himself, very excited and going over repeatedly what Dr Griffiths had said. I asked him was he satisfied with what he said to the Governor and he said: "Not very. I could not see him very well (his sight was dim now), and I could not make myself quite clear but I think he understands, I think it will be alright. I told him about Griffiths and that I would not take anything at all if they tried that trick."'

At four in the afternoon, Mary MacSwiney took over the shift by the bedside. She too noticed a great change in his demeanour even though he did begin to slowly settle down as the hours passed. He was somewhere approaching his normal self when Muriel arrived at 6.30pm. Of course, by this point, his normal self was a man struggling to make out the faces of those by his side and suffering increasingly frequent memory lapses.

The true state of his deterioration was reinforced the following morning, 20 October, Day 69. Having received Holy Communion early from Father Dominic, he complained again to the priest about Dr Griffiths threatening to make him take food, and thereafter drifted in and out of consciousness. Annie MacSwiney was alone with her brother for a while that morning and the silence inside the room was such that it was possible to hear some distant banging and clashing from the prison yard. Suddenly, her brother grew alert and animated.

'Do you hear that knocking: Do you hear it?' he asked. 'That's Griffiths' new treatment, that's what he was talking about now. You stay now and watch, listen, do you hear? What's the time?'

'Quarter past ten,' she replied.

'Show me the watch, I can tell the time more accurately than you – look it is only 13 and a half minutes past ten (it was). And today is Wednesday?'

'Yes.'

'Now, you think I am muddle-headed, but I am not.'

'No you are muddle-headed if you think that.'

'Yes.'

He grew still and stopped speaking for a few minutes, though he kept looking at her, as if trying to focus on her face. Then he was off again.

'Now you are my witness I'm a soldier dying for the Republic. Say this after me: "I Annie MacSwiney do hereby affirm that I am a soldier dying for the Republic." Now we will swear that, have you anything we could kiss?'

Annie held up the cross of her rosary beads. She kissed it herself and then gently pressed it on his lips as he lay still on the bed. Just then, she was called out of the room to take a phone call. Upon returning, her brother admonished her for leaving and failing to take note of the knocking as he'd asked.

'That's valuable evidence. It is of international importance – do not let a thing escape you – note it down.'

Dutifully, she took her pencil and inscribed upon his copy of The Gospels: '10.13 and half, Wednesday knocking'. When she stopped, he noticed and told her to keep going. She scribbled some more and then he lost concentration and succumbed to fresh delirium, throwing his arms up to hug her, talking wildly and making no sense. A nurse came over to intervene, a warder was called, and the doctor was sent for.

He lapsed in and out of clarity all that Wednesday, his fleeting and brief cameos of sense given over to poignant statements that would later have to be re-classified as goodbyes.

'Muriel, you have always stuck by me,' he said to his wife that afternoon. 'This is awful for you because you have to stay here.'

'It's a better time than we have had since we were married or since you have been Lord Mayor, because I can be with you all the time,' she said with a smile. And they both laughed.

Later, he turned to Mary, and called his sister by his pet name for her. 'Min, you are always loyal to Ireland. Stay by me and see what they do to me.' Ever-vigilant, Mary MacSwiney wasn't likely to fail him in that regard.

She complained to the authorities that his rapidly deteriorating mental state was a consequence of the threat to feed him playing upon his mind. Whatever the validity of that theory, there's no question that his brain was now succumbing after so long without sustenance. Early in the evening, she supervised the writing of wires from the family to Edward Shortt at the Home Office, and to several MPs in the Commons.

'Following Dr Griffiths' threat to force the Lord Mayor of Cork to take lime juice, delirium has set in today,' went the message to Shortt. 'The Lord Mayor has been bad all day owing to excitement caused by the threat in his prostrate condition after 70 days fast. Tonight at 6.30, Dr Griffiths announced to his sister he was going to forcibly feed the Lord Mayor. Will the representatives of the British people uphold this refinement of cruelty in prolonging the Lord Mayor's torture? After 10 days hunger strike, one prison doctor considered it dangerous to attempt forcible feeding. Dr Griffiths announces he will begin it on the 70th.'

Before Shortt had a chance to read the telegram, the substance of it was being raised in the House of Commons by Lieutenant-Commander Kenworthy, the Liberal MP for Hull who had accompanied Mary to the Trade Unions Congress the previous month. At the adjournment for the evening, Kenworthy asked the Home Secretary about the government's intention to force-feed the prisoner lime juice and other substances, and the dangers inherent in such a move.

'I can only say in perfectly general terms that the doctors will do, as they have done consistently, what they consider to be the best in the prisoner's interest,' answered Shortt. 'Their business is to try to keep him alive. They have done everything possible. He has had every possible consideration and care, and the best of nursing and everything has been done for him; but eat he will not. If the doctors think lime juice would ease him, help him to live, and give him another chance of seeing sense, they will be perfectly justified in trying to persuade him to take it, and, indeed, if necessary, in forcing it upon him.

'Whether they are doing so or not, I have not had an opportunity of ascertaining. I know that he has taken certain light medicines, like Eno's Fruit Salt from time to time, but whether he has taken lime juice or not, I have not had an opportunity of asking. I am satisfied that whatever the doctors have been doing has been done from a sense of pure mercy and consideration, and in what they consider to be the best possible interests of the prisoner himself.'

By the time Shortt delivered that response, the question was moot. During a lengthy bout of unconsciousness that Wednesday night, MacSwiney was forcibly fed with Brand's Beef Essence and drops of brandy. Upon awakening, he immediately tasted the food in his mouth and called his sister Mary, still standing sentry inside the room, to his side.

'I am afraid they have tricked me, have they?' he asked.

'I am afraid they have.'

'What did they give me?'

'Meat juice.'

'Wait a minute, we will have to keep cool now.'

At this juncture the nurse on duty came across and asked Mary to leave her brother be. He was aware enough to be angered by this.

'Go away nurse; I must speak to my sister.'

'You must not speak to her,' said the nurse.

'Go away, go away, go away, go away.'

'Nurse, please go away for a minute,' asked Mary. The nurse stepped away from the bed and she tried to calm her brother. 'It is all right now.'

'Wait a minute,' he said desperately. 'Wait a minute. Wait. Wait. Wait. Wait. Wait.'

He couldn't get anything else out of his mouth except 'wait' and then he lost his train of thought completely and descended into delirium once more.

That night, Mary and Father Dominic stayed over in the prison as the feeling grew that the end was now truly at hand. Dr Griffiths warned them that MacSwiney might not last more than twelve hours.

He endured to disprove that prognosis, but on 21 October, Day 70, he was, for the first time since his chaplain arrived in London, too weak even to receive Communion. He was unable to recognise his wife either when she arrived. Indeed, he couldn't make out anybody at all, the sight problems compounded now by the ongoing and more serious manic episodes. The vigil had reached its most painful point, the visitors agonising as they watched his mouth opening and closing as if in slow motion, his limbs twitching beneath the sheets, and the pain etched upon his face.

The body and the mind seemed to revolt against the food administered the previous day. He vomited copious amounts of green liquid and occasionally thrashed his arms around in the bed with anger and frustration. When he lapsed into unconsciousness again, however, he was fed once more: Brand's Beef Essence, drops of brandy, and Benger's Food [a liquid type of 'Complan' from that era which was usually given to the sick]. Two spoonfuls of Benger's were swallowed involuntarily but as soon as he awoke the trouble started. Ever hopeful that he might relinquish the struggle now that his fast had, by whatever means, been broken, a nurse placed a cupful at his lips.

'Will you have a little more now,' she asked, the question sending the watching Peter MacSwiney into a fury.

'It is a shame for you to ask an unconscious man that,' said Peter angrily. 'You know that if he were conscious he would say no. It is a mean thing to take advantage of a man in his condition. You had him here for seventy days and he would not take it from you. Why do you ask him a question like that now?'

Muriel MacSwiney was sitting in the room during the incident and she calmed her brother-in-law down.

In recognition of the increasing gravity of the situation, the bulletins to those waiting outside the gates of the jail were now being given every two hours.

4.30 – The Lord Mayor is still delirious and he looks much worse.

6.30 – The Lord Mayor had a violent fit of vomiting. His condition generally remains unchanged. He is now in a semi-conscious state and does not recognise anyone.

8.30 – Although his mouth, feet and hands are still subject to spasmodic working, the Lord Mayor has been calmer since the issue of the last bulletins. The vomiting has ceased but he is still retching.

10.30 – Condition is generally the same as at time of last bulletin.

Simultaneous to the prison drama, another production based around MacSwiney's case was taking place in the Commons:

MR. KENWORTHY: What is the condition of the health of the Hon. Member for Mid-Cork; and is it intended to retain him in prison?

MR. SHORTT: The condition of the prisoner is very serious. Until yesterday the doctors have given him medicines only, but yesterday, during a period of semi-consciousness, they gave him a little liquid food. I cannot speak for his friends. He will be retained in the prison hospital.

MR. KENWORTHY: Does that mean that forcible feeding against the man's will is being resorted to, and is there any legal justification for that in the case of this unfortunate gentleman?

MR. SHORTT: In this case forcible feeding consists merely in holding a cup to his lips, and the swallowing has been voluntary. In any case, forcible feeding is not only legal, but many times a duty.

MR. BOTTOMLEY: Has scientific evidence recently come to the possession of the Home Office proving that nourishment has been administered to this prisoner?

MR. SHORTT: No, that is not accurate.

Shortt knew that his description of the conditions under which MacSwiney had taken food wasn't accurate. The moment that news of how fast and loose the Home Secretary played with the truth of the circumstances of her brother's feeding reached Mary MacSwiney (and it was carried verbatim in the English newspapers the next morning), she put pen to paper.

'You are reported as having said in the House of Commons last evening that my brother, the Lord Mayor of Cork, swallowed, voluntarily, the food administered to him,' she wrote. 'That is another lie told for the purpose of discrediting my brother's position among foreign nations, who are watching his struggle with sympathy and interest. I have just seen one of the prison doctors, Dr Higson, and called attention to your statement. On his authority, I desire to inform you that my brother has been and still is quite unconscious that food is being administered to him, and that he is not in the very smallest degree responsible for anything that is being done to him. The action of swallowing is not voluntary, but reflex – a purely automatic action in which his will has no part.

'Of all the infamies possible to an individual, or a government, that of lying about an unconscious victim, who for the time being, is in their power, is the most vile. Your statement that you know that the prison doctor did not feed him till he became unconscious but that you cannot answer for what his friends are doing, is as despicable as the rest of your Government campaign of lies by implication against us. His friends, or any one of them, have never administered a particle of food to the Lord Mayor while he is on hunger strike, and you are quite aware of that fact. We have ceased to hope for any sign of honour or fair play from any member of the English government, but you will not succeed in discrediting us or the cause for which we stand – Ireland's independence among the civilized nations of the world.'

Father Dominic, Annie and Sean MacSwiney all stayed in the prison on Thursday night, fearing for and preparing for the worst. They weren't allowed in the room during those hours so they waited in the corridor outside, from where they took turns peeking through the keyhole to try to see what was happening inside. At 3 o'clock in the morning, the mayor became violent but soon fell back to sleep. He woke shortly before five when Annie, her ears to the door, overheard the following conversation.

'What is the time?' he asked the nurse by his bedside.

'A quarter to five.'

'A quarter to five in the morning or evening?'

'A quarter to five in the morning.'

'Where am I?'

When the nurse offered him a drink, he snapped at her.

'What's that?'

'Hot water.'

'Oh, hot water.' Satisfied with the answer, he sipped it down. He closed his eyes then, and at 7.30am, Annie was invited in to sit by the bed. No sooner had she sat down than her brother woke and stared back at her.

'Do you know me?' asked Annie.

'Yes,' he replied, the voice just audible.

'Who am I?'

'Annie,' he said. She paused then and he came back with questions of his own.

'What month is it?'

'October.'

'What year?'

'1920.'

'Have I been here all the summer?'

'Yes.'

'And have you been in England all the year?'

'No, only for two months.'

'But what are you all doing here?'

'Muriel, Máire [his sister, Mary MacSwiney, who was often also called Máire], and I are at the hotel.'

'What hotel?'

'The Germyn Court Hotel,' said Annie, 'and Peter too.'

'Peter?' he repeated the name in a puzzled tone, 'Peter?' He seemed to be struggling to comprehend how his brother from America was in London. After a pause, he quizzed her some more.

'But what is it all for, what are we here for?' he asked.

'Don't you remember you're in Brixton?'

He stared back at his sister as if trying to figure out exactly where he was.

'What count have they got me here for?'

'For the Irish Republic.' That answer brought something

approaching a bright smile to his wan face.

'So it is established?'

'Yes,' said Annie.

'Is it in alliance with the Allies?' he asked.

Annie wasn't sure how to play this, worrying over what response might impact on a man in such a fragile state. She gave the one she thought he'd like best.

'Yes!' she declared.

At that, he stared some more, then:

'Oh we did grand marching in the night,' he said, 'and they marched too, we made them march, but we marched better!'

That was the point when he stopped making sense and began rambling again, his eyes flitting around the room as if searching for something he couldn't find.

So began 22 October, Day 71.

Annie left in mid-morning, her place taken by Mary. Later, Muriel and Peter came on the scene and it was that pair who were by the bedside on Friday evening when Dr Griffiths came into the room. As was their custom, the family members walked out to afford him privacy to do his job. They were sitting in the corridor waiting to go back in when the warder came along. The prison officer announced that, following a conversation with Dr Griffiths, his new orders were that there were to be no further visitors. The room containing Terence MacSwiney was now off-limits to everybody.

'They now also said that we were not even to stay outside the door,' said Muriel. 'You see, when we would go outside the room before, we used to stay outside the door always. And they also stopped up every little hole or window we could see through.

The warder said we could not stay outside the door, and I said I wanted to speak to the doctor and he went down and found him. And I asked him if he was dying, if he would not want his wife to be near him. He said he would. And he said it was bad for us to be in the room, so many of us.'

During the lengthy discussion that ensued, Muriel asked whether it would be better if only one person from the family went in at a time. Dr Griffiths responded by saying that it was the nurses who wanted them all kept away from the prisoner. Eventually, he told her that she could go in whenever the nurse saw fit to allow her, and could also wait outside the door of the room at all other times. However, this proposed solution involved the rest of the family being excluded completely.

'I cannot be here always and what will we do when I cannot be here?' protested Muriel.

After Griffiths suggested that the sisters and brothers could continue to maintain their vigil downstairs, within the prison walls yet with no access to their dying brother, Muriel alleged that the doctor and his colleagues must be doing things to the patient they were ashamed for the family to see. Finally, the doctor agreed that whenever she wasn't able to attend, she could nominate a family member to take her place in the room, with the nurse's permission. At this point, she went upstairs and had it out with the nurse on duty.

'What harm have I done since I have been here with my husband?' asked Muriel.

'None,' replied the nurse. 'You do not interfere with me. You have never interfered with me when I was feeding him. But I know you are against it, and it makes me nervous.'

As Peter MacSwiney left Brixton around six o'clock that evening, he met Annie at the gate, and gave her a quick summary of the situation. She wasn't surprised then when a warder subsequently blocked her path and told her that she'd have to wait downstairs until the nurse gave the okay to go up to her brother's room. A request to wait in the corridor outside her brother's room in the meantime was also denied.

When Annie finally made it upstairs, she went to the nurse on duty and asked why she didn't want them in the room any more.

'You refused to go away yesterday when I asked you,' said the nurse.

'You asked me then would I prefer not to witness you give him food and I replied that it did not matter whether I was inside or outside the room as the pain was the same to me since I knew you were doing it. You never suggested that it was for any reason of your own, or for anything you needed to do for him.'

'Well, your brother hurt me very much yesterday,' said the nurse.

'I knew he [Peter] spoke to you,' said Annie. 'He felt how cruel it all was, and how mean it was to ask him, when he was unconscious to take food. He was sorry after he had spoken.'

'You all make me nervous and I can't do my work,' said the nurse. 'I don't like doing it because it is against his will and against your will but I have to do it, and when I feel you are all watching me I can't do it.'

The quest for an explanation for the new visiting regime involved another confrontation that Friday night between Dr Griffiths, the nurse and Mary MacSwiney. All of the discussions and debate came to naught. Although Sean MacSwiney and

Father Dominic were allowed to remain in the prison overnight, the access to the mayor that the family had retained for over two months was now placed under severe and punitive restrictions. Some of them would never see him alive again.

CHAPTER 12

A Perfect Martyr

... We know their dream; enough
To know they dreamed and are dead.
And what if excess of love
Bewildered them till they died?
I write it out in a verse –
MacDonagh and MacBride
And Connolly and Pearse
Now and in time to be,
Wherever green is worn,
Are changed, changed utterly:
A terrible beauty is born.
Extract from 'Easter 1916', WB Yeats.

On Saturday, 23 October, Day 72, WB Yeats's 'Easter 1916', arguably the most nationalist poem in his canon, was published for the first time in the *New Statesman* magazine. Originally written in the months after the Easter Rising, he had refrained from putting it in any publication or in his 1917 collection 'The Wild Swans at Coole'. Consequently, it had been available only to a privileged audience for years and was described by one academic as existing in the interim as an 'underground text'. The decision to finally go mainstream with this potentially controversial work was regarded as a deliberate and overt political gesture, and can also be viewed very obviously as a by-product of the poet watching MacSwiney's struggle over the preceding three months.

As Yeats went public with what would become one of his most oft-quoted poems, premature reports of MacSwiney's imminent death continued to whirl around London as the hunger striker began the improbable 72nd day of his fast. That very morning, a bouquet arrived at the jail from Eileen O'Leary, an old friend from Cork. 'Kindly accept these few flowers for your little altar, "brave one",' she wrote on the attached note. 'God is all-merciful and will not forsake you in your darkest hour. Chin up – Ireland (all of us are praying for you here) and masses are being said for you everywhere, brave one.'

As per the rota system the family had established for much of the previous two months to ensure that somebody was always by the bedside, Mary was the first due at the prison to relieve the night watchmen, Sean and Father Dominic. When she arrived at the gate shortly after half past eight that Saturday morning, however, there was a break from the usual protocol.

'What is your name, please?' asked the warder.

'MacSwiney,' she replied, shocked at the sudden outburst of formality after so many weeks during which the family were allowed in and out with some ease.

'Your Christian name, please?'

'Miss Mary MacSwiney.'

'I cannot admit you,' said the warder after a brief pause.

'On whose orders?'

'On the governor's.'

'May I see the governor?'

'He is not here. Now will you kindly step outside the prison gate.'

She refused to leave, instead installing herself in the nearby waiting room so she could accost every prison official and every doctor on their way in and out. Each gave the same answer to her question as to the provenance of the order banning her from entering the jail. It soon emerged that the directive to prohibit her from seeing her brother had come straight from the Home Office. Mary sat down and almost immediately dashed off a letter that Sean McGrath, a Volunteer who'd accompanied Father Dominic to the prison that morning, then delivered to Annie at the Irish Self-Determination League offices in Adam Street.

'In it she told me what had happened on her arrival, and said she was going to remain there fasting, on hunger strike too, until she saw Terry,' wrote Annie MacSwiney. 'She said the order of exclusion from Terry did not apply to me but Fr. Dominic said it did. However, I said I would go out and if prevented, would join her there, and neither of us would leave or touch food, until we had seen Terry. It was after 1 o'clock when I arrived at the prison and I was allowed inside (the outer gate), contrary to any expectation but was informed I could not see Terry, nor be allowed inside the prison.'

Annie joined her sister in the waiting room then, and there the two women sat for the rest of the day and into the evening. They refused to take food and rebuffed all efforts – even those of the prison Governor, Captain Charles Haynes – to persuade them to leave.

'The order to expel me came from my publishing Dr Higson's statement that my brother was not voluntarily swallowing,' claimed Mary as she sought an explanation for this action. 'And she [Annie] was expelled because my brother recognised her [the previous day].'

The exclusion order did not apply to Muriel MacSwiney. She'd arrived in Brixton earlier in the morning. By then Mary had already begun her protest, but the mayor's wife was allowed to go upstairs. However, when she reached the corridor leading to her husband's room, she discovered that the landscape had changed there too. The nurse on duty prevented her from seeing her husband.

Muriel's first move was to go to the telephone to call Art O'Brien with an update on what was happening so he could go public with it in the next two-hourly bulletin about MacSwiney's condition. On this day, though, that tactic was circumvented. The phone was declared off-limits by a prison clerk who explained he'd been ordered by the governor not to let the family use it. Muriel accepted a subsequent offer to take the matter up with Captain Haynes who then claimed that the decision was made because the family was using the telephone too much. She didn't believe this, pointing out that they'd only ever used it with the permission of the warder. Matters deteriorated from there.

'You must have got orders about this so that they are stopping us from going in to see my husband,' said Muriel.

'You are very well treated here,' said Haynes. 'You are using this place like a hotel coming in here any moment you like.'

'This is hardly a hotel. My husband does not wish to be here and you are keeping him against his will.'

'Even in ordinary hospitals there are visiting hours, and you are not allowed to see your friends at any time.'

'In an ordinary hospital we would have put my husband there with people whom we trusted.'

Despite her best efforts to persuade him otherwise, the phone remained off-limits. The only concession Haynes would make was an offer that any message the family wished to be conveyed outside the prison should be written down on paper and handed to a warder who would then phone it for them.

When Muriel went back to the room where her husband lay, the nurse allowed her inside for half an hour. Then she was asked to leave again. The nurse mentioned that it was time to take his temperature. Muriel suspected it was more likely time for them to force-feed him again. Either way, she was allowed back in after that for another half an hour visit with her unconscious husband.

At one point, as she sat by his bedside that Saturday afternoon, she leaned over to kiss him and thought she saw a little smile of recognition break across his face. She wasn't certain, but, as time passed, she liked to think that's what it was, because that would be the last time she ever saw him alive. Muriel departed the prison that afternoon and accompanied Art O'Brien to the Home Office to protest the restrictions being placed upon her sisters-in-law, and to ask for telephone rights to be restored. On both counts, their requests were ignored. The rules of the game, it seemed, had suddenly and irrevocably changed.

When O'Brien and the ISDL publicised the refusal to allow the sisters to visit their dying brother, and the decision to prevent family members using the prison phone, the Home Office responded by pointing out that the prisoner's delicate condition required careful nursing, the type of care that might be made more difficult by too many visitors. It also rather mischievously implied that MacSwiney's scurvy had improved due to his food intake and that this new course of action might yet prolong his life. Despite that assertion and notwithstanding the fact that the ISDL was unable to issue many bulletins that day (for the want of fresh eyewitness information) international news agencies reported at noon that MacSwiney was very near the end, being watched over by his wife and Father Dominic.

Eight hours after that byte of information hit the wires, the ISDL issued another update. 'The condition of the Lord Mayor has not materially changed. He is still unconscious and does not recognise anyone. His mouth moves at times as if he wished to speak. The Lady Mayoress was allowed to spend only an hour with him today and Peter MacSwiney was allowed to see him for only a few minutes. The refusal to allow his two sisters to see him continues, and they are still in the waiting room, refusing to leave until they see their brother.'

The sisters hadn't budged. No persuasion could move them from the cold, dank room where they had spent all day hoping that the mood might change and the authorities would relent. It didn't and they didn't. At ten o'clock that night, the matter finally came to a head when the deputy governor became the latest emissary to try to cajole them into leaving the building.

'Miss MacSwiney, it is time to lock up,' he said to Mary.

'Very well, lock up,' she responded.

'I am afraid you must go out.'

'I will not go out until I see my brother.'

'You must for it is time to lock up the prison.'

'It is strange to be locking up a place that is always locked up. If you will let me see my brother for five minutes, I will go away but not before.'

'The local police have orders to put you out by force.'

'Very well. If the local police – enough of them – come in and use force to put two women out, they can do so. But I will not go voluntarily.'

'And what do you say?' asked the deputy governor, turning to Annie MacSwiney.

'My sister expresses my views, but it is not necessary for us to say it in chorus. We won't go until we have seen our brother.'

'I just want things to be pleasant.'

'They are very pleasant aren't they when our brother is dying here and we will not be allowed five minutes by his bedside.'

The deputy then tried a different tack, pointing out he was merely following a government order and again warning that the Home Office had phoned the local constabulary, ordering them to use force to remove the women if necessary.

'You can arrest us if you like,' said Mary. 'We are only two women and cannot resist your armed force, but we will yield to nothing except force.'

The debate went on for close to an hour during which the deputy governor was eventually joined by three police inspectors. All four men argued the same point with the recalcitrant sisters. They didn't want to arrest them. They were simply carrying

Right: Archbishop Daniel Mannix of Australia and Eamon de Valera, here pictured with Father Flanagan of Boystown fame, were two outspoken supporters of MacSwiney in the international press.

Below: Bishop Daniel Cohalan entertaining WT Cosgrave and a government delegation at the Bishop's Palace, Cork. The Bishop was an old friend of MacSwiney's who travelled to London to visit him in Brixton Prison.

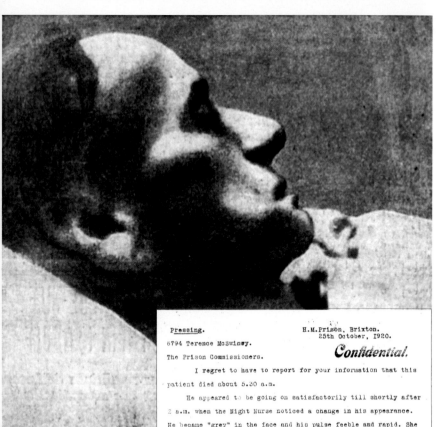

Top: The emaciated face of Terence MacSwiney, in a photograph published by a French newspaper under the heading: 'The Lord Mayor of Cork Two Days Before His Death'.

Pressing.   H.M.Prison, Brixton.
                                              25th October, 1920.
6794 Terence McSwiney.

The Prison Commissioners.   *Confidential.*

    I regret to have to report for your information that this patient died about 5.30 a.m.

    He appeared to be going on satisfactorily till shortly after 2 a.m. when the Night Nurse noticed a change in his appearance. He became "grey" in the face and his pulse feeble and rapid. She administered the remedies ordered to meet such a situation and sent for Dr. Methven who came at once. I was sent for and arrived about 3.45 a.m. He was then very collapsed. Everything possible was done. I telephoned for Dr. Beddard but the patient died just before his arrival.

    The Night Nurse reports that until the change about 2 a.m. the patient had taken his medicines and nourishment without any apparent unwillingness and that he appeared to be going on much as usual.

    In my opinion on the advent of the scurvy a definite change took place in the patient's already debilitated condition and was probably responsible for the acute mental symptoms. It was in the state of acute delirium that the patient's heart became dilated and the immediate cause of death was heart failure.

    He was quite quiet during the night.
                     (Sgd) G.B.Griffiths.

Above: The prison doctor's notification of the death of Prisoner 6794.

THE BRITISH WAY: A FUNERAL UNDER A REBEL FLAG IN THE CAPITAL OF THE EMPIRE.

LONDON AND THE FUNERAL OF THE LATE LORD MAYOR OF CORK: THE HEARSE AT THE OPENING OF THE PROCESSION CROSSING BLACKFRIARS BRIDGE ON ITS WAY IN ROUTE

Coverage of MacSwiney's funeral in *The Illustrated London News*

Above: A delegation from Cork Corporation and Cork Harbour Board travelled to London to accompany their mayor home.

Below: Crowds watch as the remains arrive in Cobh on board the *Rathmore*.

Above: The coffin arrives at the Cork quays on board the *Mary Tavy*.

Right: The remains of the Lord Mayor lie in state in Cork City Hall.

Above: Peter (left) and Sean MacSwiney help carry their brother's coffin out of City Hall.

Below: The funeral procession on Cornmarket Street, Cork.

Right:
Muriel MacSwiney went to America after her husband's death to rally support for the Irish Republic.

Left: Irish-American women protest outside the Seventh Regiment Armoury in New York.

THE BRUTISH EMPIRE

Left: The bust of Tomás MacCurtain outside City Hall, Cork.

Below: Lord Mayor Sean Martin and Máire MacSwiney Brugha at the bust of her father, Terence MacSwiney outside City Hall, 2004.

out orders from higher up, and failing to do so would cost them their jobs.

'If you had a servant and gave an order which she disliked, you would expect her to obey it no matter how much she disliked it,' said one of the inspectors, attempting to explain why they were keeping the women from seeing their dying brother.

'I'd expect her to leave my employment rather than do any dishonourable act, no matter how strong the order,' replied Annie.

The situation had become intractable. Shortly before eleven o'clock, the constables placed their hands on the shoulders of the women and the MacSwiney sisters regarded forcing the police into that physical action – constituting a technical arrest in their minds – as a victory of sorts. Then, they walked rather than were forcibly ejected from the prison. Aware of the drama that was playing out in the waiting room, Art O'Brien had a taxi waiting outside the gate to bring the women directly back to their hotel at the end of such a stressful day.

On Sunday, 24 October, Day 73, the warders had learned their lesson from the day before. When the sisters approached the outer gate that morning, they were refused admission completely. There would be no repeat of the histrionics that took place in the waiting room and there would be no softening of the government's position either. Though the bulletins about the prisoner were growing more and more grave (most news agencies continued to report at the beginning of this – Day 73 – that he was on the brink of death), Annie and Mary were denied the opportunity to visit.

'If that had happened in Germany, if two women had been

kept from their brother's death bed and made to stand on the street during the long, cold day, you would have heard a great deal about it as a German atrocity,' said Mary. 'I mention it simply because it was a British atrocity.'

Undeterred by the new stance towards them, the sisters spent the day maintaining their vigil from outside and pleading their case to the phalanx of journalists then gathered at the gates in anticipation of MacSwiney's by now imminent death.

If the sisters remained remarkably strong in the face of so much adversity, Sunday was the day when the toll finally began to tell on MacSwiney's wife. Muriel collapsed that morning, an inevitable consequence of sheer exhaustion and overwhelming grief. For more than two months, she had put on a brave face walking in and out of the prison, and fought her husband's corner in interview after interview. Now, she started to succumb to the pressure and the unimaginable stress of watching him die a slow, drawn-out death before her very eyes.

'I had kept up until then and really felt very well,' said Muriel 'But I felt ill and could not go [to the prison], and went to bed again. And in the afternoon, since I was the only person that was allowed in the room, Mr. O'Brien took me down in a taxi. I opened the door and the nurse was there and she said: "Would you wait outside for a few minutes?" They had a habit then of having a warder just inside the door. And I opened the door again in about five minutes and I asked if I could go in, and he said he would ask the nurse. And she said, no, she was taking his temperature. And in about five minutes more I sent in word again if I could see him, and she said no, I could not.'

Muriel left the prison soon after, unable to deal anymore with the constant rebuffs and the desperate politicking necessary to gain access to her husband's bedside. In its daily bulletin to the press, the ISDL blamed her weakened condition on the extra demands being imposed upon her by the Governor making things so much more difficult for the family when visiting the prison. The latest bulletin also offered a bleak account of MacSwiney's status.

'He opened his eyes occasionally, staring sometimes at Father Dominic, but gave no sign of recognition even when Father Dominic spoke to him. He lies quietly moaning as if in pain. The restrictions suddenly imposed on the Mayor's relatives, limiting or prohibiting their access to the Mayor and removing their facilities for communicating with friends outside continue in force.'

By Sunday evening MacSwiney was still unconscious and the only people allowed inside the room with him were his brother Sean and the ubiquitous Father Dominic. The situation was now very obviously grave and the pair of them stayed overnight in the prison. When he took a turn in the small hours of Monday morning they were called to the room and told to prepare for the worst. At that point, their request to be allowed to use the phone to tell Muriel and the rest exactly what was happening was refused.

'He appeared to be going on satisfactorily till shortly after 2a.m. when the Night Nurse noticed a change in his appearance,' wrote Dr. Griffiths. 'He became "grey" in the face and his pulse feeble and rapid. She administered the remedies ordered to meet such a situation and sent for Dr. Methven who came at once. I was sent for and arrived at 3.45a.m. He was then very collapsed ... The Night Nurse reports that until the change about 2a.m. the patient had taken his medicines and nourishment without any apparent unwillingness and that he appeared to be going on much as usual.'

When Father Dominic came to the bedside, MacSwiney was unconscious, with his eyes open, a condition that made a mockery of Griffiths's official description of his willing acceptance of nourishment earlier in the evening.

His priest whispered prayers into his ear as his breathing became more and more laboured. Having given up on his efforts to procure a phone from the warders, Sean MacSwiney knelt beside his brother as the priest recited the prayers for the dying.

'Depart Christian soul out of this world in the name of God the Father Almighty...'

The doctors gathered around the bed with two nurses and at the conclusion of the prayer Father Dominic and Sean retreated to another corner of the ward so the medics could go back to work. As MacSwiney received a strychnine injection that it was hoped might revive him, his brother and his priest were on their knees, saying the rosary in Irish, the type of soundtrack the avid Gaeilgeoir and devout Catholic would have appreciated.

In a matter of minutes, Dr Griffiths came to where the men were praying and announced that there was nothing more could be done. They returned to the bedside and resumed their grim vigil. Father Dominic began the prayers for the dying once more. When he'd finished, the room was completely silent but for the sound of the rosary beads he was rolling between his fingers. There was no laboured breathing now, no twitching limbs beneath the sheets, no sign of life.

After 74 days, Terence MacSwiney, Lord Mayor of Cork, Prisoner 6794, was dead.

'Everything possible was done,' wrote Dr Griffiths. 'I telephoned for Dr. Beddard [the specialist] but the patient died just before his arrival.'

Sean MacSwiney knew that his first, awful duty was to inform his sisters and sister-in-law as soon as possible. Again, even in this darkest hour, he was refused access to a telephone inside the prison. So, mere moments after watching his brother die, he was forced to walk the streets of South London in search of a payphone from which to call the Germyn Court Hotel where the women were billeted.

It was nine o'clock on Monday morning when Muriel, Mary and Annie MacSwiney arrived at the prison gates, wearing stoical expressions and remaining determinedly dry-eyed. Even in this nightmarish moment, they refused to let the authorities glimpse the impact this loss was having upon them. When they finally reached the room where the body of the Lord Mayor lay, each stooped to kiss his cold cheek and then they knelt to pray together. There were no histrionics. There were no public tears.

'While we were in England, it was a point of honour to us that the enemy should never see us cry,' said Mary.

Still, they had to take in the sight of him, lying there, an emaciated version of the man he used to be, arms by his side and a crucifix on his chest.

'He looked like a perfect martyr,' said Muriel.

Annie carried a camera and took a picture of his face in death. The camera was never used to take another photograph and was kept in safekeeping for his daughter, Máire, until she was old enough to be gifted it.

'I joined him in Brixton Jail, as a friend, as his chaplain,' said Father Dominic. 'But it was as a brother, a fellow child of St. Francis of Assisi, I bade him farewell and sent him to meet Tomás [MacCurtain] and Eoghan Roe and Joan of Arc in the company of the soldier and gentle patriot of Italy, St. Francis.'

MacSwiney was a member of the Third Order of St Francis, a confraternity consisting of lay people devoted to contributing to the good work of the Franciscans, and his dead body had been robed in the Franciscan habit. With no cincture to tie the robe, Father Dominic removed his own from around his waist and carefully cinched it around his friend, whose given religious name was Brother Columcille.

When it was all over, after the body had been removed downstairs to the mortuary, Father Dominic remained in the room just as he had done nearly every day since the middle of August. For the first time, the bed now lay empty before him. Before he turned to walk away, he bent over and unsheathed the pillow from the pillow-case. Then he folded the pillow-case neatly, like a man putting away laundry, and tucked it into his pocket. A souvenir. A keepsake. His very own Shroud of Turin.

Below stairs, a vigil of a different sort was starting. Mary and Annie went with the body to the mortuary and remained there beside their brother for most of the day. As per prison rules, the door was locked behind them as they sat in a room made of stone with the body laid out on a slab in front of them. It was late in the evening when Peter and MacSwiney's great friend, Fred Cronin, came to relieve them and to take over the night watch. The family had resolved that somebody would be with him at all times in what Annie called 'that dreadful place'.

Outside the prison, crowds from all over London had been gathering throughout the day. Eventually police roadblocks pushed them back across the roads to a safer distance from the gates. A precautionary measure, but it wasn't needed. There was no trouble. Not a hint of violence. Just a tangible sadness in the air. Many of those present brought flowers of green, white and gold. Others hawked hastily-prepared memorial cards, hoping to cash in on the immense public interest. Some prayed in unison.

One of Father Dominic's first acts after MacSwiney's death had been to send a telegram to Donal O'Callaghan, the Deputy Lord Mayor, back in Cork:

'Lord Mayor completed his sacrifice for Ireland at 5.40 this morning. Sean and myself present. Inform Bishop of Cork agus Ceann Feadhma [Heads of Operations, possibly leaders of the Volunteers in this context]. Respectfully request my fellow citizens to maintain the same calm, dignified and noble bearing as on occasion of Tomás MacCurtain. Deepest sympathy to his friends and fellow-citizens and fellow-soldiers. No vain regrets, but fervent prayers. No useless sighs, but stern resolve to emulate his patient and heroic endurance in bearing all that God requires of us in establishing the Republic on a firm basis. May his noble spirit be with us always to guide and guard us. *Ar dheis Dé go raibh a anam.*'

At nine o'clock that Monday morning, large written notices were placed outside Cork City Hall and the offices of the *Cork Examiner* informing the public of the news. Huge crowds gathered around the signs in both venues and the City Hall version also contained Father Dominic's message about the need to remain calm and dignified. A meeting of Cork Corporation was hastily convened to pass resolutions of sympathy with the MacSwiney family and to decide on a delegation to set off to London to accompany the body home.

By mid-morning people on the streets of Cork wore Republican rosettes fringed with black crepe. Flags were hanging at half-mast, all public functions were cancelled, and theatres and other places of amusement didn't open their doors. When word reached UCC, students absented themselves from lectures for the remainder of the day. The city's grief was compounded that Monday night by the death of Joseph Murphy after 76 days on hunger strike in Cork Gaol, an event unfortunately overshadowed by the reaction to MacSwiney.

'It was the first time I saw Michael Collins really upset,' said Sean McGrath of the Corkman's response to the news from Brixton. 'He talked then about shooting in England.'

There would be no reprisals in England, well, not immediately at any rate. But there would be a significant political impact. At the behest of Collins, amongst others, Arthur Griffith, acting-Priomh Aire of Dáil Éireann, ordered the nine remaining Cork hunger strikers to give up their fasting and requested 'that they should now, as they were prepared to die for Ireland, prepare again to live for her'.

Reports of MacSwiney's demise filtered through to the inmates of Dublin's Mountjoy Prison while they were in the middle of morning exercise time in the yard. As the update swept through their ranks, a game of rounders ground to a halt and every prisoner then knelt for a recital of the rosary. In Waterford, blinds were drawn at the corporation offices as soon as the news came through, and that night a procession was held to the Cathedral where the rosary was recited again. If these were typical of the immediate acknowledgments throughout the island, there were places that took the news rather differently.

In various parts of Belfast, including Duncairn Gardens, effigies of the Lord Mayor were hastily constructed and then set on fire, the conflagrations cheered by angry mobs who chanted what the Dublin papers called 'disgusting remarks' about MacSwiney. In another area of the city, the raising of a Sinn Féin flag in his memory prompted the display of two Union Jacks and culminated in a riot wherein both sides threw stones at the other.

In Campsie, Derry, Catholic residents of a predominantly Protestant neighbourhood discovered that, overnight, memorial cards had been nailed to their front doors, bearing the message: 'In loving memory of Terry, who committed suicide. He asked for bread and they gave him a stone.'

In the House of Commons that day, the only reference to MacSwiney's death came when Lieutenant-Commander Kenworthy questioned the Home Secretary about the fact that his wife and sisters had been denied access to him in the last hours of his life. During a very brief exchange, Shortt denied that the ban was an order from the Home Office, and stated that medical advice was that the women were having an adverse effect on the condition of their brother. He then added: 'The relatives will be allowed to view the body'. At that point, the house moved on to discussing Industrial Life Assurance.

Others in London were moved. Upon hearing the news, a Vietnamese dishwasher named Nguyen Tat Thanhn, working in the kitchen of a city centre hotel, reacted by bursting into tears and declaring: 'A country with a citizen like this will never surrender!' Ho Chi Minh, as he later became known, was apparently as touched by the death as any Irishman in the country.

Eamon de Valera was in Washington when he received the news, busy preparing a submission to President Woodrow Wilson formally requesting recognition for Ireland. De Valera responded by releasing the contents of a cable of condolence he had dispatched to Mrs MacSwiney and then issuing his own statement to the press. Having spent almost a year and a half visiting sites across America pertaining to that country's battle for independence from Britain, he now had one more poignant comparison to draw between that struggle and Ireland's.

'The principles that Mayor MacSwiney, like his comrade, Fitzgerald, has given up his life to uphold – the principles for which the remaining comrades are giving up their lives in British jails – are the principles of the American Declaration of Independence and President Wilson's war aims – the inalienable right to liberty, "the privilege of men everywhere to choose their own way of life and obedience". Like Patrick Henry and his comrades, these Irish patriots were forced by the tyranny that would deprive them of liberty to make death the alternative.'

In Milan that night, La Scala Opera House remained closed because the Irish soprano Margaret Burke-Sheridan felt unable to perform in light of the terrible news from London.

Shortly before the news reached Rome, Pope Benedict had received Superior General Hennessy of the Christian Brothers in a private audience. A former teacher of MacSwiney's in the North Monastery, Hennessy informed the Pontiff that the prisoner was near death and warned that his passing was likely to make the situation in Ireland deteriorate. Subsequently, Monsignor Cerretti, Papal Under-Secretary of State, delivered the final bulletin confirming that MacSwiney had died. After showing 'deep regret' at the news, the Pope then knelt and prayed for a long time. It would later be reported that Benedict was convinced that the mayor had to be receiving some sort of nourishment to keep him alive that long.

The Paris office of Sean T O'Kelly, who was Irish Envoy to both Paris and Rome at the time, was besieged by well-wishers all that day. Plans were quickly put in place for a Requiem Mass to be said at the Irish Church of St Joseph's on Avenue Hoche, and the public reaction was such that O'Kelly dispatched a telegram to Father Dominic announcing: 'People of France horrified at England's cold brutality.' He wasn't exaggerating either, as the reaction from the French press, which had so assiduously covered the hunger strike for the previous two months, was mostly sympathetic.

'One can have on the Irish question and on the campaign of the Sinn Féiners whatever opinion one likes,' wrote Jacques Marsillac in *Le Journal*, 'but one cannot but bow before a man who died for his ideal, and because he hoped, re-invigorating by his example the soul of those whom he leaves behind, to hasten the liberation of Ireland.'

CHAPTER 13

Body and Soul

The Lord Mayor condemned himself to death for the sake of a cause in which he passionately believed, and it is impossible for men of decent instincts to think of such an act unmoved, whatever they may think of the wisdom or the rectitude of the policy inspiring the sacrifice. He adopted the hunger strike as the last political weapon at his disposal in a fight against constitutional authority. It is, in our judgment, an unfair weapon- it is an attempt to coerce by lacerating the feelings of one's adversary. It should not be allowed to succeed. It need not be said that we recognise the quality of spirit in his determined endurance and respect it.
The *Daily Telegraph*, 26 October 1920.

The inquest was fixed for Brixton Prison at 11o'clock on Wednesday morning, 27 October. The night before, the family heard rumours that the coroner was intent on bringing in a verdict of suicide. There was a suggestion that such a finding would allow the authorities to hold onto the body indefinitely. Alarmed at this talk, Mary MacSwiney's first instinct was to contact Sir Norman Moore, President of the

Royal College of Physicians, and to ask him to appear as a witness. She wanted the doctor to testify that, from the evidence of his examination back in September, the mayor didn't want to die. This would seriously weaken the case against suicide, but Moore refused the invitation.

There were other worries about the inquest. After her husband's death, Muriel MacSwiney had retired to bed at the hotel, distraught. That was where she was when the government issued her a notice to come to the prison to identify the body and to appear as a witness. Obviously, her brothers and sisters-in-law were concerned at the negative impact such a traumatic event might have on her in such a weakened state. Sean was mentioned as a possible surrogate, but in the end it was decided that Muriel would have to summon up what was left of her strength for the task at hand.

She entered the Coroner's Court that morning, walking past a scrum of photographers outside the prison gates, clad entirely in black, a dark veil almost obscuring her face. Inside, the jury (which newspapers described as culled from 'Brixton's middle-class and businessmen'), and the coroner himself were sat around a long table which ran down the centre of the carpeted room. Even this early in the morning, a blazing fire was going, the warmth and light from which was out of step with the mood among the Irish contingent.

Apart from Sean, Peter, who'd spent the night with the body in the prison morgue, Annie and Mary MacSwiney, there was Art O'Brien, Father Dominic, Florence McCarthy (town clerk of Cork), W Hegarty (Lord Mayor's secretary) and Donal J Galvin, Cork city solicitor. As she lifted her veil to be sworn in,

Muriel spoke in a low voice that betrayed her weakened condition. Yet, from somewhere, she found the resolve to deliver a performance of courage and wit in the witness box.

The dichotomy between the norms of English society and the contemporary Irish situation was illustrated by the first question. The Coroner, Dr G P Wyatt, opened by asking her to state her name and address for the record. The second part of that request was a tad difficult. The MacSwineys had no actual address because they always had to keep one step ahead of potential assassins.

'Cork,' replied Muriel, her face once again concealed beneath the dark veil.

'Cork is a big place,' quipped Wyatt, hoping for more detail.

'4 Belgrave Place,' said Muriel, giving the home of her sisters-in-law.

'Terence MacSwiney was your husband?'

'Yes.'

'Is that his full name?

'Terence James.'

'How old was he?'

'Forty years.'

'What was your husband in occupation?'

'An Irish Volunteer.'

'What does that mean? Did he make his living at it? Had he any trade?'

'He was a teacher years ago.'

'A school teacher?'

'Yes.'

'Can you call that his occupation?'

'He has done nothing for years except to work for his country
– Ireland.'

'I do not know how you can describe that exactly as an occupation.'

'You can describe him as an Irish Volunteer,' said Muriel, this
time with a certain coldness in her tone. 'I do not see why you
cannot. You have an army of your own, I think, and he was in
our army.'

'You can't call that an occupation.'

'I think you call that of your own officers in your own Army
an occupation.'

'Yes, a Regular Army. But it is a different thing altogether, is it
not?'

'I see no difference.'

'Shall I call him a Volunteer officer?'

'Yes.'

'Was his life insured?'

'I think so.'

'You are not sure?'

'No.'

'Do you know when he died?'

'Yes.'

'What was the date?'

'Monday the 25th.'

'At this prison.'

'Yes.'

'You have seen him since he has been here?'

'Yes.'

James Heyman McDonnell, solicitor for the MacSwineys,

rose to speak. He began by asking Muriel about the charges upon which her husband had been court-martialled. Wyatt objected, claiming that the task of this jury was simply to ascertain the cause of death and nothing else.

'May I respectfully suggest it was in consequence of his arrest and trial that his death has taken place,' said McDonnell. 'If you do not object, I will speak slowly.'

There ensued a brief legal debate between himself and the coroner about the parameters of the inquest and the question of motive. Claiming that the charges were central to MacSwiney's state of mind and his subsequent death, McDonnell wanted the charges read into the record, but this request was denied. So he took another tack.

'Had the Lord Mayor any wish to die?' he asked Mrs MacSwiney.

'No, none whatever. He told everyone he did not wish to die but to be unconditionally released.'

'Why, as far as you know, did he go on hunger strike?'

'Because they had no right to arrest him. He went on hunger strike as a protest against being arrested. It was an offence against the laws of the Irish Republic.'

'You mean the arrest was an offence against the laws of the Irish Republic?'

'Yes, certainly.'

To counter this evidence, Captain Charles Haynes, Governor of Brixton, produced the warrant for the detention of MacSwiney as evidence of the legality of his presence in the prison. Still, it was the performance of Muriel which caught the eye of the journalists seated in a row along the wall of the room, and of her in-laws too.

'I thought then and shall always think that Muriel's quiet dignity was just the tribute Terry would have wished – her simple statement that he was a soldier of the Irish Republican Army, and that his occupation was to work for his country,' wrote Annie MacSwiney. 'What is essentially simple does not bear description, its simplicity is lost sight of in the attempt – it's as if one were to try and probe an axiom – and the atmosphere created by Muriel there was felt by its simplicity and its finality.'

Dr Griffiths, as senior medical officer of the prison, was up next. He testified that he'd been away when MacSwiney first arrived in Brixton so had only taken over his care as of 1 September. By then the prisoner was in a weak condition, betraying signs of pulmonary tuberculosis, and utterly refusing to take food of any kind.

'Was he doing it with the idea of killing himself or only as a means to try to get away?' asked Wyatt.

'He told me he would get out of prison dead or alive,' replied Griffiths.

The questioning then moved on to the endgame, to the last week of MacSwiney's life.

'Symptoms of scurvy became worse and he had an attack of acute delirium on October 20th,' said Griffiths. 'He became very restive in his delirium and struggled violently. It was necessary to get two male nurses to keep him in bed. After that he had periods of semi-consciousness, unconsciousness and turns of delirium ... I should have said that when he became delirious I gave him food; when he became unconscious or semi-conscious.'

'That you were bound to do?' suggested Wyatt.

'Yes, and that I told him I should do,' said Griffiths. 'He was fed with considerable nourishment, and took a very fair quantity of it.'

Griffiths went on to recount how, between two and three o'clock on the morning of 25 October, he was roused from his bed and told he had to attend to the prisoner.

'I got there about three in the morning. I found his breathing was laboured, his pulse very fevered and quick. I did what I could, but having got to the end of my resources and seeing he was going to die I told the priest who came to see him. He died at 5.30 on the 25th. In my opinion his death was due to heart failure, following scurvy, due to exhaustion arising from prolonged refusal to take food.'

At this point, a member of the jury raised his hand with a question. 'He could and would have been fed had he wished at any time during his imprisonment?'

'I repeatedly asked him to take food. He always refused.'

'Did he say why?'

'Yes, I think I have said that. He said he would get out of prison alive or dead.'

James McDonnell then rose to conduct a cross-examination. 'You say you told the Lord Mayor that when he became delirious he would be fed. Do you remember the reply?'

'I explained to him and his wife that the reason he was not fed then was that he was not fit,' said Griffiths, reading from his notes, 'but that after he became collapsed or unconscious or incapable of exercising his will power and of struggling, I should use every means in my power to revive him by giving him anything that I thought fit. They both agreed that was the proper course. I told him I could not stand by with my hands in my pockets and let him die.'

'Did he agree that you should feed him?'

'He agreed it was the proper course for me as a doctor to take. I should add that he told me when he became conscious again he would refuse food but he agreed it was my duty as a doctor to do it. He did not agree to take food but agreed that it was my duty.'

'He said when he became conscious again, he would again refuse to take food?'

'I can give you the exact words. He said: "On regaining consciousness I should then refuse and it would only be prolonging the agony."'

'In your opinion and from the various conversations you have had, if the Lord Mayor had been released, he would have done his best to recuperate his health?'

'Yes, he said that if he was released he would take food.'

At this point, Sir Richard Muir, one of two counsels appearing for the Crown, rose to question Griffiths further. After clarifying again that the doctor had missed the first two weeks of MacSwiney's incarceration, he wanted to verify that on 20 August, Dr Treadwell had read the following statement from the Home Secretary to the deceased: 'Terence MacSwiney. I am directed by the Secretary of State to solemnly warn you that you will not be released and that you alone will be responsible for any consequences that may ensue from your persistence in refusing to take food.'

'I am cognisant of that statement,' said Griffiths.

'The prisoner's reply was: "I have been told this in Cork."' said Muir. 'In your opinion would it have prolonged or shortened Mr.

MacSwiney's life to have forcibly fed him?'

'I think it would have killed him almost at once.'

In his summing up to the jury, Wyatt told them they had three questions to ponder: Did MacSwiney deliberately take his own life by refusing food? Did refusing food unbalance his mind to such an extent that he didn't realise what was happening? Did he refuse food hoping that to do so would lead to his release, only for his body to give up during the protest? He also pointed out that the third option represented returning an open verdict.

In the end, this was the one they chose. After going out for fifteen minutes, the jury returned to declare it had found that: 'The deceased died from heart failure consequent upon his refusal to take food.' They also expressed the unanimous opinion that all the prison officials carried out their duties in distressing circumstances to the best of their ability. The Coroner amplified the verdict to read: 'Death was due to heart failure, dilated heart, acute delirium, following scurvy, due to exhaustion from prolonged refusal to take food.' For the family, the only thing that mattered was that there was no verdict of suicide.

The courtroom drama hadn't finished yet. James McDonnell asked the coroner about the body and the proposed burial in Cork. Before Wyatt could even answer, Sir Richard Muir was on his feet, pointing out that the coroner's jurisdiction was limited to England so he couldn't grant a certificate of release for burial if the body was to be buried somewhere else. There ensued an almost comical exchange

'Will you give me a certificate for burial?' asked McDonnell.

'I cannot, if you tell me he is going to be buried out of the country,' replied Wyatt.

'I withdraw that. I do not know where he is going to be buried.'

'But you have already told me he is going to be buried in Ireland, and I have no power to issue an order out of my own jurisdiction.'

'Can you give me an order for burial here?'

'I cannot, if you tell me he is not going to be buried here.'

'It would be the same if he was buried in Scotland then?'

'No doubt. I am not quite sure about Scotland without looking it up.'

McDonnell then asked that a certificate be issued so that the body could at least be taken from the prison and removed to Southwark Cathedral. That, too, was shot down. After more legal posturing, no solution was found to the problem so it was decided that Muriel, accompanied by Art O'Brien and McDonnell, would go directly to the Home Office and demand the body. After that trio departed the prison, Mary and Annie returned to the morgue, to continue to keep vigil over their brother's remains.

At the Home Office, McDonnell went inside first as the official legal representative of the family. When he returned to the taxi, he came bearing an offer from the government. As long as the body was taken directly to Cork, with no stopover in Dublin, a ship would be provided, free of charge, to make the trip. This course of action had been recommended by Hamar Greenwood, the Irish Chief Secretary, who felt that the shortest route was the method least likely to cause more trouble in Ireland.

O'Brien told the solicitor to go back in and to tell the Home Secretary, Edward Shortt, that the funeral arrangements had already been made. Terence MacSwiney would return to the Irish capital for a state funeral en route to his hometown and eventual resting place. He was also told to inform Shortt that Muriel MacSwiney would like to meet with him.

When Muriel entered the Home Secretary's office, accompanied by O'Brien, she had her game face on, her abrupt manner and steely demeanour apparently putting Shortt on the back foot.

'I understand that there was a technical difficulty about my husband's body coming with us, but I supposed there would be no difficulty.'

'I know nothing at all about it.'

'I suppose I can go and take my husband's body then.'

'Oh you cannot do that. There may be some law against it.'

'Well, will you find out what the law is? How long will it take you to do it?'

'I cannot tell you how long it may take – an hour or more. I don't know.'

'Do you refuse to give me my husband's body?'

'Oh, no, I cannot say that. There are legal points.'

When Shortt claimed that he merely needed time to clarify his powers with regard to the body, Art O'Brien spoke up.

'Your powers are exactly what they were when Richard Coleman died in Usk, and when Pierce McCan died in Gloucester.'

Coleman and McCan were Irish Volunteers who had died from pneumonia and influenza in English prisons in 1918 and 1919, and their bodies had been released without difficulty to their next of kin. O'Brien didn't stop there. He also demanded that Shortt speed up the process, given how much pain and grief he had already caused the MacSwiney family. When Shortt still refused to give a timetable for sorting out the bureaucratic snafu, obviously hoping he could still get them to agree to the plan for direct transport to Cork, it was agreed that his visitors would return in an hour, regardless.

'When Mrs MacSwiney, Mr Art O'Brien and Mr MacDonnell came to the Home Office and saw the Secretary, it was perfectly plain no such bargain was possible,' wrote Edward Troup in an account of what happened. 'They had made all the arrangements for the funeral in London and simply demanded the body should be given them. As there was now no question that they were entitled to it, the Secretary (after communicating formally with the Coroner who said he was quit of the case and did not care what he did) decided that the body must be given up.'

By the time their taxi had taken them to O'Brien's office at 3 Adam Street, the Home Office had already called ahead, requesting that McDonnell return. When he did, Shortt informed him that the family could now take the body. Furthermore, the Home Secretary also conveyed a message to Muriel MacSwiney, expressing his regret for the delay and trying again to explain it away as a legalistic complication. From his tone, it almost seemed like he was trying, at last, to be conciliatory and sympathetic in light of what the family had endured.

While all this negotiating was happening, the sisters remained by their brother's side, growing more and more concerned about the fate of his body as the hours passed. In the absence of any update from the Home Office or from the solicitor or from prison officials, Mary and Annie just sat there, stewing. By the time the afternoon had given way to the oncoming darkness of early evening, their minds were starting to consider all sorts of awful scenarios.

'While we watched by his dead body in that awful place, we wondered what evil malice more the English government was planning,' wrote Annie. 'That they should pursue him with their spite to the grave we felt in keeping with their reputation but their final brutality we did not dream of. Min and I talked of the different possibilities, first that probably they would not let us take him back to Ireland, in which case we would embalm his body and bring him home later; secondly, that they should keep his body in the prison and that we should not even be permitted to visit his grave. Our one thought was that he was beyond their power, they could hurt him no longer, much as they wished to do.'

Word finally reached the sisters in the morgue around 6 pm that the release was imminent. Within an hour, the body was being carried from the chapel at Brixton Jail on the shoulders of six Irishmen who were also imprisoned there at the time. With twelve of their incarcerated compatriots forming an honour guard, they placed the coffin in a hearse waiting in the prison yard, draped it in the tricolour, and saluted their comrade. Then, the sextet turned and marched back inside, from which vantage point they watched MacSwiney's body being driven away towards St George's Roman Catholic Cathedral in Southwark, the church of Bishop Peter Amigo.

For nearly two months, Amigo had campaigned tirelessly on MacSwiney's behalf, firing off letters to the Home Office, Bonar Law, and to Lloyd George. He had become friendly with the family and, given the fact that the nearest church to the prison was obviously not going to be big enough to hold the crowds that would come to see the body, he'd long ago offered the use of his cathedral.

'After careful consideration, I came to the conclusion that Mr MacSwiney did not intend to commit suicide but had every wish to live,' said Amigo. 'He exposed his life and eventually lost it for what he considered a national cause; though we may not agree with him in this, I certainly could not refuse him the Sacraments as I did not consider him guilty of suicide and he has been a daily communicant for years. His relatives approached me about his body being brought here. Again, I could not deny this request. He was an excellent Catholic and a Lord Mayor. He had every right to be treated with honour by the Church, which, while respecting nationality, is the Church of all.'

Obviously conscious of his own position, Amigo asked only that 'no political demonstration should take place and no unseemly incident.'

By the time the cortege reached Southwark that night, an estimated five thousand people had already gathered to witness its arrival. Somehow, word had swept through London and, from all corners of the city mourners had started to take seats from 6pm onwards. With a heavy police presence eventually ringing the church, decades of the rosary were recited for the repose of MacSwiney's soul as the crowds waited patiently for the coffin to be formally received by Amigo, Archbishop Mannix, Dr William Cotter, the Cork-born Bishop of Portsmouth, and nearly a dozen other priests.

The coffin was shouldered up the aisle by six members of Cork Corporation (a twenty-one-strong delegation having travelled over to London with their colleagues from the Cork Harbour Board) to accompany their mayor home, flanked by an escort of Volunteers from Cork. Once placed upon the cata-falque, it was ringed by the Volunteers who would stand sentry by it for the duration of its stay in St George's.

After the triumvirate of prelates led the congregation in another decade of the rosary, the lid was removed from the coffin to reveal a glass pane, allowing the family one more painful chance to gaze upon the remains. This also allowed mourners, who spent the next four hours filing past, paying their last respects, to see the emaciated face of MacSwiney, his head rest-ing on a cushion. Some of them wept, others leaned over to kiss the glass, mothers held up their smaller children so they could see the body beneath.

An hour before midnight, it was finally announced that the doors would have to close and would reopen at seven in the morning to try to accommodate all who wished to pay homage.

When the church had finally emptied, there remained the honour guard of Irish Volunteers who'd vowed to stay beside their comrade until morning. They did this and more. Despite Bishop Amigo having been promised that MacSwiney would be buried wearing the habit of the Third Order of St Francis, the uniform of a Brigadier-General of the Irish Republican Army was produced and placed upon the corpse over the holy robes. That was only one contravention of the agreed terms. Unbeknownst to Amigo, the coffin now also contained an overtly political inscription on the lid, written in Irish. After MacSwiney's name and position, the inscription recorded that he was:

Murdered by the Foreigner

in

Brixton Prison, London, England

on

October 25th, 1920

The fourth year of the Republic

Aged 40 years

God have mercy on his soul. [Translation]

Whether or not the epitaph was in Irish out of deference to MacSwiney's love of the language or out of knowledge that the English authorities surely wouldn't decipher its true meaning until it was too late isn't clear.

What is certain is that in the hours before the Requiem Mass began at 11 o'clock on Thursday morning, tens of thousands more made their way to Southwark to try to see the body. Many were Irish or of Irish extraction. Most were sympathetic to his plight. Major Clement Attlee, a future British Prime Minister and then Mayor of Stepney, was among five local leaders who turned up to pay their respects. The British Labour Party was represented by its leader William Adamson, JH Thomas arrived on behalf of the Trade Union movement. The turnout was so impressive that the papers compared it in size and stature to the lying in state of General William Booth, the founder of the Salvation Army, back in 1912.

All around the coffin lay wreaths and messages regarding the lives he had touched. From the actor Arthur Sinclair and the Irish players at the Ambassador Theatre. From the staff at Furnival House in Highgate 'who would consider it their greatest privilege to follow his holy and glorious example'.

On the coffin, beside the hat of a commandant in the Irish Volunteers, there was the white widow's cross. There was, however, no widow. Muriel MacSwiney was too ill to be present in Southwark that morning or to travel back to Ireland with her husband's body. With his wife absent and his sisters Margaret and Kit (both nuns) unable to travel from America and Tokyo respectively, the chief mourners were Mary, Annie, Sean and Peter, accompanied by Fred Cronin, and Mac Swiney's cousins, Mrs Foley and Miss O'Sullivan.

At around ten o'clock, police had been forced to link arms in the doorways to prevent the thousands stranded outside from trying to push their way in. Admittance for the actual mass was supposed to be restricted to those with tickets. Just before Bishop Cotter began the formal rite, a taxi pulled up outside St George's carrying six men wearing long coats.

They presented tickets to the policemen manning the doors and walked inside. Then, the sextet threw off their long coats in a rather dramatic gesture and revealed the green uniforms of the Irish Republican Army. They duly replaced their non-uniformed colleagues as the honour guard by the coffin. The 'Dead March' from *Saul* by Handel sounded on the organ, the congregation stood and the mass began.

At the conclusion of the service, Bishop Cotter, Bishop Amigo and Archbishop Mannix delivered absolutions to the congregation while Chopin's 'Marche funèbre' was played on the organ. Then, they stopped and talked a while with the MacSwiney family as the pews emptied and the people left outside could now file in to pay their last respects too.

If the atmosphere outside was generally one of hushed

solemnity, hawkers had also set up pitches around the church grounds. Amongst other paraphernalia, they were selling yellow and white chrysanthemums, emerald green badges, Lord Mayor handkerchiefs, and 'In Loving Memory' cards. The sound of Cockney accents trying to cash in on Irish tragedy was no more bizarre than a corner of London being turned into the staging ground for what one London paper described as 'a funeral under a Rebel flag in the heart of the Empire.'

Shortly before 2.30pm, Sean and Peter MacSwiney, accompanied by four Volunteers, bore their brother's coffin onto their shoulders and carried it outside. They did so to the soundtrack of pipers wailing out 'Slán le Corcaigh'. As they loaded it into the funeral carriage, Archbishop Mannix sprinkled holy water. Then, the elaborate procession was somehow organised and set off across the Thames towards Euston Station.

The funeral cavalcade stretched for more than a mile. A body of mounted police led from the front, accompanied by six of their colleagues on foot. If the London bobbies were on duty, placed there by their superiors, they treated the task they'd been given with the utmost respect, marching in ceremonial step all the way and evincing what one English journalist called an air of 'great solemnity'. Behind them walked a group of Irish Volunteers, a band of pipers wearing saffron-coloured kilts, and then rows upon rows containing several hundred priests.

Following a hearse filled to the brim with wreaths and flowers came the carriage carrying the coffin. Four Volunteers marched alongside, and behind it strode the MacSwiney brothers and Father Dominic, a distinctive figure in his brown Capuchin robe. Then came cars containing Archbishop Mannix, Bishop

Cotter and the MacSwiney sisters. Behind that was a veritable sea of dignitaries from the Dáil, Cork Corporation, Dublin Corporation, and what seemed like every Irish association in the British Isles. This was the spectacle that headed over crowded Blackfriars Bridge.

Spectators were packed five rows deep on both sides, as kilted pipers played 'Let Erin Remember'. Many of those on the bridge had been waiting for over an hour to witness its passage. The cavalcade moved along the Embankment, up Norfolk Street and across the Strand. At every turn, men bared their heads once the carriage bearing MacSwiney came into view. All the while, a respectful silence hung over the streets. Even the thousands of curious spectators leaning out of windows and watching from the rooftops of buildings did so quietly and in keeping with the mood.

'Some of the men looked comfortable and prosperous; the women were more often poorly-clad and hardened,' wrote The *Times* of London of the mourners. 'In one respect, however, both men and women were wonderfully alike. Both presented a great variety of Irish types. The Irish peasant was there, with broad face and uptilted nose; the lantern-jawed, mystical Irishman; the swarthy, dark-eyed Irishman, own brother to the Spaniard. These and others could be recognised from their prototypes in Irish story, drama, and art. Even the Irishman who is said to exist only in the Englishman's imagination was to be discovered without much search.'

Apart from those in the vanguard, many of the policemen charged with the task of supervising the funeral as it wended its way through the streets wore black gloves. Almost all formally saluted the coffin when it passed them. The respect afforded the whole affair by the constabulary may explain why it went off seamlessly and without incident.

After two hours, the procession reached Euston Station where barriers had been erected to keep the main part of the court there empty. The train scheduled to take MacSwiney's body and the legion of mourners intent on travelling with it to Holyhead was waiting on the Number 6 platform. There, as the coffin was placed in the funeral van of the train for the start of the long journey home, Archbishop Mannix recited Psalm 130, 'De profundis': Out of the depths I cry to you, O Lord …

CHAPTER 14

The Long Journey Home

Still 'The Funeral'. Motty came down before lunch to tell Anderson that Cabinet had ratted, presumably on Macready's wire, that Body is to be put on a special boat at Holyhead and sent direct to Cork. Seems to be the right course but a pity decided so late. 'London' has declined to inform the relatives of this change or make it public in London so we are not able to put anything in the evening papers here – the result will be that stacks of people will be assembled before they read the morning papers and I should think a row may ensue. One cannot resist the inference that London's only care is to get quit of MacSwiney without trouble there, against which the increasing of our difficulties here does not weigh at all. Even Shinns are entitled to be told tonight if tomorrow's circus is off, apart from policy – to rob them of their meat at the last minute may provoke a far bigger row than the funeral itself.

Diary of Mark Sturgis, liaison officer, Dublin Castle, Thursday 28 October.

The first sign that something nefarious was afoot came at Euston Station. Once the body had been loaded onto the funeral van of the train around 4.30pm, the Station Master announced that the train would leave at 4.45. The family and the seventy others who planned to accompany the body back to Ireland from Holyhead had all been booked on the 6.20pm train. When they heard about the proposed timetable change, Mary and Annie remained by the coffin, accompanied by Archbishop Mannix, and declared that they would be taken wherever it was taken. In due course, Art O'Brien negotiated a settlement of sorts and a new departure time of six o'clock was agreed upon.

The second sign of trouble came aboard the train itself. Carriages, compartments and aisles were full of policemen. By some estimates, nearly 100 officers were on board. According to others, the figure was closer to 300. Initially, the MacSwineys didn't think this presence too odd because, as they said to each other, they had grown accustomed to being shadowed at every turn. Not to mention that there would probably be some crowd control requirements at the docks in Wales. This was something different, though. They realised that much when, after leaving London behind, one of the detectives came to O'Brien and said that the Police Inspector on board wished to speak to him in private.

The Inspector wanted to know what members of the family were travelling and, in particular, if the Lady Mayoress had been able to make the trip. He had in his possession a letter that he'd been instructed to deliver to Muriel MacSwiney after the train passed Crewe, the Cheshire town that marked about the two-thirds point of the journey. When O'Brien asked why the missive couldn't be handed over to the family before that, the Inspector told him he was due to receive further instructions from his superiors at Crewe.

Whatever the orders were, the Inspector sought out O'Brien and Sean MacSwiney shortly after the train left Crewe and advised that the letter from Sir Hamar Greenwood, Chief Secretary of Ireland, be opened as soon as possible. The funeral plans had been changed.

'I am advised that the landing and funeral of the late Lord Mayor in Dublin may lead to demonstrations of a political nature,' wrote Greenwood. 'I regret therefore that the Irish government [the Dublin Castle administration] cannot allow disembarkation of remains of the late Lord Mayor in any other port of Ireland except his native City of Cork. In order to save you further inconvenience the Government has directed the London Northwestern Railway Co to provide a suitable steamer to carry the remains directly to Cork from Holyhead. This steamer will also convey you and twenty of your friends if you so desire.'

Mary and Annie MacSwiney had just turned down the light in their compartment when they were roused with this news that the guarantees from the Home Office about a funeral without restrictions had been reneged upon. The terms of the funeral were now being dictated by the British, anxious to circumvent the stop in Dublin for fear of the troubling atmosphere it might promote in the capital. As they reeled from the impact of the letter, the sisters and their brothers considered their options.

They tried to effect a holding action of sorts, claiming that they could not move the body from Holyhead until Muriel was apprised of the situation and given her say about what should happen next. The Inspector was having none of that. His orders were to proceed to Cork with the body and he intended to do this by whatever means necessary, with or without their permission. If he had to employ force to fulfill his obligations, so be it.

Sean MacSwiney assured him that the family would resist in such a way that force would be very definitely necessary. They had no intention of boarding the *Rathmore*, the steamer charged with the task of sailing the coffin directly to Cork. Furthermore, he reminded the officer that the only person eligible to receive the body in Cork was the Lord Mayor's two-year-old daughter Máire.

The intransigence of the Inspector was underpinned by his knowledge of the back-up he and his men had waiting for them in the Welsh port. When the train pulled into Holyhead station, stopping short of the pier itself, shortly before midnight, it was greeted by an estimated 100 Black and Tans, newly-crossed from Kingstown, supplemented by a large number of the Cheshire Regiment. Several hundred onlookers had also gathered near the station house to witness what they (correctly) presumed might turn into a spectacle.

Not everybody in the Irish party knew about the attempt to divert the body, and when the train stopped, some were almost fooled by the officials into immediately boarding the 'Rathmore'. The MacSwineys themselves had gone straight to the funeral van of the train where the coffin lay, still surrounded by the wreaths which had travelled alongside the mayor since he departed St George's Cathedral. However, the solemn atmosphere that had pervaded the scene then was long gone.

There was tension in the night air as Mary and Annie positioned themselves on either side of their brother's remains. As they had back at Euston when they first got a sense of something awry, their policy was that the coffin would go nowhere without them. Their brothers and Art O'Brien argued the case with the Station Master, AW Taylor. O'Brien even waved the contract that the London North-Western Railway had signed to transport the body from London to Dublin.

'All the time that the discussion was going on, the Black and Tans, and others of the same ilk, were glowering through a window in the part of the van near where we stood by Terry's body, and to my dying day, the horror of those evil faces will be before me,' wrote Annie MacSwiney. 'They were muttering through their clenched teeth, glaring at us and at the coffin, showing their teeth in their diabolical fury, that the sight of them made us shiver with horror.'

At one point, Station Master Taylor left the van to make a phone call but was waylaid by the Inspector who reminded him that the orders to remove the body and sail it to Cork came from the highest level of government. This, Taylor then told the family, was enough for him to ignore the contract in which O'Brien had tried to place so much store.

After a stand-off, somebody at the end of the van near the door muttered 'they're coming' as a group of railway workers made their way down the platform, seemingly bent on extracting the coffin. They began by removing the wreaths, during which operation Father Dan Walsh berated the Station Master: 'I thought the age of body-snatching was gone.' When it came time to go for the coffin itself, the railwaymen found themselves facing a cordon around it, all of the MacSwineys, Father Dominic, Art O'Brien and others, their hands clasped together, united and determined they would not be moved.

'You shall not take my brother's body away,' shouted Mary. 'You will have to go over my body first.'

'Don't dare touch it, we forbid you to touch it,' shouted Annie.

The railway workers thought better of the task, telling the police gathered outside: 'We are forbidden to touch the coffin.'

It was about then the order was given for the police to move in. With an inspector bellowing 'Clear out!' they rushed the van and all hell broke loose. Sean McGrath, one of the London Volunteers, stood away from the others, directly in front of the coffin, and met the invasion head on. He ended up tumbling out of the train and onto the platform during a lengthy bout with two officers. The rest was a melee.

'Sean [MacSwiney] and Min [Mary] got the brunt of it,' said Annie. 'They were dragged from the coffin. Min was lifted off her feet and thrown out of the van. Sean tried to protect her – he had his arm around her, and three huge police attacked him in front. One of them struck Min in the face, while a military officer jumped at him from behind, caught him by the collar and tried to choke him ... I was pushed from behind away from the coffin, and having nothing to catch onto, they got me easily away. I tried to get back again, but a cordon of police surrounded the coffin, and it was impossible ...'

All those who placed themselves around the coffin were manhandled until the police and military had cleared the van and begun the process of lifting MacSwiney's coffin onto the back of a lorry. It was speedily brought to the pier, wrapped in sackcloth, and hoisted onto the *Rathmore* by a crane. Once safely aboard, it was quickly surrounded by British soldiers.

As the *Rathmore* chugged out of the harbour shortly after one o'clock that Friday morning, some of the soldiers were spotted sitting on the coffin, playing cards and smoking cigarettes. The entire travelling party knelt on the docks watching the departure. There, Father Dominic led them in a recital of 'De Profundis' and more decades of the rosary. When the vessel was out of sight and their prayers had ended, they marched quietly to the Admiralty Pier to catch the mail boat to Kingstown [Dun Laoghaire].

'If they took my brother's remains away from us by force and then we went on the ship, it would have been a tacit consent to their action,' said Mary MacSwiney. 'Some people have seemed to think we were very hard-hearted to let my brother's remains travel like that without any of his friends. We did what we knew he would have liked us to do – what would be for Ireland's good first.'

Ireland awoke that Friday morning to the grim reports of what had transpired in Holyhead late the previous night. Now deprived of the body of Terence MacSwiney, it was decided that the Dublin leg of the funeral would still go ahead as planned. Dáil Éireann had called for a day of mourning and almost every business in the capital had complied with this request. The trams stopped running at ten, the butchers shut down for the day shortly after. The city was so quiet and still that very often the only traffic noise that morning came from the motor lorries full of 'Black and Tans' prowling the streets.

At 11 o'clock, the Pro-Cathedral on Marlborough Street was filled to overflowing for the Requiem Mass. Having arrived in Kingstown just hours earlier, Mary, Annie, Sean and Peter MacSwiney took their seats in front of the high altar that had been draped in black. Archbishop William Walsh presided, and, in a sign of the troubled times, one of his assistants, Fr Augustine Hayden, had rushed to the church direct from visiting death row inmate Kevin Barry. The eighteen-year-old Volunteer, who was a medical student at UCD, was in Mountjoy Jail waiting to be hung for his part in an ambush of British soldiers back in September. Within three days, he would be dead too.

After the mass had ended, the mourners gathered behind a hearse drawn by four black horses. Instead of a coffin, it was piled high with wreaths. Behind it came carriages drawing the family and the clergy, followed by the members of Dáil Éireann marching in twos, and then a procession of tens of thousands of people from all walks of life. The procession extended back so far that reporters estimated it took half an hour to pass by spectators who'd gathered at all points to doff their caps and to kneel in prayer.

'The dockers marched in their dirty working clothes, unwashed and collarless, just as if they had come from unloading ships,' wrote the *Manchester Guardian*. 'The newsboys left their papers, and in a ragged group, with bare feet and exposing many inches of shirts in unusual places, formed fours and took their place. As a revelation of democratic sympathies, one could have found nothing outside Ireland to compare with these marching thousands, the majority of whom wore Sinn Féin colours and walked with quick, martial step and erect bearing.'

Their route to Kingsbridge Train Station took them along Sackville Street, across O'Connell Bridge and then down the quays, their every step tracked by a military plane flying overhead. The affair did not quite pass without incident, however. Near Grattan Bridge, two lorries of soldiers tried to drive straight through a part of the parade made up mostly of members of Cumann na mBan. It was a poor decision. They were turned back by the women.

At the station itself, where thousands had gathered in anticipation of the arrival of the empty hearse, many were appalled at the presence of an armoured car. Its sights were trained on the crowd, machine-gun turrets at the front, and, at the back, men with their revolvers pointing out through slits in the armour.

Shortly before two o'clock, the family and those travelling on to Cork with them boarded a train for the final leg of their awful journey. Almost at that very moment, the *Rathmore* was pulling up to the dock in Queenstown [Cobh]. Several hundred locals had gathered on the pier to view this peculiar sort of homecoming, and they were joined by a contingent of Cameron Highlanders, an obvious sign that the authorities remained concerned about the potential for trouble.

The commanding officer of the *Rathmore* came ashore and invited Queenstown Town Clerk EF O'Reilly and Dr Robert Browne, Bishop of Cloyne, to receive the body. Both men declined this invitation. Nobody else was willing to do so either. Every person approached by the military on the pier offered the same well-rehearsed answer: 'No one has the authority to receive the Lord Mayor's body in the absence of the Lord Mayor's relatives.'

That was to be the recurring rejoinder of the day and left the officers in charge with a new problem. Who would take the body off their hands? Eventually, it was decided that Cork city was a more likely location to yield a solution, so the coffin, wrapped in tarpaulin and carried by sailors, was soon transferred from the *Rathmore* to the *Mary Tavy*. On the deck, it was covered in wreaths of white and yellow flowers and, as the smaller tug began the short trip up the harbour, its blue ensign flag had been placed at half-mast.

When the *Mary Tavy* docked at Custom House Quay that Friday evening, 29 October, six lorry-loads of soldiers and two armoured cars secured all immediate access points to the surrounding area. Again, an enormous crowd soon gathered but, in the absence of the MacSwiney family, no one would step forward to sign for the coffin, which was taken off the ship, covered in tarpaulin and guarded on the dock by Cameron Highlanders and RIC Auxiliaries.

At nine o'clock that night, three British Army officers knocked on the door of the MacSwiney house in Belgrave Place. They had a note declaring that the mayor's body was at Custom House Quay, ready to be handed over to the next of kin. Mary told them that the family, barely in the door from Dublin, would be along immediately. Within an hour, they were down by the river where their brother's coffin remained, still surrounded by a cordon of soldiers.

'Guarded in death by the English military,' said Annie.

This then was the place where they took possession of their brother, and took charge of his funeral rites again. A large contingent of Irish Volunteers had accompanied the family, marching in formation through the gates of the Custom House, and six of them hoisted their comrade up on their shoulders and began the long, slow walk back up the river towards the City Hall.

It was dark and the town was quiet as the Lord Mayor made his last trip to the place whence he had been plucked less than three months earlier. His brothers and sisters strode behind his coffin, satisfied at last that now at least his remains were in their control. There was a sense too among them that this is what he would have wanted, returning to the job he'd thrown himself into, and the scene of the crime perpetrated against him.

When the City Hall opened to allow the public to come and pay their respects on Saturday morning, a huge crowd had already assembled outside. Word had swept through the city and surroundings and, in spite of a rain that fell all day, the queue was soon large enough that the minimum wait to get inside was an hour. Nobody minded. They stood there in near silence for as long as it took. Men, women and children. Some passed the time with prayers. Others just whispered lest their voices interrupt the solemnity of the occasion. All stopped talking completely when their turn came to walk in single file through the doors.

Inside, black drapes hung from the railings of the balconies, each marked with a white cross. The casket lay on a catafalque in the centre of the room, draped in the Republican flag, surrounded by flowers, lit by candles, and flanked at all times by four Irish Volunteers (among them a young Sean O'Faoláin) in civilian clothes, the British authorities having forbidden them to wear uniforms. The large organ at one end of the hall was slowly disappearing beneath the growing mountains of wreaths being stacked there by the constant stream of visitors.

In the coffin, MacSwiney wore the IRA uniform put on him in Southwark, one last act of defiance. His face was inevitably drawn and hollow and every mourner commented on the sheer whiteness of his skin, paler than any corpse they'd ever seen. Some thought he looked strangely beautiful lying there with a marble sheen to his face. Others reckoned that he was unrecognisable from before, too many pounds of flesh having been planed from his body over the previous months.

'The first glimpse of his dead face, from far off, was unmistakably Terry, a flashing glimpse, as it were, then as you went nearer, it seemed to get unlike him, until you were right up at the coffin head,' wrote his friend PS O'Hegarty. 'And then suddenly you understood. The face was almost the face of a bronze statue but that was not the unfamiliar thing about it. The lines were different, for it was a face in which all the tissue had gone, in which everything had gone but the fundamental things. It was a face, in fact, in which the real Terry, the fundamental Terry, first appeared, and what was left now was a warrior face ... As one looked at the face, stern and set, one's mind instinctively leaped to the word "Samurai".'

When the crowds had passed through by late Saturday night, Mary and Annie chose to remain all night by their brother's side after the doors had been locked. He had, to their mind, spent too many nights away from them. This was a last chance to be with him. It was also an eerie reprise of the very same vigil he'd kept in the very same place by the body of his friend Tomás MacCurtain just seven months before.

Sunday dawned brighter and drier but with a sense of

foreboding in the air too. The mourning drapes that hung over the entrance to the City Hall had been torn down during the night. They were later discovered, ripped up and thrown over the wall into the nearby River Lee. From dawn, armoured cars and lorries full of British soldiers had left Victoria Barracks and taken up prominent positions all over the city.

The army had agreed not to interfere with the proceedings and to maintain a respectful distance at all times in return for certain guarantees. They wanted assurances that the actual funeral procession wouldn't extend for more than a quarter of a mile; that there would be no overt militaristic formations in it, and that the only Republican flag on view would be the one draping MacSwiney's coffin.

That accord still allowed for the army to be visible on the streets, but a heavy military presence didn't dissuade more citizens from trekking to City Hall to say goodbye to their mayor. From early that Sunday morning, they continued to make their way to the city centre to view the body and to pay their respects.

'Mother and I,' wrote the writer Frank O'Connor, 'were among those who filed past his coffin as he lay in state in the City Hall in his volunteer uniform; the long, dark masochistic face I had seen only a few months before as he chatted with [Daniel] Corkery by the new bridge.'

At ten, the doors were closed to the public and preparations made for the removal. One hour later, an organist sat down in the City Hall and began to play 'The Dead March' from Handel's *Saul*. That was the soundtrack as six more Irish Volunteers, wearing Republican rosettes touched with black, lifted the now-closed coffin up onto their shoulders and began to carry him out of the place he'd last left under armed guard. In the vestibule, a pipe band, with muffled drums, played the music of 'Wrap the Green Flag' as the family and a phalanx of clergy and political leaders walked behind the casket towards the front doors.

On Anglesea Street, a lorry full of armed soldiers watched over proceedings, and an armoured car with twin machine guns poking from its turrets trained its sights upon the procession. The commander of the troops ordered his men to attention as the coffin passed and he himself saluted. British soldiers paying respect in this way was to be a feature of the day. Once the cortege made its way across Parnell Bridge and down the South Mall, the army sped off to take a faster route towards the North Cathedral and their next position.

All along the Mall and Patrick Street, thousands lined the route towards the church, policed most of the way by dozens of Volunteers. Men bared their heads as the carriage bearing MacSwiney's coffin, now wrapped in a tricolour, passed by. Women dropped to their knees and prayed on the spot, their whispered supplications often the only noise as, once the funeral went by, a weird hush would descend upon the normally bustling streets of the city.

'More troops and another armoured car were waiting on the steep road that dominates St. Patrick's Bridge,' reported the *Manchester Guardian*. 'The officer in command insisted on keeping the roadway clear at the foot of the hill, and his efforts at persuasion were reinforced by a handful of soldiers. They fixed bayonets but were not aggressive. The procession crossed the bridge, turned along the quay and slowly climbed the steep road that leads to the Roman Catholic Cathedral.'

The military maintained a high profile around the church itself too. Although they stopped short of travelling menacingly alongside the procession, as they'd done for the funerals of the other hunger strikers, Joseph Murphy and Michael Fitzgerald, twenty lorries and seven armoured cars were still stationed along the approach roads to the church. At one point, a group of schoolchildren from MacSwiney's alma mater, the North Monastery, wearing Gaelic costume, and carrying a large floral cross, marched past the gauntlet of soldiers and into the chapel to deliver the flowers.

Just before twelve, the cortege arrived. The coffin was carried in the main entrance and placed on a bier, draped with black and embroidered with crossed bones and a skull, in front of the High Altar. Four Volunteers stood by it throughout the service.

The cathedral was full, the crowd spilling over to fill the grounds and the nearby streets. From behind the altar, three archbishops (two from Australia), five bishops, and a handful of priests emerged to participate in the Requiem Mass. Archbishop Harty of Cashel presided but the chief celebrant was Bishop Cohalan. His pre-eminence was fitting. His relationship with MacSwiney went way back. He'd visited Brixton Prison, had publicly advocated on the mayor's behalf, and some of those present thought the strain of the past few months was evident in his own physical appearance. Indeed, just two days earlier, Cohalan had even written a panegyric to the deceased in the *Cork Examiner*.

'I ask the favour of a little space to welcome home to the city he laboured for so zealously the hallowed remains of Lord Mayor Terence MacSwiney. For the moment, it might appear he has died in defeat. This might be conceded if there were questions merely of the individual, but it is not true when the resolve of the nation is considered. Was Lord Edward Fitzgerald's death in vain? Was Robert Emmet's death in vain? Did Pearse and the other martyrs for the cause of Irish freedom die in vain? We are the weaker nation in the combat … periodically, the memory of the martyr's death will remind a young generation of the fundamental question of the freedom of Ireland … Terence MacSwiney takes his place among the martyrs in the sacred cause of the freedom of Ireland. We bow in respect before his heroic sacrifice. We pray the Lord have mercy on his soul.'

At one point during the mass, the midday sunlight came slanting through the windows of the church, and briefly lit across the heads of MacSwiney's brothers and sisters as they sat listening to the augmented choir music that punctuated the Requiem. When it was all over, Peter and Sean MacSwiney led the mourners behind the hearse as it departed the North Cathedral for the long trip across the city to St Finbarr's Cemetery in Glasheen.

Father Dominic strode right alongside the brothers, a reflection of how close he and the mayor had grown during the hunger strike, and after that came a sea of clergy. The striking purple robes of the archbishops and bishops in the vanguard, followed by wave upon wave of black soutanes, and the speckling throughout of the distinctive brown of Capuchins in their sandals. Politicians of every stripe and from every county took their places in the procession too.

This then was the cavalcade that slowly wended its way through a town where every shop was closed and every curtain drawn. At various junctures along the route, local pipe bands had taken up positions. As the procession rounded the bend along Patrick Street, the strains of 'The Dead March' wafted over the crowd, accompanied by the drumbeat of the feet of the marchers. All along the way, Volunteers acted as marshals, keeping order and ensuring that nobody did anything retaliatory that might besmirch the pristine mood of the day.

'The people who crowded both sides of the streets and roads felt the tragedy of the moment, but while many an eye was dimmed, and many a hand stole upwards to wipe away the tears that could not be kept back, there was also something that was resolute and unflinching in the attitude of the populace,' wrote the *Freeman's Journal*. 'There was indeed something of triumph as well as regret in the marvellous demonstration of affectionate sorrow. The tribute was unique in the earnestness and dignity of its manifestation.'

Beyond Washington Street, the parade inched its way along the Western Road, past the gates of University College Cork, from where MacSwiney had graduated with a degree in Mental and Moral Science back in 1907. Juggling a full-time job at Dwyer and Co with his studies back then, he used to go to bed at 8pm and rise at 2am to get the course work done. It was on that very campus many years before that he'd confessed to his friend and teacher, Professor William Stockley, that he'd love to spend the rest of his life in the college library, lost among his beloved books. Neither man could have guessed then that their last meeting would take place in a prison in London.

An even more poignant landmark came just along the road. Cork Jail. Beyond MacSwiney's own stays behind its bars, there was the symbolism of his colleagues still imprisoned there, and of it being the place where Fitzgerald and Murphy had died.

It was ticket only at the graveyard. There was no other way to ensure that those who deserved to be there could get in. Still, the crowds came and took up vantage points in the hinterland of the cemetery around Glasheen from early afternoon. They had a long wait. The cortege didn't loom into view until half past four, by which time the contingent of British soldiers, an armoured car and six lorries had moved back so far from St Finbarr's that they were almost out of sight of most mourners.

At the gates, the ranks of Cork firemen were standing to attention in helmets and uniforms, and the last leg of the journey was made through a canyon of Volunteers clearing a path and holding back the spectators.

The grave had been dug next to that of Tomás MacCurtain in an area of the cemetery that was by then becoming known as the Republican Circle, so-called because it was reserved for those who had died as 'soldiers of the Irish Republic'. Apart from MacSwiney's predecessor as mayor, it was also the burial place of Fitzgerald and Murphy, and of Seamus Quirke, killed by the Black and Tans in Galway the previous month.

The archbishops and the bishops led the prayers. 'Benedictus' – the song of thanksgiving uttered by Zachariah on the birth of his son John the Baptist, was chanted, 'Miserere' (Psalm 51) and 'De Profundis' were recited before the coffin was lowered into the ground. As a selection of the 600 wreaths he'd received was placed on top of the grave, Father Dominic led a saying of the rosary in Irish.

'No hand but a comrade touched his grave,' wrote Annie.

'Those who had worked and fought with him laid him there, then they covered his coffin with the earth of the land he died for, and when finally they laid over him the fresh green shamrock sod, and resting on it, the Volunteer hat that he had worn last as he followed Tomás to his grave. We felt indeed that the end had come.'

The tricolour that had draped his coffin was given to Annie. She placed it with the cross that had lain on his breast, his copy of *The Imitation of Christ* from the prison, and she found solace in just receiving these items that had been so close to him in the worst time. After the obsequies had ended, Arthur Griffith, acting Priomh Aire of the first Dáil, delivered an oration by the graveside.

'We, his colleagues of Dáil Éireann, stand by the graveside of Terence MacSwiney in sorrow but in pride. He laid down his life to consolidate the establishment of the Irish Republic, willed by the vote of the people of Ireland. His heroic sacrifice has made him in death the victor over the enemies of this country's independence. He has won over them because he has gained by his death for Ireland the support and sympathy of all that is humane, noble and generous in the world. Remember forever his words to our people of Cork when seven months ago he stepped into the *Bearna Baoghael* [the 'gap of danger' referred to in the National Anthem, Amhrán na bhFiann]– that triumph is not to those who can inflict the most but to those who can endure the most. He has exemplified that truth to all mankind. He endured all that the power of England could inflict upon him, and in enduring triumphed over that power. His body lies here, his soul goes marching through all the ages. He is not dead;

he is living forever in the hearts and consciences of mankind. Mourn for him, but let your mourning be that for a martyr who triumphs. Ireland has lost a noble son, as France lost a noble daughter when St. Joan of Arc perished in the English bonfire. The sequel will be the same. St. Joan of Arc has, in him, welcomed a comrade to heaven.'

Once the archbishops and other dignitaries had left, the barriers keeping the public back were taken down so that everybody could come in to see the final resting place. It was about then that six Volunteers stepped from the crowd, produced revolvers, and fired three volleys of shots in the air. When their guns had been put away, a sustained outburst of applause reverberated around the graveyard.

CHAPTER 15

In Living Memory

A prophet nearer home, St. Terence MacSwiney the Martyr, left us some very sacred canons of conduct as to choosing the public servants of Ireland. I venture to prophesy St. Terence will turn in his grave when the spoils of Ireland's victory come to be divided up.
George Bernard Shaw, 27 December 1921, *New York Times.*

On 31 October 1920, 40,000 people filed into the Polo Grounds, a baseball field that was then New York's largest open-air stadium, to hear Eamon de Valera commemorate MacSwiney's death. An estimated 10,000 more were stranded outside as the city's Irish community gathered to mourn his passing, carrying tricolours and a collective wish to pay tribute to his sacrifice. They were joined in this by many of other nationalities who had simply been touched by the story over the 74 days during which he had refused food.

'As de Valera stood with bowed head amid cheering that already had lasted five minutes, three turbaned Hindus darted across the baseball field, waving a large Irish flag and the flag of their own aspirations,' wrote the *New York Times*. 'They rushed to the platform and draped the flags about de Valera's shoulders. The cheers were renewed, and although de Valera waved for order, ten more minutes had elapsed before a band struck up "Soldiers of Erin" and the crowd chanted the Irish Republican hymn.'

The spectacular and awful circumstances of MacSwiney's demise had energised the expatriate constituency in America once more and also brought out an impressive roster of New York politicians and clergymen. A hastily-arranged affair, four separate stages had been erected to cater for the huge crowd and this led to the cheers from one section often making it difficult to hear a word in another. Still, as keynote speaker, de Valera captured the mood.

'Terence MacSwiney did not die to put spirit into his own people,' said de Valera whose hoarseness didn't help amid the cacophony. 'He knew that they had spirit; that they were willing to make sacrifices as he did. In other lands, patriots have had to teach other people the spirit of sacrifice by such an example but MacSwiney knew that his people had spirit … We are not complaining at MacSwiney's death. He did as much for American principles as he did for Irish principles.'

This point was echoed by Marcus Garvey.

'Hundreds and thousands of Irishmen have died as martyrs to the cause of Irish freedom …' said the leader of the United Negro Improvement Association. 'They compelled the attention of the world and I believe the death of McSweeney [*sic*] did more for the freedom of Ireland today than probably anything they did for 500 years prior to his death.'

There were protests all across America that whole weekend. A gigantic parade of people of all ethnic groups marched behind three empty caskets draped in the Irish flag that snaked their way through the streets of Philadelphia as accompanying bands played funereal music. The crowd for a very similar obsequy in Chicago was estimated to be 50,000, and eye-witness reports from Boston suggested that 30,000 turned out there to march behind symbolic hearses. Even in Jersey City, 8,000 solemnly walked behind a tricolour-clad carriage packed with wreaths and flowers.

'Please convey to the Lady Mayoress my profound sympathy in her great bereavement,' wrote Reverend James J Troy, Chaplain-General of the United States Army of Occupation, Coblenz, Germany, in a telegram. 'Lord Mayor MacSwiney died for the things we thought we fought for in the world war, and his name shall go down the ages as an immortal who did not quake before the tyrant but whose soul was grand as the ideal for which he died. I have said Mass for him and the other martyrs of Cork Gaol, and will do the same on the Feast of All Souls. Their names will forever be treasured, not merely in Ireland, but wherever the word and reality of freedom are loved and honoured.'

The same sentiments were being echoed around England. In Manchester, forty thousand marchers came onto the streets of the city for a mock funeral on a cold Sunday in Lancashire. Having met up at Stevenson Square, they walked to Moston Cemetery in a cavalcade containing sixty taxi-cabs and carriages, and a hearse containing the obligatory empty coffin, draped in the Irish tricolour. There were so many of them that the first walkers arrived in the graveyard before the tail-enders had even left the square.

'A squad of girls and women accompanied the hearse, some in semi-uniform, while an industrial school played Saul's Dead March and Chopin's Funeral March,' according to one account. 'There were also Irish pipers playing in the march. As many as forty branches of the Irish Self-Determination League were present, carrying tricolours, and many marchers wore armbands in the same colour.'

At one point that afternoon, a small group of 'Orange' protesters tried to disrupt the procession but were prevented from doing so by the police. It's not known whether that group was motivated by the common belief among spectators en route that MacSwiney's body was actually in the coffin on the way to Moston. At the cemetery, where thousands were stuck outside the gates due to overcrowding, priests led the congregation in prayers as wreaths were placed at the memorial to the Manchester Martyrs.

In Newcastle, there was another coffin, another tricolour, and a procession to Town Moor where 15,000 had gathered to listen to eulogies and political orations about MacSwiney. Four thousand more turned out in Bradford for another march in sympathy.

At the other end of the world, the tributes were equally political in tone. In the Melbourne suburb of Richmond, a mass meeting, at which Australian MP Hugh Mahon was the most strident voice, passed resolutions condemning the British government for its role in MacSwiney's death.

'Never in Russia under the worst rulers of the Czars had there been such an infamous murder as that of the late Alderman

MacSwiney,' declared Mahon before stoking the crowd into pledging its support for, amongst other things, the establishment of an independent Australian Republic. Within weeks, Australian Prime Minister William Morris Hughes was endeavouring to have Mahon thrown out of parliament for his comments. If this sort of empathy for MacSwiney was predictable down under, especially given Archbishop Mannix's proximity to the mayor during the hunger strike, the country also had a more tangible link with the entire episode.

In 1885, Terence's father John had emigrated to Australia where he died ten years later, thousands of miles from his wife and children, from diabetes and pleurisy. No proper headstone had ever been put on his grave, something that obviously stirred comment because, by the time of the first anniversary of his son's death, the Gaelic League in Melbourne organised a 'Pilgrimage to the Grave of Terence MacSwiney's Father.'

Several hundred men, women and children attended a ceremony where the rosary was led by Father James O'Dwyer, some of the call and response prayers were recited in Irish, and a floral Celtic cross of green, white and gold was placed upon the elder MacSwiney's final resting place. This previously neglected plot soon became a focal point for the city's Irish Diaspora. Within two years, a more permanent monument, a stone Celtic cross, was erected over the grave, with two inscriptions in Irish on the base. They translate:

'In memory of John MacSwiney, born in Cork, Ireland, and died in Melbourne on 19 October, 1895 at the age of 59. May God have mercy on his soul.'

'And also in memory of his son Terence MacSwiney, Lord

Mayor of the city of Cork and leader of the Irish Republican Army who died for the sake of the Republic in Brixton Prison, England, on 25 October, 1920. May his soul rest at God's right hand.'

There were other international responses too. A session of the Indian Nationalist Congress in Nagpur adopted a resolution paying homage to the memory of Terence MacSwiney, and sent a message of sympathy to the Irish people in its struggle for independence. In recognition of a man who had sacrificed himself 'that he might help to liberate Ireland', a huge demonstration in Montreal tendered the 'truest sympathy and most profound condolence to Mrs MacSwiney in this hour of her supreme sorrow.'

The range and scope of the worldwide reaction was such that over the coming decades, MacSwiney's protest would be cited as an influence by Nelson Mandela and the African National Congress, by Mahatma Gandhi, and, nearer home, by Bobby Sands in the midst of his own fatal fast in 1981. Indeed, MacSwiney's story would crop up wherever a people were struggling to free themselves from an oppressor.

Witness the *Irish Times* journalist Conor O'Clery sitting down with Zviad Gamsakhurdia, the leader of the Georgian independence movement, in the midst of the break-up of the Soviet Union. During the interview in Tbilisi, Gamsakhurdia, a history professor, told O'Clery that among the heroes on whom he based his own efforts to break from Moscow were Roger Casement and Terence MacSwiney. Seven decades earlier, Gamsakhurdia's father Konstanine, a novelist, had written a brazen letter to Vladimir Lenin, pointing out that 'Georgia

would one day have its own Casements and MacSwineys', on its
way to gaining full autonomy.

Perhaps nowhere though was the reaction to MacSwiney's
passing as animated, as immediate and as impactful as in Barcelona. Like most of the world, the Catalans had followed the
hunger strike in their daily newspapers, but when it ended they
went into full mourning. Women in the region were invited to
wear crepe and black ribbons, flags were hung at half-mast, and
around midday on 27 October, some 500 protesters arrived at
the British Consulate-General in the city. They were waving a
Sinn Féin flag and chanting: '*Viva Irlanda, muera Inglaterrra.*'

Eventually, a deputation of seven went to the door and
demanded to see the Consul-General. He was out at the time
and when staff told them that any complaint they had should be
made in writing, the demonstrators left. About ten minutes
later, the stoning of the building commenced. While workers
inside tried in vain to get the shutters up, the crowd flung anything they could lay their hands on and succeeded in breaking
just about every window in the place. By the time the police
arrived, the street outside was empty but for a carpet of shards of
broken glass.

'The square in front of this building is now guarded by a
strong force of police and Guardia Civil who shall remain until
the local excitement over the so-called martyrdom of MacSwiney has subsided,' wrote the Consul-General to his superiors in
London.

In Ireland's struggle for independence from London, the
denizens of Barcelona apparently saw their own quest to break
from the control of Madrid. From that empathy grew

enthusiasm for all things Irish nationalist, and the willingness of Cork's mayor to starve himself to death to prove a point brought the admiration to a whole new level. Several masses were said for MacSwiney in the days after his death, many of them drawing local political leaders such as the mayor and deputy mayor of Barcelona, and the speaker of the Provincial Legislature.

The presence of official representatives dismayed the English representatives in the city. Cue the following message from the consul on 4 November.

'... the Ayuntamiento of this city [Barcelona], in session yesterday, unanimously voted a message of sympathy to the widow of the late Mayor of Cork, in order to bear testimony to Cataluna's appreciation of her husband's heroic martyrdom. This act on the part of the Town Council is deplored by many Catalans and some have affirmed to me that it is little short of the town identifying itself with last week's hostile demonstration in front of this office. I paid a visit to the mayor yesterday morning regarding responsibility for the damage done but the mayor curtly told me that it was none of his business and possibly I had better apply to the Civil Governor.'

The English diplomats were in a tizzy because the city was aflame with pro-Irish passions. On 1 November, the CADCI trade union had organised a public meeting to commemorate 'Terence MacSwiney and the illustrious Catalan dead'.

Máire ní Bhriain, Sinn Féin's official representative in Spain, was the guest of honour, and the balcony where she sat was draped with a tricolour upon which a black band of mourning had been placed. This then was the set-up for a celebration of Catalan independence movements, laced with occasional expressions of sympathy to MacSwiney and the Irish cause.

'The highlight of the evening's proceedings was the recital by the well-known nationalist poet, Ventura Gassol, of the poetic homage to Terence MacSwiney he was commissioned to compose by the CADCI,' wrote Terence Folley. 'Adapting for the occasion the traditional Catalan folksong, 'La Presó de Lleida' [Lleida Prison], Ventura Gassol dedicated his version to the example of Terence MacSwiney. The poet's patriotic convictions added intensity to his recital of the poem which had a profound emotional effect on a listening public already highly receptive to the sentiments being expressed.'

At regular intervals during Gassol's rendition, the audience broke into sustained applause. It was a fitting response to this homage because during this gathering the trade unionists had granted MacSwiney entry to the pantheon of Catalan nationalism.

The Town Council of Figueres, birthplace of Salvador Dali, also passed a resolution expressing: 'emotion and admiration of the glorious death of the Lord Mayor of Cork and other patriotic Irishmen who have died in English prisons, that our adhesion to the liberty of people and the inviolable rules of justice may be proclaimed.' The Mayor of Villafranca del Panades sent a letter on behalf of his own town to Lloyd George, expressing sympathy for the cause for which MacSwiney died. The British requested that the Spanish government reprove the municipality for what it called this 'impudence'.

With the Catalans even going as far as to send a doll to MacSwiney's two-year-old daughter, Máire, then still billeted at her grandmother's house in Cork city, English officials in

Barcelona were anxious to bring to the attention of the Foreign Office in London how much the mayor's death had affected British standing in the community.

In a dispatch to the Foreign Office, Esme Howard of the British Embassy in Madrid wrote: 'The fact is perhaps worthy of our Lordship's attention that not a single newspaper except "La Epoca", which used the incident to support its campaign for a strong government in Spain, has printed anything to indicate in the slightest degree that it approved of the conduct of His Majesty's Government in the treatment of the late Alderman MacSwiney.'

The correspondence between Barcelona, Madrid and London in the weeks after 25 October betrays a panic in the ranks, the representatives in Spain anxious for those at home to understand how unpopular the decision to allow MacSwiney to die in prison had been in that region. Although some diplomats tried to play down the incident at the consulate as 'devoid of importance', it generated frenetic and sometimes coded traffic with London about the wider impact, the need for compensation and the Spanish reaction.

Several pro-MacSwiney newspaper columns from the local press were translated and sent back as proof, and also mentioned was the fact that in Bilbao, the Basque flag had flown at half-mast as a mark of respect on the day of the funeral. There were similar stories in British outposts all over the world, as diplomats expressed concern at the burgeoning public and press support for the Irish cause.

'The worldwide reaction to the hunger strike brought the British government to its knees,' says MacSwiney's daughter,

Máire MacSwiney Brugha. 'We have the proof of that in the British archives now. I didn't know anything until the archives were opened years later that these type of things were there in the archives. It exposed them worldwide for their activities in Ireland.'

On the January day we meet at her home in South Dublin, it's going on ninety years since the Catalans gifted her that doll. She in turn passed it on to the Cork Public Museum, anxious for it to be part of their display about her father. The little girl is an old woman now, in the late autumn of quite an extraordinary life, a tale told in her own memoir *History's Daughter*. There could be no more appropriate title for her autobiography than that.

During the hunger strike, Terence MacSwiney had requested that, in the event of his death, both Muriel and Mary would share custody of Máire Óg, as she was known then. Whether motivated by worries about his wife's health or the impact his passing might have upon her, he had unwittingly created the circumstances for terrible future drama. Despite the fact that both women travelled together to Washington DC in December, 1920, where they gave heartrending and powerful testimony about the hunger strike before 'The American Commission on Conditions in Ireland', the rift between them widened over the next few years.

After Muriel subsequently brought Máire to live in Europe and sent her to boarding school in Germany, her Aunt Mary came to visit and dramatically spirited her back to Cork without her mother's permission. By then fourteen years old, Máire told the judge during the bitter custody battle which ensued in the Dublin courts that she wished to remain with her aunt. He took this on advisement, and after delivering a judgment in favour of

Mary MacSwiney, mother and daughter never spoke again.

One of the stipulations of the verdict was that the child be kept away from the Republican movement. This order was strictly adhered to by her aunts but, in one of life's great ironies, she grew up to marry Ruairí Brugha, scion of another historic dynasty, in 1945. He was the son of Cathal Brugha, her father's comrade and friend, the man he'd written such a poignant good-bye to while lying on a bed in Brixton Prison, a man later assassinated during the Civil War.

'I only began to realise my own father's impact worldwide when I started to travel in the fifties,' says Máire MacSwiney Brugha. 'Going to Rome in 1950. When we crossed over from France to Italy we got into a little station and our spiritual guide, a very nice priest, produced these badges. Each of us had to wear a badge called Irlanda. We were never to take off Irlanda. When the ordinary working people of the station saw this, they came over to us and said: "Irlanda, that's where Terence MacSwiney came from." That's all they knew about Ireland.'

There is no question that MacSwiney's incredible feat of endurance and his death magnified Ireland's cause in the international arena. Just over a year before his fast began, an Irish delegation couldn't gain a credible hearing at the Versailles Treaty negotiations and this fact barely raised a murmur. Once the mayor arrived in Brixton however, the world's press turned his strike into front page news in a way that brought the wider issue of the struggle for independence into focus.

From the evidence of the communications between Barcelona and London in the immediate aftermath, the British government was definitely spooked by the spontaneous outpourings of sympathy for and expressions of solidarity with MacSwiney. How much all of this influenced subsequent British policy in Ireland can be debated but that it seriously impacted in the short-term can hardly be doubted. Yet, MacSwiney's posthumous role has been diminished by the passage of time, something his daughter has witnessed over the course of her own life.

'Somebody gave me a book called the definitive history of Ireland and my father got one line it,' says Máire MacSwiney Brugha. 'The Free State came in and wrote him out of history. I think they had to write him out. How could they justify what they did, what they threw away with the Treaty in 1921. They couldn't afford to have him looked upon as a hero because he had achieved what they had thrown away.

'Was his sacrifice worth it? It certainly was worth it in that he brought the British government to its knees. It wasn't in vain. It was only rendered in vain by the subsequent Free State government blotting him out. But, you know, people still remembered him abroad. He might not have been remembered too much in Ireland but whenever I travelled in Europe, I realised how everybody there knew what he did.'

She is not the only person to subscribe to the view that he, in many ways, became the most neglected man of that period of Irish history.

'The seventieth anniversary of his death in 1990, for example, drew no mention in the pages of his city's paper, the *Cork Examiner*, nor in other Irish publications,' wrote Francis J Costello upon publication of his excellent biography of MacSwiney in 1995. 'Nor was there a civil ceremony of any note held in Ireland. The omission was noteworthy, especially when just a week earlier considerable attention had been focused on the 100th anniversary of the birth of Michael Collins.'

If the redrafting of the Irish political landscape caused MacSwiney's contribution to be downsized, and to prove the point, Costello's book has been the first and only major study of him over the past half century, he has led a longer cultural after-life, commemorated by artists great and small.

Brian O'Higgins was digging potatoes in a field near Kilmain-ham Jail on Monday, 25 October 1920 when he learned about MacSwiney's death. A veteran of the Easter Rising, O'Higgins sat down where he was working that afternoon and wrote a trib-ute. That evening, he sent the sheet of paper down to the *Irish Independent* where it appeared the next morning.

Shed we no tear for you Terence MacSwiney!
God set the seal of his love on your brow,
Gave you to Ireland - a saint and a soldier,
Who can be fitter to plead for her now?

Joy for the valiant heroic heart of you!
Joy for the soul of you whiter than snow,
Joy for the Cause that has claimed your allegiance,
Your death is its challenge to friend and to foe!

Raise we no 'caoine' [keen, mournful cry] for you Terence MacSwiney,
High is our pride in your name and your deed,
Humble our prayer to the great God of Battles,
That we, too, will be strong in this dark hour of need.

Joy for your love and your faith and your courage,
Glowing and glad to the last anguished breath,
Thanks be to God for you Terence MacSwiney,
Thanks be to God for your life and your death!

O'Higgins was only one of the first wave to be artistically inspired by the events at Brixton Prison. Dozens more would be similarly affected over the weeks, months, years and decades that followed his hunger strike.

Just four days after MacSwiney had breathed his last, WB Yeats wrote again to Lennox Robinson about *The Revolutionist*, MacSwiney's play that had been under consideration by the Abbey Theatre before the hunger strike. Yeats was critical of the quality of the work and, in particular, female characters who he considered proof that MacSwiney had not yet fulfilled his talent. Yet, he was smart enough to recognise the commercial potential of a posthumous production while Ireland still grieved for the suddenly-revered author.

'The more however the play is kept close to its political story the better & the more it remains in the men's hands,' wrote Yeats. 'It is not a good play but it certainly increases one's respect for the Lord Mayor. He had intellect & lived & died for it. One feels that he died because he would not disappoint himself. I think the last pages would greatly move the audience who will see the Mayor in the play's hero.'

In February, 1921, the play opened at the Abbey Theatre and was a tremendous success. Muriel MacSwiney attended the premiere and Lady Gregory told her that the theatre was honoured to perform the play for the first time because it felt like 'we were laying a wreath upon the grave'. At a point in the production where the hero Hugh O'Neill attacks Father O'Connor for meddling in politics, the crowd broke into cheers and applause.

Seven months later, almost on the anniversary of MacSwiney's death, Yeats's own play *The King's Threshold*, played at the same venue. As he'd first envisaged back during the days of the hunger strike itself, he wrote a new and more tragic ending where, instead of triumphing, the fasting poet Seanchan dies because of King Guaire's intransigence. According to one critic, the new denouement reflected 'the light of MacSwiney's unalterable faith in himself, of the nobility of the impulse that drove him to the course he took.'

In 1970, the Abbey commissioned Francis Stuart to write a play to commemorate the fiftieth anniversary of the hunger strike. *Who Fears to Speak?* was controversially cancelled in rehearsals for what were perceived in many quarters to be 'political reasons'. A stage-reading of the work held in Dublin's Liberty Hall later that year received mixed reviews from the newspapers. Around the same time, the Cork writer Robert O'Donoghue also wrote a verse play about MacSwiney.

The list of writers who have cited MacSwiney's fatal strike in their work is long, distinguished and varied; from Samuel Beckett in *Malone Dies* in one era to Roddy Doyle in *A Star Called Henry* in another. If it's to be expected that he would feature in the creative imagination of Irish authors, he also crops up in unlikely places, such as William Kennedy's novel *The Ink Truck*.

In Kennedy's book, after four days without food on a picket line, a character named Bailey suffers hallucinations and imagines himself going to meet 'Alderman Terence MacSwiney, Lord Mayor of Cork'. Bailey tries to express his admiration for MacSwiney's achievement, and when the mayor raises a glass to him, says: ' … saints shouldn't toast mortals.' As the conversation progresses, MacSwiney eventually dismisses Bailey as one of 'those play actors'.

The substance of the story is less important than the simple fact that a major American author, one most usually associated with his native city of Albany in upstate New York, used MacSwiney's protest as a plot device. Especially since Kennedy wasn't even born until nearly a decade after the whole thing played out in London. There are more exotic literary references too.

Anne Spencer, a voice most usually associated with the Harlem Renaissance of the 1920s, wrote an eponymous poem about MacSwiney that ends with the couplet: 'Terence, Terence, in glory forever, now lovers have another name to die by.'

In 1989, Sri Lankan author Gopal Gandhi published *Refuge*, a novel set in the tea estates of Sri Lanka. One of the plantations is named after the Irish town of Cork and Gandhi mentions that it is the place where 'the great Irish nationalist Terence MacSwiney was mayor'. Almost seven decades after his death, one more indicator of his enduring legacy in the international community.

It wasn't just writers who, in different ways, sought to pay tribute to or to commemorate his feat. Aside from Albert Power's stunning death mask, there is the equally impressive contribution of John Lavery. The Belfast-born painter, for whom the British Royal Family had sat in 1913, captured MacSwiney's funeral in an oil on canvas piece called 'Southwark Cathedral, 1920 (Terence MacSwiney)'. In 1921, Lavery, formerly Official

War Artist to the Royal Navy, created a portrait of Muriel MacSwiney entitled 'The Widow'.

In Old St Patrick's Church on West Adams Street in Chicago, a place of worship originally built by Famine-era emigrants from Ireland, Thomas A O'Shaughnessy fashioned a Triptych of stained glass windows in 1922. It was titled 'Faith, Hope & Charity' but is known as the Terence MacSwiney Memorial. In a city he'd never visited, in a country he'd never seen, it stands there still.

A pipe band in Manchester, a branch of the Ancient Order of Hibernians in Rockland County, New York, and in his native Cork, a quay (abutting the City Hall), and a secondary school have all been named in his honour. In 1958, one of the chapels in the newly-refurbished St George's Cathedral in Southwark was dedicated to St Patrick in memory of MacSwiney. In 1970, the Department of Posts and Telegraphs issued a stamp bearing his image to commemorate the fiftieth anniversary.

Aside from these very different types of monuments, one of MacSwiney's most recurring appearances in Irish public culture and the way subsequent generations have learned of him is probably via a folk song. An adaptation of a tune first written about a Confederate soldier dying far from home in the American Civil War, 'Shall my soul pass through old Ireland' has been a lament favoured by Cork exiles all over the world.

In a dreary British prison where an Irish rebel lay,
By his side a priest was standing ere his soul should pass away,
And he faintly murmured 'Father' as he clasped him by the hand,
'Tell me this before I die: shall my soul pass through Ireland?"

CHORUS: 'Shall my soul pass through old Ireland, pass through Cork's old city strand?
Shall I see the old cathedral where St. Patrick took his stand?
Shall I see the little chapel where I pledged my heart in hand?
Tell me this before you leave me: shall my soul pass through Ireland?

'Twas for loving dear old Ireland in the prison cell I lie.
'Twas for loving dear old Ireland in this foreign land I die.
Will you meet my little daughter? Will you make her understand?
Father, tell me if you can: shall my soul pass through Ireland?'

With his soul pure as a lily and his body sanctified,
In that dreary British prison a brave Irish rebel died.
Prayed the priest 'that wish be granted' as in blessing raised his hand
'Father, grant this brave man's wish. Let his soul pass through Ireland.'

It can be argued that not one of the various songs, sculptures and stories have ever reached as wide an audience or has touched as many people as some of the words Terence MacSwiney himself uttered the night he was elected Lord Mayor of Cork. In that lengthy speech, one profound line was destined to figure wherever pithy quotations were gathered between the covers of a book, wherever a public speaker trying to rouse the downtrodden was in search of an inspirational line.

'… it is not they who can inflict most but they who can suffer most will conquer …'

Its enduring impact became a posthumous fulfilment of his literary ambitions, its continuing relevance to every human struggle a fitting epitaph for his truncated life.

BIBLIOGRAPHY

BOOKS and PAMPHLETS

Bayor, Ronald H and Meagher, Timothy J. (editors) *The New York Irish*, Baltimore, The John Hopkins University Press, 1996

Callwell, CE, *Field Marshall Sir Henry Wilson*, New York, Cassell, 1927

Chavasse, Moirin, *Terence MacSwiney*, Dublin, Clonmore and Reynolds, 1961

Clifton, Michael, *Amigo- Friend of the Poor*, Leominster, Fowler Wright Books, 1987

Costello, Francis J, *Enduring the Most: The Life and Death of Terence MacSwiney*, Dingle, Ireland, Brandon Press, 1995

Coyle, Albert, *Evidence on Conditions in Ireland*: The American Commission on Conditions in Ireland, Washington DC, Bliss Building, 1921

Ellmann, Richard, *James Joyce*, New York, Oxford University Press, 1992

Fallon, Charlotte H, *Soul of Fire – A biography of Mary MacSwiney*, Cork, Mercier Press, 1986

Foster, RF, *WB Yeats: A Life Vol 2*, New York, Oxford University Press, 2003

Foxton, David, *Revolutionary Lawyers, Sinn Féin and crown courts in Ireland and Britain, 1916-23*, Dublin, Four Courts Press, 2008

Garvey, Marcus, The Marcus Garvey and Universal Negro Improvement Association Papers, Volumes 2 and 10, Los Angeles, University of California Press, 1983

Hannigan, David, *De Valera in America; The Rebel President's 1919 Campaign*, Dublin, The O'Brien Press, 2008

Hart, Peter, *Mick- The Real Michael Collins*, New York, Penguin, 2006

Hopkinson, Michael, *The Irish War of Independence*, Dublin, Gill and Macmillan, 2002

Hopkinson, Michael, *The Last Days of Dublin Castle*, Dublin, Irish Academic Press, 1998

Jones, Thomas, *Whitehall Diary Volume 1 – 1916-25*, London, Oxford University Press, 1969

Keogh, Dermot, *The Vatican, the Bishops and Irish Politics, 1919-39*, Cambridge, Cambridge University Press, 1986

Krimm, Bernard G, *WB Yeats and the Emergence of the Irish Free State*, Troy, The Whitston Publishing Company, 1981

Laffan, Michael, *The Resurrection of Ireland: The Sinn Féin Party, 1916-23*, Cambridge, Cambridge University Press, 1999

MacSwiney Brugha, Máire, *History's Daughter; A Memoir from the Only Child of Terence MacSwiney*, Dublin, The O'Brien Press, 2006

MacSwiney, Terence, *The Revolutionist: A Play in Five Acts*, Dublin, Maunsel, 1914

MacSwiney, Terence, Principles of Freedom, Dublin, Talbot Press, 1921

McConville, Sean, *Irish Political Prisoners, 1848 -1922*, New York, Routledge, 2003

Murphy, John A, *Cuimhe Dha Laoch: MacCurtain and MacSwiney*, Cork, 1995

O'Connor, Frank, *An Only Child*, London, Pan Books, 1961

O'Connor, Frank, *The Big Fellow*, Dublin, Poolbeg Press, 1979

O'Donoghue, Florence, *No Other Law*, Dublin, Irish Press Ltd, 1954

O'Faolain, Sean, *Vive Moi*, London, Sinclair Stevenson, 1993

O'Hegarty, PS, *A Short Memoir of Terence MacSwiney*, Dublin, The Talbot Press, 1922

O'Malley, Ernie, *On Another Man's Wound*, Boulder, Colorado, Roberst Rinehart Press, 1999

Paulin, Tom, Minotaur: Poetry and the Nation State, Cambridge, Harvard University Press, 1992

Rhodes James, Robert, *Memoirs of a Conservative*, London, Weidenfeld and Nicolson, 1969

Rose, Kenneth, *King George V*, London, Weidenfield and Nicolson, 1983

Street, CJ, *The Administration of Ireland, 1920*, London, P Allan and Co, 1921

White, Gerry and O'Shea, Brendan, *Baptised in Blood – The formation of the Cork Brigade of the Irish Volunteers 1913 -1916*, Cork, Mercier Press, 2005

Wilson, AN, *After the Victorians,* London, Hutchison, 2005

JOURNAL ARTICLES

Corkery, Daniel, 'Terence MacSwiney Lord Mayor of Cork', *Studies: An Irish Quarterly Review*, Vol. 9, No. 36 (Dec., 1920), pp. 512-520

Folley, Terence, 'A Catalan Trade Union and the Irish War of Independence, 1919-22,', *Saothar* 10, Journal of the Irish Labour History Society, 1984

Hart, Peter, 'Operations Abroad: The Irish in Britain, 191-23', *The English Historical Review*, Vol. 115, No. 460 Feb, 2000

MacGreevey, Thomas, Old Ireland, 26 November 1921, pp. 570-571

Mews, Stuart, 'The Hunger Strike of the Lord Mayor of Cork, 1920: Irish, English and Vatican Attitudes', The Ecclesiastical History Society, 1989

Neville, Grace, 'The Death of Terence MacSwiney, A French Perspective', *The Journal of the Cork Historical and Archaeological Society*, Vol 106, 2001

Noonan, Gerard, 'The Eyes of the World are watching – Sinn Féin Hunger Strikes in Britain, 1920', Trinity College Dublin

O'Gorman, Kevin, 'The Hunger Strike of Terence MacSwiney', *Irish Theological Quarterly*, Vol 59, Issue 2, 1993

Reynolds, Paige, 'Modernist Martyrdom, The Funerals of Terence MacSwiney', *Modernism/modernity* Volume 9, No. 4, 2002

Wooding, Jonathan M, 'Monumental Commemorations and Corporeal Relics in 1920s Irish-Australia', *History Australia*, Volume 4, Number 2, 2007

NEWSPAPERS

Irish Press (Philadelphia), *The Freemans Journal, The Guardian, The Cork Examiner, The Irish Times, The Observer, The Daily Telegraph, New York Times, The Daily Mail, The Evening News* (London), *The Atlantic Monthly*

ARCHIVES

Dáil Debates

Hansard (House of Commons Debates)

MacSwiney Collection, UCD

MacSwiney Collection, Cork Public Museum

McGarrity Collection, Villanova University, Philadelphia

National Archives, Kew, England

WEBSITES

http://www.martindardis.com/id217.html

http://radicalmanchester.wordpress.com

SOURCE NOTES

PROLOGUE

'The circumstances of the vacancy in the office of ' – HO 144/1038, National Archives, London

CHAPTER 1

'But it is because they were our best and bravest ...' – MacSwiney Brugha, p291

'Meals were snatched hurriedly and ...' – O'Hegarty, p81

'I saw my husband sometimes, because ...' – Coyle, p282

'A British raid on local mails ...' – O'Donoghue, p89

'I rushed upstairs to warn the Lord Mayor ...' – Chavasse, p143

'When I got to the top of the wall ...' – HO 144/10308, National Archives, London

'It was clear that MacSwiney had ...' – O'Donoghue, p92

'I would rather die than part with it ...' – O'Hegarty, p85

'At midnight that [Thursday] night, two military – Coyle, p307

'What could I do?' – Ibid, p283

'I saw him in Cork Gaol that Saturday morning ...' – Ibid, p308

'A big military lorry came up, a very large one ...' – Ibid, p284

'First of all, they took him up very high ...' – Ibid, p284

'While waiting in the shed ...' – Chavasse, p144

All courtroom dialogue is taken from the official court transcript – HO 144/10308, National Archives, London

'None of us dreamed that it would be a month ...' – Coyle, p288

'This thing is rather important to us ...' – Ibid p310

CHAPTER 2

A pilgrim from beyond the sea ... – *Irish Independent*, 23 August 1920

'This man is not to be released ...' MacSwiney Papers, Cork Public Museum

'He [Dr Treadwell] impressed on me the gravity...' P48c/325, UCDA

'I have just seen him and his condition ...' – *Freemans Journal*, 21 August 1920

'Do you mean that you are ...' – *The Irish Times*, 21 August 1920

'You will see your husband ...' – Coyle, p289

'I saw my husband then ...' – Ibid, p290

'I found the Lord Mayor considerably...' – *Freemans Journal*, 23 August 1920

'I have received your letter of the 20th instant...' – Ibid

'After a bit he did not like to be there ...' – Coyle, p290

'His spirit is as strong as ever ...' – *Daily Mail*, 23 August 1920

'He has appealed to the weapon of the hunger strike ...' – *The Times*, 23 August 1920

'Could sane Englishmen do nothing to ...' – *The Irish Times*, 26 August 1920

'Just returned from Terry ...' – *The Times*, 24 August 1920

'I am for ever saying them to myself ...' – Chavasse, p18

'He lies on a prison bed in pain and restless ...' – *Freemans Journal*, 25 August 1920

'But if you Englishmen of the better hopes ...' – *The Manchester Guardian*, 26 August 1920

'My brother, Lord Mayor of Cork ...' – *The Times*, 25 August 1920

'I have received several communications here ...' – *The Manchester Guardian*, 26 August 1920

'I made no appeal to you for exceptional ...' – *New York Times*, 27 August

'He is facing death with a brave ...' – *The Manchester Guardian*, 26 August 1920

'Lord Mayor much weaker ...' – *Irish Independent*, 26 August 1920

'excitement might have been ...' – *The Times*, 28 August 1920

CHAPTER 3

SEE, though the oil be low... – *The Times*, 31 August 1920

'We, the undersigned, being members of ...' – *The Manchester Guardian*, 27 August 1920

'I am receiving appeals from ...' – McConville, p745

'I am very sorry that we differ ...' – Rhodes James, p98

'The issue became a major ...' – Costello, p163

'The King feels that the probable results ...' – Rhodes James, p98

'I have for some days been trying ...' – *Irish Independent*, 11 September 1953

'Even if the King were in favour ...' – *New York Times*, 1 September 1920

'In thanking you for your telegram ...' – *New York Times*, 26 August 1920

'The King is an old coward ...' – Wilson, p228

'Your lordship, my conscience ...' – *The Times*, 30 August 1920

'... the offences imputed to the Lord Mayor...' – *The Times*, 30 August 1920

'... the Christian conscience of this country...' – *The Times*, 30 August 1920

'If released alive he will have won...' – Hopkinson (*War of Independence*), p86

'Terence MacSwiney is as calm...' – *Irish Independent*, 30 August 1920

'I told the doctor that nothing ...' – *New York Times*, 29 August 1920

'I am convinced I will not be released...' – *The Times* 30 August 1920

'Greetings to all my comrades...' – *New York Times*, 1 September 1920

'You claim to be a Celt!' – *Freemans Journal*, 2 September 1920

'I should not be surprised if I were...' – Ibid

'I feel that the end is near...' – *New York Times*, 3 September 1920

'None of the mercy which some seek...' – *New York Times*, 23 September 1920

'To compare his case with that...' – *Irish Independent*, 2 September 1920

'The Cork Martyr has filled the stage...' Hopkinson, p35

'Since when has it become...' – p48b/427, UCDA

'The policy of the government has been...' – *Irish Independent*, 6 September 1920

'An insult to freedom, honour, truth...' – *New York Times*, 7 September, 1920

CHAPTER 4

'I have your letter and as desired...' – p48b/417, UCDA

'He's dying fast,' she said...' – *Freemans Journal*, 7 September 1920

'The doctors said: "The food is always...' – Coyle, p316

'Although some people say that the desire...' – *New York Times*, 7 September 1920

'That this council do now adjourn...' – *The Irish Times*, 11 September 1920

'I am positive he will...' – *Irish Press*, 11 September 1920

'Now the majority of public opinion...' – *The Observer*, 5 September 1920

'It is amazing that your government...' – *New York Times*, 7 September 1920

'I have watched this case with pain...' – *New York Times*, 9 September 1920

'I make this offer in the hope that...' – *The Times*, 9 September 1920

'I think the decision to allow...' – *The Times*, 9 September 1920

'In the course of conversation with him...' – Costello, p192

'If he would only take a spoonful...' – *Irish Press*, 10 September 1920

'No such order will come from...' – *New York Times*, 10 September 1920

'This Congress, representing six and...' – *The Times*, 10 September 1920

If any of you think for...' – Fallon, p48

'I did not want to urge...' – Coyle, p322

'I do not think it is a...' – *Cork Examiner*, 10 September 1920

'When I said it was Friday...' – *Irish Press*, 10 September 1920

'Lord Mayor grows weaker...' – *Irish Press*, 10 September 1920

'He thought their present experience...' – Costello, p179

'The matter may prove in the...' – McConville p747

'Mayor MacSwiney is entering the danger...' – *New York Times*, 10 September 1920

'Then began the insinuations...' – Coyle, p316

'He is very bitter and says that...' – Costello, p192

'The Lord Mayor is very...' – *Freemans Journal*, 12 September 1920

'Will you take food?...' – Costello, p193

'The Lord Mayor of Cork is no longer...' – *The Observer*, 12 Sunday 1920

CHAPTER 5

'Our organisation, consisting of eight thousand – *Saothar* 10 (1984), p 60

'Taking the matter under advisement would...' – *New York Times*, 29 August1920

'Will you stand back and see MacSwiney...' – the scenes on the dock are collated from the *New York Times*, *Irish Press* (Philadelphia), Nelson, p 26-35, and Meagher and Bayor, p365-373

'Few if any developments in the entire history...' – Nelson, p30

'Well, we did it...' – Meagher and Bayor, p367

'The whole case is epitomised...' – *New York Times*, 27 August 1920

'If I were in MacSwiney's place...' – *New York Times*, 28 August 1920

'He [MacSwiney] is acting as a...' – Ibid

'If MacSwiney dies...' – *New York Times*, 2 September 1920

'As Mayor of New York...' – *Irish Press*, 11 September 1920 'its deep indignation and protest…' – Ibid

To President Wilson, Washington… – *Freemans Journal*, 6 September 1920

To Mrs. Wilson, White House, Washington… – Ibid

'I beg to inform you that…' – The *Times*, 7 September 1920

'Convey to McSwiney [*sic*]…' Garvey, p649

'the declarations made by the…' – *Irish Independent*, 25 August 1920

'About 8.30 p.m. on the 31ˢᵗ – Documents on Irish Foreign Policy, No. 46 1125/13

'Has not every human being…' – *Irish Press*, 25 September 1920

'Over in Brixton in a cold…' – Ibid

'There is a man dying for…' – Ibid

'The case of the dying…' – Ibid

'By taking him to London, he…' – Coyle, p313

'Yesterday he was unknown outside…' – *Freemans Journal*, 30 September 1920

'*Uno stoicismso superbo…*' – Keogh, p249

'Your excellency, I take the liberty…' – *Irish Press*, 18 September 1920

'About this time Father…' – Chavasse, p161

'If the present tragedy is allowed…' – *Freemans Journal*, 14 September 1920

CHAPTER 6

What good is it to live a … à Kempis, Chapter 23, Book 1

'See, then, dearly beloved…' – Ibid

'I want it to be a simple…' – *Freemans Journal*, 16 September 1920

'Do you think I'm going to give way…' – *New York Times*, 16 September 1920

'a final appeal to you to…' – *Freemans Journal*, 15 September 1920

'Can the American people not force…' – *New York Times*, 14 September 1920

'An important message from our…' – *The Times*, 14 September 1920

'Dáil Éireann, assembled in full session...' – Dáil Debates, 17 September 1920

'found him sitting up in bed...' – Costello, p193

'In the afternoon, he was able to sit up...' – The *Evening News*, 20 September 1920

'At the commencement of the struggle...' – *New York Times*, 25 September 1920

'We did not court publicity when...' – Ibid

'There is no foundation for the...' – Ibid

'The Home Office is simply trying...' – *New York Times*, 20 September 1920

'Everybody is asking who is feeding...' – *Sunday Times* of London, 19 September 1920

'Statements, at various times, in the British...' – O'Hegarty, p93

'He is becoming sulky and...' – Costello, p194

'He [the Medical Commissioner] confirmed the report of...' – p48c/325, UCDA

'Edith Cavell became an English martyr...' – *The Manchester Guardian*, 20 September 1920

'With lots of the peasants...' – Sturgis, p59

'Tomorrow I shall have completed forty...' – *New York Times*, 20 September 1920

'Not that we know of...' – *New York Times*, 20 September 1920

CHAPTER 7

Corkmen in Dublin extend... – *New York Times*, 11 September 1920

'If any of the Irish political prisoners die...' – The *Observer*, 22 August 1920

'Men have gone across last night...' – Costello, p161

'I was very much alarmed at his appearance...' – Ibid, p162

'As Terence MacSwiney's ordeal...' – Hart (Operations Abroad) p71

'While MacSwiney was dying...' – O'Connor *The Big Fellow*, p115

'The English press is swinging…' – Sturgis, p

'The Premier intended to test…' – *Atlantic Monthly*, April, 1922

'When I got to Art O'Brien's office – Costello, p186

'As Bishop of many Irish…' – Clifton, p74

'… the dying man has no power…' – Ibid, p75

'The Irish can be won, but never…' – Ibid, p73

'Your Eminence knows that my…' – *New York Times*, 2 October 1920

'Daily he received with edifying…' – O'Hegarty, p95

'Even if those who think …' – Clifton, p75

'Personally, from my reading…' – *The Tablet*, 4 September 1920

'I would remind your reverence…' – *Freemans Journal*, 3 September 1920

'As I write these lines, there lie…' – O'Gorman, p116

'So many discussions…' – Chavasse, p157

'Practically the entire church has…' – *Freemans Journal*, 30 September 1920

'You may be sure that if…' – Mews, p399

CHAPTER 8

We grieve with you in the tension… – Irish Press, 2 October 1920

'A last line in case I don't …' – p48c/322, UCDA

'His cheeks and temples are…' – *Irish Press*, 2 October 1920

'I am having him [MacSwiney] sprayed…' – MacSwiney Papers, Cork Public Museum

'The prolongation of life…' – Costello, p185

'I find him to be a veritable miracle…' – *Irish Press*, 2 October 1920

'The doctor says he finds…' – *Freemans Journal*, 27 September 1920

'He is very much exhausted…' – *Irish Press*, 2 October 1920

'I have made another enquiry…' – MacSwiney Papers, Cork Public Museum

'I cannot predict how long…' – *Irish Press*, 2 October 1920

'We got the most eminent…' – Coyle, p315

'They [the sisters] seem more…' – MacSwiney Papers, Cork Public Museum,

'Because of her public posture…' – Fallon, p50

'Doctors, my wife and…' – Coyle, p316

'Of course, my brother did not…' – Ibid, p317

'She made occasional trips…' Costello, p185

'We never had anything like…' – Coyle, p290

'Dr Griffiths was a very capable…' – Ibid, p313

'While the doctors and nurses…' – O'Hegarty, p

'If MacSwiney were to…' – *Irish Press*, 2 October 1920

'I am quite used up…' – Ibid

'He complains of tingling pains…' – MacSwiney Papers, Cork Public Museum

'It may be given to him…' – *Freemans Journal*, 30 September 1920

'The death of MacSwiney risks…' – Ibid

'Terence MacSwiney, in the prime of his…' – *New York Times*, September 1920

'The relatives of the Lord Mayor…' – P48b/428, UCDA

CHAPTER 9

KING: … *He has chosen* – WB Yeats, *The King's Threshold*

'If I can make a few hours…' – Paulin, p144

'If I feel I can…' – Ibid

'He practised literature for the…' – *Studies*, December, 1920

'Tell them nothing matters…' – MacSwiney, *The Revolutionist*

'Your letter went to my heart…' – p48c/323, UCDA

'His sufferings no pen could…' – O'Hegarty, p93

'We wanted someone who was entirely…' – *New York Times*, 2 October 1920

'My mind is made up…' – *Irish Press*, 9 October 1920

'I don't know how to – RTÉ.ie Radio 1/Cork Moments

'If I may not return, and my place…' – p48b/443, UCDA

'The Lord Mayor's…' – *Daily Mail*, 4 October 1920

'During all the time he kept…' – O'Hegarty, p93

'The position here with regard…' – p48b/418, UCDA

'On your 56th day I greet you…' – *Irish Press*, 23 October 1920

'One of the latest [rumours] is…' – *Daily Telegraph*, 6 October 1920

'I hurried over here hoping…' – *Irish Independent*, 7 October 1920

'Here is a man dying…' – Ibid

'If it was a question of Englishmen…' – Ibid

'After a bit, he did not…' – Coyle, p290

'Ireland is the victim of England's…' – p48b/431, UCDA

CHAPTER 10

I visited Brixton Prison… – *Irish Press*, 16 October 1920

'Please give these flowers…' – *Freemans Journal*, 8 October 1920

'Your comrades in Cork Jail…' – Ibid, 9 October 1920

'We want to send the message…' – Ibid, 8 October 1920

'I'm only 12 years old…' Ibid

'Religious friends had been…' – Coyle p317

'I feel very weak…' – *Freemans* Journal, 9 October 1920

'Terry very weak this…' – *The Irish Times*, 11 October 1920

'He also made it clear…' – Costello, p197

'I am quite played out….' – *New York Times*, 14 October 1920

'The paragraphs which have…' – *Irish Independent*, 11 October 1920

'I wish you to convey an…' – p48b/444(1), UCDA,

'England's treatment of Ireland…' – *Irish Independent*, 13 October 1920

'Lord Mayor MacSwiney's remarkably…' – *Evening News* (London), 12 October 1920

'JT Davies [Private Secretary to Lloyd George] read me…' – Callwell, p265

'He [the ISDL informer] said that MacSwiney…' – National Archives London, CAB/24/112

'One marvels that men of scientific…' – p48b/430, UCDA

'My brother is confident that his…' – *New York Times*, 16 October 1920

'It was during the silly season…' *Sunday Independent*, 17 October 1920

'I am content,' said MacSwiney…' – *Irish Press*, 23 October 1920

'Terence is the sole occupant of a…' – Ibid

CHAPTER 11

'Terence MacSwiney's hunger…' – O'Malley, p229

'Not tears but joy for…' – *Irish Independent*, 19 October 1920

'On behalf of the Lord…' – p48b/432, UCDA

'I assure you Miss MacSwiney…' – Coyle, p323

'In his present state of extreme…' – *Irish Press*, 23 October 1920

'I'd give a thousand…' – O'Hegarty, p94

'…even more cruel and no less fatal…' – *Freemans Journal*, 20 October 1920

'Is it true as reported in the…' – Hansard, 19 October 1920

'When I went in I found him…' – p48b/421 (3), UCDA

'Do you hear that knocking…' – Ibid

'Muriel, you have always…' – Coyle, p324

'Following Dr Griffiths' threat…' – *Freemans Journal*, 21 October 1920

'I can only say in perfectly general...' – Hansard, 20 October 1920

'I am afraid they have…' – Coyle, p324

'Will you have a little…' – p48b/421 (3), UCDA

'What is the condition of the health...' – Hansard, 21 October 1920

'You are reported as having said…' – p48b/433, UCDA

'What is the time…' – p48b/421 (3), UCDA

'They now also said that we…' – Coyle, p 294

'What harm have I done…' – Ibid

'You asked me then would I prefer…' – p48b/421 (3),UCDA

CHAPTER 12

... We know their dream... – WB Yeats, 'Easter 1916'

'Kindly accept these...' – UCDA, MacSwiney Papers

'What is your name...' – Coyle, p325

'In it she told me what had...' – p48b/421 (3), UCDA

'The order to expel me...' – Coyle, p326

'You must have got orders about...' – p48b/421 (3), UCDA,

'The condition of the Lord...' – *Irish Press*, 30 October 1920

'Miss MacSwiney, it is time...' – p48b/421 (3), UCDA

'If that had happened in Germany...' – Coyle, p327

'I had kept up until then ...' – Ibid, p297

'He opened his eyes occasionally...' – *Irish Press*, 30 October 1920

'He appeared to be going...' – HO 144/10308, National Archives, London

'Everything possible was...' – Ibid

'While we were in England...' – Coyle, p306

'He looked like a perfect martyr...' Ibid, p298

'I joined him in Brixton...' – O'Hegarty, p95

'Lord Mayor completed his...' – *Cork Examiner*, 26 October 1920

'It was the first time I saw...' – Noonan, p62

'The relatives will be allowed...' – Hansard, 25 October 1920

'A country with a citizen...' – Mews, p389

'The principles that Mayor MacSwiney...' – *New York Times*, 26 October 1920

'One can have on the Irish...' – *Irish Independent*, 29 October 1920

CHAPTER 13

The Lord Mayor condemned... – *Daily Telegraph*, 26 October 1920

'Cork,' replied Muriel....' – HO 144/10308, National Archives, London, all dialogue from Coroner's Court is taken directly from official transcript.

'I thought then and shall...' – p48b/421 (3), UCDA

'I understand that there...' – Ibid

'When Mrs MacSwiney...' – McConville, p751

'While we watched by his dead...' – p48b/421 (3), UCDA

'After careful consideration, I came...' – Clifton p79

Scenes in Southwark Cathedral collated from contemporary reports in *Irish Independent, New York Times, Manchester Guardian, Irish Times, Freeman's Journal, The Times,* and *Irish Press* (Philadelphia), 29 October 1920

'Some of the men looked comfortable...' – *The Times,* 29 October 1920

CHAPTER 14

Still 'The Funeral'. Motty came down before lunch to tell... – Sturgis, p61

'I am advised that the landing and funeral...' – *New York Times,* 30 October 1920

'All the time that the discussion was going on...' – p48b/421 (3), UCDA

'You shall not take my brother's body away...' – Ibid

'Sean [MacSwiney] and Min [Mary] got the brunt of it...' – Ibid

'If they took my brother's remains away...' – Coyle, p328

'The dockers marched in their dirty...' – *Manchester Guardian,* 30 October 1920

'Guarded in death by the English military...' – p48b/421 (3) UCDA

'The first glimpse of his dead face...' – O'Hegarty, p96

'Mother and I...' – O'Connor, *An Only Child,* p148

'More troops and another armoured car...' – *Manchester Guardian,* 1 November 1920

'I ask the favour of a little space to welcome home...' – *Cork Examiner,* 29 October 1920

'The people who crowded both sides of the streets...' – *Freemans Journal,* 1 November 1920

'No hand but a comrade touched his grave...' – p48b/421 (3), UCDA

'We, his colleagues of ...' – Ibid

CHAPTER 15

A prophet nearer home… – New York Times, 27 December 1921

'As de Valera stood with bowed head…' – *New York Times*, 1 November 1920

'Terence MacSwiney did not die to put spirit…' – Ibid

'Hundreds and thousands of Irishmen have died…' – Garvey (vol 10) p lxxvi

'Please convey to the Lady Mayoress my profound sympathy…' – *New York Times*, 31 October 1920

'A squad of girls and women accompanied…' - http://radicalmanchester.wordpress.com

'Never in Russia under the worst rulers of the Czar…' – Wooding, History Australia, p39.3

'The square in front of this building is…' FO 3715497/014, National Archives, London

'…the Ayuntamiento of this city [Barcelona], in session…' FO 3715497/037, Ibid

'The highlight of the evening's proceedings was…' – Folley, p63

'The fact is perhaps worthy of our Lordship's…' – FO 3715497/029, National Archives, London

'The worldwide reaction to the hunger strike…' – interview with author

'I only began to realise my own father's…' – Ibid

'Somebody gave me a book called…' – Ibid

'The seventieth anniversary of his death…' – Costello, p13

Shed we no tear for you… – *Irish Independent*, 26 October 1920

'The more however the play is kept…' – Foster, p182

'the light of MacSwiney's unalterable…' – MacGreevey, p570

'In a dreary British prison where…' – http://www.martindardis.com

HISTORY'S DAUGHTER
BY MÁIRE MACSWINEY BRUGHA

A Memoir from the only child of Terence MacSwiney

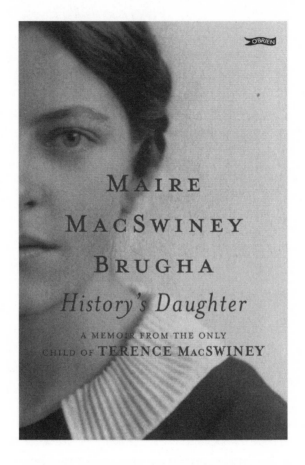

'One of the most fascinating and important stories in
the nation's biography' *Irish Independent*